Freud's Dream

Freud's Dream

A Complete Interdisciplinary Science of Mind

Patricia Kitcher

A Bradford Book
The MIT Press
Cambridge, Massachusetts
London, England

First MIT Press paperback edition, 1995

© 1992 Massachusetts Institute of Technology

This book was set in Palatino by DEKR Corporation and was printed and bound in the United States of America.

Library of Congress Cataloging-in-Publication Data

Kitcher, Patricia.
    Freud's dream : a complete interdisciplinary science of mind /
Patricia Kitcher.
       p.   cm.
    "A Bradford book."
    Includes bibliographical references and index.
    ISBN 0-262-11172-1 (HB), 0-262-61115-5 (PB)
    1. Freud, Sigmund, 1856–1939—Contributions in interdisciplinary
approach to knowledge. 2. Interdisciplinary approach to knowledge—
Case studies. 3. Cognitive science—History. 4. Psychoanalysis—
History. I. Title.
BF109.F74K58 1992
001—dc20   92-15126
                                              CIP

For G.F.W. and A.Y.W.

Contents

Acknowledgments

A number of people and institutions have made substantial contributions to this project. In 1988 I was invited by the Mind Association and the Aristotelian Society to give a presentation at their joint meeting. The resulting paper, "What Is Freud's Metapsychology?" (Kitcher 1988), served as a pilot project for the book and is the basis for much of chapter 3. I am grateful to both organizations for their hospitality and to Peter Clark and Crispin Wright for their encouragement. Most of the book was written during 1989–90, when I was the beneficiary of a grant from the National Endowment for the Humanities and a University of California President's Research Fellowship in the Humanities. I thank both organizations for their support. I would also like to thank the Committee on Research at the University of California, San Diego, for providing me with a research assistant and Warren Dow for his conscientious help.

Patricia Churchland and Stephen Stich read some early material and provided advice and encouragement. Owen Flanagan, Frank Sulloway, and Philip Kitcher read the penultimate draft and offered many thoughtful suggestions. Clark Glymour sent pages of useful criticism, which I wish I had been able to deal with more effectively. Peter Machamer annotated the penultimate draft with hundreds of large and small ideas and corrections, almost all of which changed the final version. I am deeply grateful to these kind and clever people for providing me with so much help.

My colleagues at UCSD have been very encouraging, and I would especially like to thank Patricia and Paul Churchland for their constant support. As always, I am extremely grateful to my husband, Philip Kitcher, for his patience and for his philosophical and practical help in making the book possible. As he has done so often, my father supplied esoteric books from Yale's Sterling Memorial Library when needed. On the occasion of their fiftieth wedding anniversary, I would like to dedicate the book to my parents for so many years of love and encouragement.

PART I
Freud's Interdisciplinary Theory

Chapter 1

Freud and Interdisciplinary Cognitive Science

Two Goals

Over the last decade there has been a dramatic shift in the approach of the mental (now "cognitive") sciences. Psychologists, philosophers of psychology, linguists, computer scientists, neurophysiologists, anthropologists, and others have converted to the view that progress in any of the cognitive sciences requires an interdisciplinary perspective. Since neural, developmental, computational, linguistic, psychological, and social factors are all involved in cognition, a complete cognitive science must include them all. Hence, these disciplines must learn from each other and coevolve. Psychological experiments and theories must be informed by an understanding of neuroanatomy and neurophysiology; computer simulations of mental capacities should take advantage of what is known about the organization of the brain and, at the other end of the spectrum, what is known about the social structures in which individual minds function; psychology and neuroscience should be aware of what has been learned about computational processes from computer science; and so forth. It is a measure of the strength and influence of this movement that it is even moving educational institutions. Many universities have established or are establishing interdisciplinary departments of cognitive science.

Philosophers of psychology have played two complementary roles in this intellectual revolution. They have wholeheartedly endorsed the interdisciplinary approach and have tried to fathom the implications of its early results for traditional philosophical conundra. These discussions have been overwhelmingly positive. Interdisciplinary studies have been seen as making important contributions to issues ranging from induction and the nature of inner representations to free will and the unity of the self. The results are seen as confirming the positive a priori estimate of the approach. On reflection, integrating work from different disciplines seems demanded by the complex interrelations among mental, physical, and social phenomena—and the proof is in the results.

Beyond pointing out obvious virtues of an interdisciplinary integration and canvassing, or, perhaps, synthesizing implications of work in other disciplines, I believe that philosophers ought to undertake a further task in this grand joint venture. They should provide some more detailed assessment of the interdisciplinary perspective now driving research in cognitive science or—not to beg a central question—the cognitive sciences. Are the virtues as shining as they first appear? What are the substantive commitments of the approach? Does it have inevitable weaknesses? Are there specific errors to which interdisciplinary theory construction is less, or more, vulnerable than other approaches?

The assessment might be done in different ways. Philosophers could peruse contemporary work in cognitive science itself, looking for evidence of good or ill effects of interdisciplinary approaches. Alternatively, they could abstract from the particular case and consider the logical form of interdisciplinary theories and arguments. Or, they could try to achieve a better understanding of the potential strengths and weaknesses of interdisciplinary methodology by examining a historical case. My approach is going to be the last. It is perhaps somewhat early to judge the effects of interdisciplinary integration on cognitive science, and it is often extremely difficult to reduce a methodological perspective to a set of logical relations. Still, I have no reasons of principle for objecting to other approaches or for preferring the case study method. I use this method because there is a wonderfully rich and complete historical case of interdisciplinary theory construction available for study. Moreover, it is a case of interdisciplinary work in the mental sciences and is so close in time that its relevance can hardly be doubted. The case is Sigmund Freud.

The rise and fall of psychoanalysis[1] has many claims to be the ideal case study for this purpose, but it also has a notable drawback. If social conservatives bridle and high school students snicker at the sound of Freud's name, the reaction of intellectuals is hardly more sophisticated. They almost divide into two exclusive and exhaustive groups: those who read "Freud" as "fraud" and those who read it as "joy" (its meaning in German). To the first contingent, any new study will be greeted as hagiography masquerading as intellectual history. Conversely, Freudians will fear yet another instance of a popular form of syllogism: Freudianism involves X; therefore, X is methodologically flawed, false, or somehow bad.

Although these attitudes have some warrant, there is a growing body of work that takes Freud seriously, but not, so to speak, obsessively. Outstanding examples are Henri Ellenberger's (1970) erudite study of Freud's psychiatric precursors, Frank Sulloway's (1979) masterful treatment of the biological roots of psychoanalysis, and Adolf Grünbaum's (1984) thorough demolition of arguments from putative cures. Given its influence on science and culture, a sound understanding of Freud's work is needed, whether one's initial impulse is love or hate. The development of psychoanalysis can provide an extended case study in interdisciplinary theory construction. However, understanding its interdisciplinary supports can also provide a more accurate assessment of Freud's account of mental life. So the book has two goals. I hope to extract lessons about an important contemporary approach from Freud, and I hope to use the recently articulated idea of interdisciplinary coevolution to illuminate an important episode in intellectual history.

Part I makes the case for Freud's being the first interdisciplinary cognitive scientist and shows how interdisciplinary concerns guided the construction of his theories. Freud's program is clearly on the wane. Whether one laments or rejoices in this fact, there is no doubt about its truth (see the beginning of chapter 6). Although the faithful may remain, the number of new converts has declined precipitously. Part II makes two interconnected points about the collapse of psychoanalysis: In large measure, its evidential base weakened because of its interdisciplinary commitments; its intellectual respectability also declined, in part because Freud used faulty interdisciplinary reasoning to try to maintain his position. Since this attempt at interdisciplinary theory construction ended in failure, we see the approach as it labored under great strains, and there are many more examples of potential pitfalls than of potential strengths. Thus, the picture that emerges is somewhat one-sided. Since philosophers have chorused the praises of interdisciplinary integration, however, a cautionary tale provides balance to the overall assessment. I should say explicitly that, despite the caveats that will emerge, my purpose is not to argue against the interdisciplinary perspective. I regard this approach as essential to cognitive science for the familiar reasons already given. My hope is that by understanding some of Freud's misadventures in interdisciplinary theory construction, contemporary cognitive scientists can find a steadier and surer path for themselves.

Objections and Replies

Before turning to Freud, I offer replies to some likely objections to the project. These will also serve to clarify my interpretive strategy. Three potential criticisms seem especially obvious. First, in appealing to Freud, I am proposing to explain the obscure by the more obscure. Second, even if Freud's work and contemporary cognitive science are both interdisciplinary, the particular disciplines and their states of development matter. Finally, it is naive, or worse, to try to extract general principles from a single case.

Although the value of Freud's work has been fiercely debated, this is not generally the result of disagreements about what he says. Freud is no Kant. His prose is eloquent, direct even as it overflows with illustrative examples and helpful imagery. There are interpretive controversies, but I need enter only two: whether Freud significantly changed his approach to theorizing about mental functioning over the years and whether his "metapsychology" is detachable from psychoanalysis proper. I will argue that he did not change and that metapsychology provided the unchanging blueprint for the construction of psychoanalysis. Since my approach is somewhat novel, I use two means of establishing the interpretation. First, I extract Freud's interdisciplinary attitude and interdisciplinary commitments from his major theoretical works and show how these shaped the emerging theory. The central tenets of psychoanalysis—the pleasure and reality principles, the unconscious system, libido and repression, psychosexual development, and the Oedipal complex—all turn out to have been firmly rooted in programs and results of various nineteenth-century social and natural sciences. Second, I try to confirm the hypothesis of Freud's interdisciplinary theory construction by showing how it enables us to understand otherwise surprising aspects of *The Interpretation of Dreams*, the book he considered his masterpiece.

I take the hallmark of interdisciplinary research to be simply that workers in one discipline intend their theories to be informed and influenced by theories in what have traditionally been separate disciplines. This attitude makes sense only on the assumption that the phenomena dealt with by the different disciplines are in some way interdependent. The dependence relations might be so strong as to permit a reduction of one of the sciences to another. On the classical model, one science can be reduced to another if the laws of the first science, or reasonable approximations of them, can be derived from the laws of the second science, plus biconditional or one-way bridge laws linking the terms of the two sciences.[2] Since reduction is rarely possible, philosophers have also described a somewhat weaker relation, that of "supervenience" between sets of properties. Supervenience holds just in case the properties captured in one science alter if and only if there is some change in the properties characterized by a second science.[3] However, phenomena may be interdependent even in the absence of these rather strong relations. The phenomena described by two sciences are interdependent just in case some changes in the properties mentioned by one science alter a significant range of properties mentioned by the second. Failing such connection, there is no reason to believe that being informed about the phenomena dealt with in one science can directly assist progress in another science.[4]

If interdisciplinary research is committed to an order of being—to claims that some properties or relations depend on others—then there may be significant differences across such programs as a result of their different ontologies. The second objection is that, even if Freud did use an interdisciplinary approach, his problems with it may have been a function of his vision of the order of nature and, so, of the cast of disciplines he tried to unite. At one level, the disciplines that were to contribute to Freud's complete cognitive science will seem quite alien. No contemporary cognitive scientist would look to the history of civilization or to comparative mythology for enlightenment. Still, from Comte onward, there has been widespread agreement on the rough order of being and of the sciences, with mathematics as the most basic, followed by astronomy, physics, chemistry, biology, and sociology (Fletcher 1971, vol. 1:175). Freud was as much a part of this tradition as contemporary cognitive scientists are and amended Comte's list, as they do, by inserting psychology between biology and sociology (and also psychoanalysis between biology and psychology).

Even if Freud ordered the disciplines in essentially the same way that contemporary theorists do, the disciplines have made dramatic progress in the last fifty to one hundred years. Thus, the objection can still be pushed, but in a slightly different direction: Contemporary scientists know so much more than Freud's cohorts did that his problems were probably quite different from anything they are likely to face. I try to meet this obvious criticism in several different ways. First, questions of approach concern not what is known, but how to pursue the unknown. My focus will be not on what Freud knew, or even thought he knew, but on his appeals to interdisciplinary considerations to deal with his vast areas of ignorance. Since contemporary cognitive scientists take an interdisciplinary perspective, they also make interdisciplinary assumptions in approaching the unknown, so there is at least a potential for illumination.

Further, in most cases, I will demonstrate the relevance of Freud's interdisciplinary errors directly. Having seen clearly in this historical context that a particular type of interdisciplinary reasoning is fallacious, I will often point to what seem to be contemporary instances of the same fallacy.

Finally, I will consider two significant differences between Freud's intellectual milieu and our own. First, tracing lines of historical development was a major effort of almost all nineteenth-century sciences. In the twentieth century, science has sought to develop synchronic as opposed to diachronic theories. Second, computer science is the heart of current cognitive science, and it is a twentieth-century science.[5] To use a nineteenth-century expression that still enjoys some currency, the "zeitgeist" of contemporary work differs from that of the mental sciences as Freud wrote: nineteenth-century mental sciences were evolutionary, today's cognitive science is computational. These differences are important, and many problems of psychoanalysis stemmed from the fading of diachronic science. Again, however, my interest is in Freud's interdisciplinary reasoning in the face of changes in the disciplines. Further, the differences between current attitudes and those of nineteenth-century mental scientists can be turned to advantage: We will be able to see the interaction effects of interdisciplinary research and zeitgeist quite clearly and extract a lesson that can be applied to today's computationally dominated attitudes.

Part of my reply to this objection may appear to support the third potential criticism, that nothing can be learned from a single historical example. If I need to demonstrate the relevance of studying Freud by finding parallels in contemporary work, then why duplicate effort? Why not follow one of the other strategies mentioned and simply canvas current work for instances where interdisciplinary integration has been valuable or baneful? As noted, I have no objections of principle to this strategy, and it has the advantage of automatic contemporary relevance. However, there are also great advantages in proceeding historically. The most obvious is that the past is done. Freud's interdisciplinary approach involved assumptions about how the disciplines would develop, as does the approach of contemporary cognitive scientists. In his case, however, we know what happened next. We are able to see the consequences of his assumptions, something we cannot do in the contemporary case. Perhaps we *ought* to be able to spot fallacies in interdisciplinary reasoning without the advantage of hindsight, and we probably can in some instances. But that hardly implies that hindsight is not an advantage.

A second advantage of a historical case is that it presents insights about interdisciplinary research in a coherent frame. We can see how, in a particular set of circumstances, a methodological assumption may have seemed attractive, or plausible, or at least not unreasonable, and then went awry. Further, Clio happens to be a good teacher. This fact was celebrated in classic defenses of liberal education: Children should study history, because its dramatic examples of wisdom and folly cannot fail to impress tender minds. Recent work suggests a somewhat different take on this point. Apparently, minds of all ages are much more easily impressed by vivid cases than by more reliable, statistical data (Nisbett and Ross 1980:43ff.). Whether this is an infirmity or a blessing, vivid examples are clearly an effective way to impart information, although not information that is statistically valid.

I do not appeal to Freud to establish universal or statistical claims about the consequences of certain types of interdisciplinary reasoning. It is one example and is only meant to be illustrative. My purpose is to explore the potential strengths and weaknesses of different kinds of interdisciplinary reasoning, by showing their good or ill effects on the development of psychoanalysis. What we can learn from this case is not "Whenever one makes interdisciplinary inference X, the effect on one's theory is inevitably or probably Y." Rather, it is "When one engages in type X reasoning, one makes one's theory vulnerable to Y."

Historians may object to even this modest project. One of J. H. Hexter's three cardinal principles for doing history is that one cannot learn about the past if one is trying to make a case for present action or a prediction about the future (Hexter 1979:251). Hexter's targets were Marxist historians bent on social action. Still, my intention to examine Freud to enlighten current methodology may seem dangerously close to enlisting history in the service of a contemporary cause.

My defense is partly autobiographical. I began studying Freud fifteen years ago in order to use historical theories in a philosophy of psychology course. I kept reading Freud, as interdisciplinary attitudes were taking hold in the cognitive sciences. Against this background, I began to realize that Freud's goal was a complete interdisciplinary science of mind and that many of the strengths and weaknesses of his program flowed from this fact. It was not worries about contemporary approaches that led me to Freud, but the study of Freud that led me to see that, for all its obvious virtues, interdisciplinary research has dangers of its own and should be evaluated more critically.

Second, I believe that I am using—and not abusing—history, because, although my approach has a novel twist, others have documented the intimate connection between psychoanalysis and other disciplines. David Rapaport sketched the basic scientific background to psychoanalysis thirty years ago; Frank Sulloway has shown in great detail how Freud's theories were informed and shaped by the biology of his day; Peter Amacher, Karl Pribram and Morton Gill, and Raymond Fancher have all demonstrated the sophistication of Freud's knowledge of (then) recent work in neurophysiology and its influence on his theories; Edwin Wallace has described Freud's knowledge of anthropology and the integration of anthropology and psychoanalysis in *Totem and Taboo*.[6] My work builds on these studies, arguing that the examples are part of a larger pattern: Freud drew on these and other disciplines in an attempt to construct a complete theory of human mentality and—for better and for worse—this goal guided the development of psychoanalysis.

Chapter 2
The Disciplines and Their Relations

In a Postscript (1927) to *The Question of Lay Analysis*, Freud specified the subjects that he considered essential to the practice of psychoanalysis. Psychoanalytic training "must include elements from the mental sciences, from psychology, the history of civilization and sociology, as well as from anatomy, biology and the study of evolution" (S.E. XX:252).[1] Presumably these fields were also essential to psychoanalytic theory. Although very helpful, Freud's list is not completely transparent to modern readers. History of civilization would include anthropology, prehistoric archaeology, comparative mythology, comparative philology, and the history of religion and philosophy. The anatomy indicated is obviously brain anatomy and, in Freud's own education, neurophysiology was taught along with "higher" anatomy (Bernfeld 1949:163–96).

Freud's curriculum may seem a strange amalgam of natural science, social science, and the humanities. As will be clear in this and the next two chapters, however, he did not recommend these subjects in order to train psychoanalysts who would also be well-rounded individuals. On the contrary, because he was committed to various doctrines and projects, including recapitulationism and genetic psychology, he regarded these fields as essential contributors to the science of psychoanalysis.

Without attempting to be comprehensive, this chapter will give some sense of what these subjects were like in the thirty years prior to the emergence of psychoanalysis, roughly the period from 1870 to 1900. In particular, I will indicate features that influenced that construction. Before considering the disciplines themselves, I take a closer look at how Freud's more distant and immediate predecessors and mentors saw relations among different fields of study.

How the Disciplines Are Related: Differing Views

Inevitably, I begin with Auguste Comte. Freud studied with Ernst Brücke, who was a close intellectual ally of Hermann Helmholtz, who was a student of Comte's. Although the chain of influence is quite direct, the students did not always maintain their teachers' views. Comte's hierarchy of the sciences rested on interrelated metaphysical and historical claims: The most basic sciences had this status because the phenomena they dealt with were the most simple and general. More particular and complex phenomena depend on these, and so their sciences depend on basic sciences. These metaphysical facts explained and were confirmed by the historical order in which the sciences developed, from the most basic to the most specific and complex, namely, the science of sociology that Comte wished to found (Fletcher 1971, vol. 1:163–96).

Comte claimed further that morals, roughly, the study of individual psychology and ethics, could pass beyond its more primitive theological and metaphysical stages to be a positive science only by being grounded in this hierarchy (Fletcher 1971, vol. 1:179–80). Figure 2.1 presents Comte's hierarchy, with morals occupying its potential place at the top. Although Comte's historical claims were quickly and effectively attacked, the metaphysical argument has been more persuasive. This is presumably because it is an interdisciplinary application of a standard view of science: To understand a complex phenomenon, analyze it into its simplest components and then explain the whole by synthesizing features of the components.

John Stuart Mill reversed Comte's ordering of individual mental science (psychology) and sociology. He reasoned that since human

[Morals (individual psychology and ethics)]

Sociology

Biology

Chemistry

Physics

Astronomy

Mathematics

Figure 2.1
Comte's hierarchy

beings remain so, even when joined in society, the laws of society can be nothing but the laws of individuals united together (Mill 1843:572). Freud translated four of Mill's social essays, cited *A System of Logic*, and referred freely to the principle of the complication of causes (*The Psychopathology of Everyday Life*, 1901, S.E. VI:60–61), so he was probably familiar with this discussion. Positively, Mill's position on the relations among the disciplines can be captured in five claims.

1. Although it is highly probable that every mental state has a nervous state for its immediate antecedent and proximate cause, since we know nothing of nervous states, we must study mental states directly. Since presently, and perhaps always, it is not possible to deduce mental laws from laws of physiology, psychology is a distinct and separate science.
2. Nevertheless, since the laws of mind may be derivative from laws of physiology, "the relations, indeed, of that science to the science of physiology must never be overlooked or undervalued."
3. The laws of psychology are established through observation and experiment, following "Mill's methods."
4. We can find empirical laws of sociology. An empirical law holds true of all known phenomena, but we cannot be certain that it holds beyond that, because although we know that it is true, we do not know why it is true. Ideally, this defect would be remedied by deducing sociological laws from psychological laws. Even with sociological laws, exact prediction is highly unlikely, since we rarely know all the antecedent conditions.
5. Ethology, the science of the formation of character, is a deductive science, whose principles follow from psychological laws, plus sociological laws (Mill 1843:556–97; citation from 556).

Mill also attacked Comte for a crude reduction of psychology to physiology.

[Many eminent physiologists] contend that a thought (for example) is . . . the result of nervous energy. . . . According to this theory, one state of mind is never really produced by another; all are produced by states of body. When one thought seems to call up another by association, it is not really a thought which recalls a thought; the association did not exist between the two thoughts, but between the two states of the brain or nerves. . . . On this theory the uniformities of succession among states of mind would be mere derivative uniformities, resulting from the laws of succession of the bodily states which cause them. . . . [M]ental science would be a mere branch, though the highest and most recondite branch, of . . . Physiology. M. Comte, accordingly, claims the scientific cognizance of moral and intellectual phenomena exclusively for physiologists; and not only denies to Psychology or Mental Philosophy properly so called, the character of a science, but places it, in the chimerical nature of its objects and pretensions, almost on a par with astrology. (Mill 1843:556)

Although it is not clear that Comte was a reductionist, Mill's reading has been a standard one.

Regardless of its justice to Comte, Mill's criticism brings out some of the complexity in the question of which sciences are more basic. Comte believed that physics was more basic than biology in two senses. It was *ontologically* more basic, because the objects of biology were made up of the objects of physics; it was *epistemologically* more basic, he held, because it was impossible to discover biological laws before discovering physical laws. Mill criticized Comte for maintaining that physiology was also *explanatorily* more basic than psychology, that is, for holding that the laws of physiology explained why observed psychological phenomena were as they were. Other than reversing the positions of psychology and sociology, they agreed on the ontological ordering. In claims 1 and 3 above, Mill rejected Comte's claim for the epistemological priority of physiology to psychology. However, claims 2, 4, and 5 suggest that Mill believed that the laws of psychology might be derivative from and hence explanatorily dependent on laws of physiology, that sociology was probably explanatorily dependent on psychology, and that ethology was definitely explanatorily dependent on psychology and sociology. In brief, Mill believed that psychology should be informed by physiology, but that this might never lead to reduction. By contrast, he believed that if real laws were possible in social science, that is, laws that afford assurance that they hold beyond the realm of past experience, it would only be because they were deducible from laws of psychology (Mill 1843:562, 597). Mill's position is represented in figure 2.2.

The views of Comte and Mill were elaborated in the methodological reflections of two scholars whose work Freud studied, sociohistorian Henry Thomas Buckle (1821–62) and anthropologist Edward B. Tylor (1832–1917). Both Comte and Mill had stressed the need to pursue sociology by historical and comparative methods. Buckle began his two-volume *Introduction to the History of Civilization in England* by announcing that the laws of social evolution were to be found inductively through history. He was particularly concerned to show the effects of physical forces on intellectual development and concluded that violent physical conditions outside Europe conspired to make non-Europeans

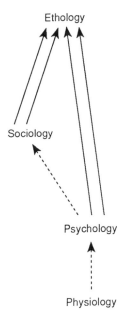

Figure 2.2
Mill's view. The bottom-to-top layout indicates ontological priority. Double solid arrows indicate explanatory dependence and deductive support, and run from the explaining to the explained disciplines. Dotted arrows indicate the weaker epistemological relations of support, inspiration, and possible deductive support (but not, pace Comte, order of discovery), and run from the supporting to the supported disciplines.

imaginative and to weaken their reasoning faculties (Buckle 1857–61: vii). Such naive Euro-ethnocentrism may raise doubts about Buckle's intellectual stature. But he was the epitome of the English cultural historian and his *History* made him an instant celebrity.

Tylor is widely regarded as the father of modern anthropology, the individual who turned this tradition of semiprofessional cultural reflections into a discipline, by defining its central concept, "culture," and by clarifying its methods (Stocking 1968:72–77). Like Mill, Tylor saw the study of human life as a branch of natural science and social action as the result of many individual actions. Although he recognized hereditary variations across individuals, he believed that human beings could be treated as uniform, but situated at different "levels" of civilization. To discover laws governing the evolution of culture, he thought it necessary to reconstruct states of previous civilization. The key to such reconstructions was prehistoric anthropology, but it was possible to appeal to directly expressive language, art, religion, mythology, and "survivals," elements of previous civilization that have somehow endured to the present day (Tylor 1891, vol. 1:chap. 1, passim).

Although Tylor's views were more developed, he drew on Buckle, and their positions were sufficiently close to be captured in a single account. Figure 2.3 illustrates their view of how the disciplines were related. With so many resources to assist in finding laws of cultural evolution and improving the human condition, Tylor was optimistic: "It is our happiness to live in one of those eventful periods of intellectual and moral history, when the oft-closed gates of discovery and reform stand open at their widest" (Tylor 1891, vol. 2:452).

Turning to more immediate influences, Franz Brentano published *Psychology from an Empirical Standpoint* (1874) while Freud was his student. It opens with a discussion of relations among the disciplines (bk. 1, chaps. 1 and 2, passim). Brentano accepted Comte's underlying principle that some disciplines deal with simpler phenomena and so developed first and were the basis for sciences of the complex, including psychology. He sided with Mill that psychology was the foundation of the study of character (ethology), adding that it was also the

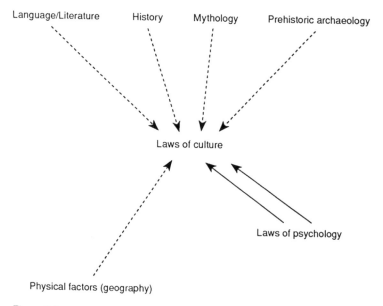

Figure 2.3
Buckle's and Tylor's view. Again, the bottom-to-top layout indicates ontological priority, double solid arrows indicate explanatory dependence and deductive support, and dotted arrows indicate the weaker epistemological relations of support and inspiration.

basis of political economy, the study of the acquisition and consumption of wealth.

Although Brentano accepted Mill's view that psychological laws were not basic and probably needed grounding in laws of physiology, he resisted any suggestion that psychology should be studied physiologically. His opposition rested on reasons of principle and of practice. On the principled side, he asserted that it was clear from what he characterized as our nonintrospective perception of inner states that they were different from anything physical. More plausibly, he argued that the wrong lesson has been abstracted from the standard examples of the dependence of physics on mathematics and biology on chemistry. No one believed, on reflection, that the laws of physics could be deduced from the principles of mathematics, despite the enormous importance of the latter to the former. Further, although organic compounds may be made out of the same constituents as inorganic, it was not possible to carry out the work of organic chemistry by deductions from inorganic. From the practical standpoint, Brentano embellished Mill's complaint. Physiology was just not sufficiently advanced to offer real enlightenment. Worse still, the analogies and insights that had been offered by physiologically minded psychologists were so crude and premature that they probably caused more harm than good. Thus, despite the ontological dependence of psychology on physiology, the former was neither explanatorily nor epistemologically dependent on the latter.

Brentano's discussion is a good example of the way these methodological disputes have tended to be carried out both in Freud's time and currently. Champions of physiology point out how very little has been accomplished in two thousand years of studying the mind without an adequate understanding of the brain; advocates of more traditional methods retaliate that, for all their promises of insight, the physiologists have delivered very little. Although Brentano's hierarchy would look very like Mill's emendation of Comte's (so I omit it), his conception of the disciplines had a somewhat different emphasis. Granted that complex sciences were grounded in the more basic, each science should largely be pursued on its own. In particular, since premature physiologizing produced theoretical chaos, psychological research should not be "surrendered to" or even "mixed with" physiological research (Brentano 1874:64).

Several of Freud's other teachers appear, in word or deed, to have taken the opposite view. Emil Du Bois-Reymond explained Brücke's (and his own) attitude.

Brücke and I pledged a solemn oath to put in power this truth: "No other forces than the common physical chemical ones are active within the organism. In those cases which cannot at the time be explained by these forces one has either to find the specific way or form of their action by means of the physical mathematical method or to assume new forces equal to dignity to the chemical physical forces inherent in matter, reducible to the force of attraction and repulsion." (cited in Bernfeld 1949:171)

After leaving Brücke's Physiological Institute to pursue medical studies, Freud did part of his residency in Theodor Meynert's Psychiatric Clinic (Amacher 1965:21). Since Meynert regarded specific cortical cells as representing specific ideas (Fancher, ms.), Freud appears to have heard the reductionist as well as the antireductionist side of the issue.

Frank Sulloway argues that it is an oversimplification to picture Freud as torn between the ideologies of physiological and "pure" psychology, and this is probably right. As he notes, the attempt to reduce physiology to physics and chemistry (the "biophysics" program) was no longer flourishing when Freud took up his studies (Sulloway 1979:66). Further, much of Meynert's reasoning went from psychology to physiology: Look for association fibers in the cortex, because the law of association is true, according to psychology. Even if these views did not amount to schools and even if the extreme positions were more subtle than sometimes portrayed, Freud saw a range of attitudes toward methodological relations among the disciplines.

Perhaps the most subtle and authoritative view was that of Wilhelm Wundt, one of the founders of modern psychology. Among many other topics, Wundt wrote about dreams, slips, and taboos. Freud cited him frequently and with deference, if not always agreement. Wundt is often said to have been the last person to have mastered all of human knowledge. However, he was not an interdisciplinary scholar merely in the sense of being a Renaissance individual. In the *Principles of Physiological Psychology* (1874), Wundt was explicit that psychology depended on anatomy and physiology and he observed that physiologists had long depended on psychology. He complained that, by contrast, psychologists had only recently become intimately acquainted with physiological efforts (Wundt 1874:2). His book was intended to promote this interchange, even though he admitted that the foundations he was proposing for his new science of physiological psychology—anatomy and physiology—were "in certain respects, themselves very far from solid" (Wundt 1874:iii; my translation).

Wundt described the goal of physiological psychology: It was to determine how physiological processes affected the objects of psychology. This was indicated in the name, "in the fact that the proper objects of our science are those named by psychology, and the physiological standpoint is added only as further determination" (Wundt 1874:2; my translation). Although he believed that higher capacities (those of the cerebral hemispheres) were so complex that one could only have the crudest conception of the distinctive properties of the physiological function of a particular part of the brain whose accomplishments were being expressed, he argued for the importance of being aware of the general principles governing brain anatomy and physiology (Wundt 1874:223). Further, he suggested that psychologists borrow and adapt the experimental methods of physiology. Wundt's view of the relations among the disciplines was complex. Anatomy and physiology were ontologically more basic than psychology, so any principles of the latter science had to be consistent with basic principles of the former. On the other hand, physiology could not explain complex psychological phenomena. Further, both sciences needed to learn from one another, because it was important for psychology to understand the relations between determinant physiological conditions and states of consciousness, and important for physiology to offer hypotheses about the brain on the basis of determinate mental symptoms (Wundt 1902:2).[2]

Beyond physiology and the experimental method, Wundt claimed other sources of objective psychological knowledge in the products of mental life: language, myth, and custom. These were partly determined by historical conditions, but also by universal psychological laws. Cultural artifacts due to the latter could be investigated by a special branch of psychology, ethnic psychology (*Völkerpsychologie*). Ethnic psychology was to be the chief source of information about the general psychology of complex mental processes, but it was also possible to glean useful information from child and animal psychology. Together, ethnic, animal, and child psychology could address issues of psychogenesis, how human mentality developed (Wundt 1902:5–6). As illustrated in figure 2.4, Wundt's conception of disciplinary interrelations was distinctive in both its richness and its commitment to mutual dependence.

From this brief survey, it is clear that, as Freud developed his theories, he faced almost the same range of opinion about the relations among the disciplines taken to be relevant to mental life that is available today. At a superficial level, most agreed on the relative ontological ordering of the disciplines and on the need for several to contribute to a science of mind. Beneath this surface ecumenicism lay major

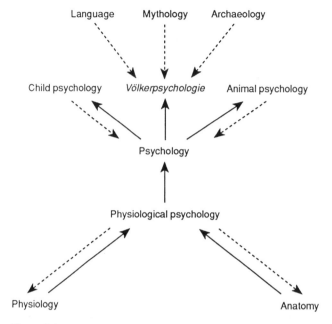

Figure 2.4
Wundt's view. The bottom-to-top layout again pictures ontological dependence. As noted, Wundt felt that this sometimes implied that higher disciplines were constrained by consistency with lower ones, a feature indicated by (single) solid arrows running from the constraining to the constrained disciplines. Dotted arrows again indicate sources of inspiration and support.

differences in attitude concerning explanatory and epistemological dependencies. For example, two theorists could have agreed that ethnic psychology and physiology were both needed, even though one believed that ethnic psychology was more advanced than physiology or that only ethnic psychology could be the source of mental laws and so would contribute the vast majority of the solid, usable results in understanding the mental, whereas the other's expectations were exactly the reverse. Few said that they believed that, given physiology, psychology was unnecessary, or that discoveries about the brain were largely irrelevant to understanding the mental. These sharp characterizations were left for opponents to supply. Nevertheless, research emphases and bibliographies revealed where various theorists placed their serious bets. Although Mill and Brentano conceded the importance of the brain, they made no real efforts to learn about it. And, as Wundt complained, when materialists invoked psychology, it was often just a crude version of the traditional doctrine of association (Wundt 1902:9–10).

Freud had a further model of mental research that is no longer available today. Scholars like Buckle and Tylor looked to the study of history, civilization, and, especially, history of civilization to discover laws governing social evolution. Like Wundt, they believed that knowing how civilization arose and developed would provide important clues to understanding the development of human intelligence and its current complexity. Finally, in this array of approaches, there was at least one example of a genuinely interdisciplinary strategy. Wundt did not merely say that many disciplines had to work together to develop a scientific psychology. He supplied anatomical and physiological information needed to advance the cause of psychophysics in *Principles of Physiological Psychology* and devoted his five-volume *Völkerpsychologie* to analyzing and interpreting language, art, mythology, and religion (Wundt 1916).

Before turning to the various branches of knowledge themselves, I should take note of one well-known position that has not yet been considered. Wilhelm Dilthey began a long and important methodological controversy when he distinguished between *Naturwissenschaft* (natural science) and the social or humanistic sciences, *Geisteswissenschaften* (literally, the sciences of the mind or spirit). As Grünbaum observes, some recent discussions have attempted to reinterpret Freud's work as a *Geistes-* rather than a *Naturwissenschaft* (Grünbaum 1984:chap. 1, 2, 3, passim). Given his many appeals to literature and mythology, this strategy has a superficial plausibility. However, it faces insuperable textual obstacles. Freud obviously knew about this distinction; among many other possible sources, Wundt referred to it (Wundt 1874:4–5). But in all his discussions of the relations between psychoanalysis and science, he cast his work in the mold of a natural science and he explicitly described psychology as a natural science (e.g., *An Outline of Psycho-Analysis*, 1938, S.E. XXIII:158). Further, a crucial assumption of Dilthey's opponents was that humanistic disciplines contain natural laws, because there are laws of human psychology. Nothing in Freud's development or defense of psychoanalysis makes any sense without the underlying assumption that, despite the appearance of chaos, human mental life is governed by laws (Sherwood 1969).

The Progress of the Disciplines

Views about relations among the disciplines were part of the background to the construction of Freud's theories. So were developments in particular areas.

Brain Anatomy and Physiology

A major neurophysiological controversy was resolved in the 1890s, as Freud began his speculations about mental functioning. From the work of Waldeyer and Ramón y Cajal, it appeared that neural matter was not continuous, but made up of discrete neurons. Neurons consisted of nerve cells with branch-like arrangements of fibers emanating from them. Although in close proximity, the fibers of one neuron did not actually touch those of other neurons. Ramón y Cajal first reported observations supporting gaps between fibers in 1888. In 1891, Waldeyer offered a review of the literature and supported Ramón y Cajal's position. From 1901 to 1903, Ramón y Cajal bombarded his neurophysiological colleagues with evidence favoring the discontinuity of neural matter (Bullock 1977:103). Although neurons were discrete, signals were somehow propagated across the gaps. Neurons were thus the basic morphological and functional unit of the nervous system.

Neural conduction was known to be accompanied by electrical and chemical changes, but its specific nature was unknown. Wundt cautioned that one should assume only that basic neural processes were some type of movement processes, governed by the general laws of motion (Wundt 1874:235–36). Reflex experiments suggested that central elements of neurons appeared to offer greater resistance to incoming excitations than the nerve fibers, but were also able to develop larger amounts of stored energy. Excitation could come from external or internal sources. From the perspective of nerve substance, however, both exogenous and endogenous stimuli were external. The term "reflex" had been introduced by Marshall Hall in 1833. According to Hall, the reflex was a basic principle of action in animals that connected sensory impression to motor activity, but he limited its scope to the spinal cord system (Clarke and Jacyna 1987:114–24). A number of German investigators, including Johannes Müller, argued that the reflex concept should be extended to include cerebral reflexes, thus opening the way for a unified concept of the reflex as the basic unit of neural action (Clarke and Jacyna 1987:124ff.).

An important and still unresolved question was whether different regions of the cerebral cortex had differing structures. Meynert argued for uniformity of structure, whereas Ramón y Cajal defended specific differences. Wundt offered a thoughtful compromise: What Ramón y

Cajal himself has shown is an extraordinary degree of similarity in the structure of various regions. Indeed, he has shown that motor, sensory, and association functions are connected to definite cell and fiber systems that are found in all parts of the cortex. Further, the differences among these systems depend on the direction of conduction, and so on the modes of connection of different neurons and not on the specific character of structural elements (Wundt 1902:224).

On the basis of lesion studies and other considerations, Wundt argued further that neurons began in a functionally indifferent state. Peripheral neurons acquired different activities (modes of connection) as a result of the specific stimuli they received because of their location. Thus, localization of function developed among the peripheral neurons; the different regions that subserved different sensory modalities became structurally differentiated. Applying the principles of original indifference and differentiation through differing external and internal conditions, Wundt suggested that neurons subserving different aspects of central processing could be thought of as relatively localized. At a time, particular functions would be spatially localized, but this would vary as the surrounding functional conditions (patterns of connection) varied.

Beyond this general sketch, provided by Wundt (1902:chap. 2, passim, and 57–58, 88, 322–23, 328–29), three particular contributions, made by Meynert, Fechner, and Jackson, offer insights into the bases of Freud's theories. An influential anatomist and psychiatrist, Theodor Meynert (1833–92) was also a devout associationist. He speculated that experience created a structure of associations in the nervous system, which he called the "primary ego (*Ich*)." This structure was built up when, for instance, a child experiencing the pain of hunger had a nipple put into its mouth and experienced the satisfaction of eating. Henceforth, the sensation of hunger would call up images of the nipple and the child would seek it. Associations forged by trial and error followed by pain or relief from pain became the primary ego; the ego was expanded by secondary perceptions of friends, property, and skills that were added to it. Meynert described the primary ego as the "nucleus of individuality" and claimed that, however complex, all human actions had the motive of avoiding greater pain (Amacher 1965:34–35).

The great psychophysicist Gustav Fechner (1801–87) maintained that all conscious impulses were related to pleasure and pain, which were themselves related to conditions of stability and instability in the nervous system. On this hypothesis,

every psychophysical motion rising above the threshold of consciousness is attended by pleasure in proportion as, beyond a
certain limit, it approximates to complete stability, and is attended
by unpleasure in proportion as, beyond a certain limit, it deviates
from complete stability. (cited by Freud in *Beyond the Pleasure
Principle*, 1920, S.E. XVIII:8)

Freud was explicit that his constancy principle (which maintained that
the nervous system strove to get rid of energy or to keep it at the
lowest possible level) was intimately related to Fechner's hypothesis
about the relation between pleasure and pain and neural equilibrium.[3]

Nineteenth-century preoccupations with evolution were reflected
in the anatomical and physiological views of the well-known British
neurologist John Hughlings Jackson (1835–1911). Freud read Jackson
and cited his views with approval (e.g., "On Aphasia," 1891, S.E.
XIV:207n.). Jackson argued that the nervous system was composed of
different levels that represented different levels of evolutionary development and that were able to perform increasingly complex tasks.
According to his theory of "nervous dissolution," in mental illness,
higher levels were impaired, so thinking was taken over by lower,
older, and more primitive thought processes. He regarded his method
as "anatomical" and "physiological," in contrast to a psychological
method that "explained" aphasia, for example, by noting that patients
had lost their memory for words. However, he also contrasted this
method with those who looked just at nerve fibers and cells. A crucial
explanatory level was required between cells and behavioral effect,
namely, a level that divided the whole apparatus into units based on
evolutionary and functional considerations (Jackson 1873ff.:3–118,
passim).

This was an exciting time in brain research. For the purpose of
understanding Freud, the most important developments were the
establishment of the neuron doctrine, the possibility of a unified theory of reflex action for all neural processes, and the connection between pleasure and pain, which had often been regarded as regulating
behavior, and conditions of equilibrium and disequilibrium in the
nervous system. As we will see in chapter 4, the issue of localization
and the evolutionary approach to the components of the brain were
also decisive influences on the development of psychoanalysis.

Evolutionary Biology
The nineteenth century was "Darwin's century," at least in terms of
influence. That influence was so pervasive across the life sciences that
it became "invisible," as Frank Sulloway puts it. Like all educated

people, Freud not only read Darwin firsthand, but also encountered his ideas in innumerable secondary sources, very often without explicit citation (Sulloway 1979:238–39). I note just five key contributions: sexual selection, instincts, Lamarckian inheritance, the biogenetic law, and the "primal horde."

Sex was at the center of Darwin's story of the origin of species (Sulloway 1979:252ff.). A novel physical structure would have no effect on the course of evolution if its possessors failed to reproduce themselves. Hence, Darwin devoted much of *The Descent of Man and Selection in Relation to Sex* to discussing unusual varieties of plumage and antlers designed to win the battle to reproduce (Darwin 1874). Many of these structures, he noted, weakened the organism's capacity to survive. Further, he concluded that many mental qualities, from courage and perseverance to imagination and reason, were probably partly the result of sexual selection (Darwin 1874:559). Darwin's work also made so-called sexual perversions an important scientific subject: Given that behaviors such as exclusive homosexuality thwarted reproduction, how could they have been introduced or maintained in the human population?

It did not require Darwin's insight to see that people are driven by self-preservative and sexual urges. However, his theory put common wisdom on a firm scientific foundation (Sulloway 1979:252). Darwin never claimed that the instincts to survive and reproduce were the primary determinants of animal behavior, but he supplied premises from which others drew this conclusion: Instincts impel instinctive actions, that is, actions which people would require experience to perform, but which can be performed by animals without prior experience, and which many individuals perform in much the same way (Darwin 1859:207). Some instincts are stronger than others (Darwin 1874:104). Human beings have fewer instincts than other animals, but they do share some, such as self-preservation, sexual love, love of the mother for newborns, and so forth (Darwin 1874:64). Many structures and instincts must have evolved through sexual selection (Darwin 1874:206). It is untenable to claim that social instincts have greater strength than those of self-preservation, hunger, lust, or vengeance (Darwin 1874:108). Natural and sexual selection account for the evolution of the vast majority of characteristics of animal species. Taken together, these claims amount to the position that there are sexual and self-preservative instincts, which are likely to be stronger than other instincts, and that, other things being equal, evolution would have favored creatures with stronger rather than weaker sexual and self-preservative instincts.

Darwin believed that most instincts evolved through natural selection, by accidental variations that produced slight deviations in bodily structures that could be passed on to progeny. But he did allow that some instincts could be acquired by habits formed in one generation and transmitted to the next (Darwin 1859:209). More generally, he allowed a limited role to a process normally associated with his alleged rival, Lamarck: the inheritance of acquired characteristics. This is evident in his speculative account of blushing, which I will summarize rather than cite in full.

> 1. Blushing cannot be produced by physical stimuli. It is involuntary and does not require experience, since Laura Bridgman, blind and deaf since birth, blushes. Moreover, it is restricted to human beings and women blush much more than men. Blushing generally only affects the face, ears, and neck, although some blush down as far as their collarbones or even farther.
> 2. How might this odd phenomenon have come about? Suppose that, when attention is paid to any part of the body, it interferes with the tonic contraction of the small arteries of that part, which therefore fill with blood. The face is considered the seat of expression and of beauty; therefore, it will have been the subject of self-attention more than any other bodily part. Further, whenever we feel others are deprecating us, our attention is directed toward our faces. Thus, the face will be subject to more self-attention than any other bodily part and, over generations, its capillary vessels will become very susceptible to being affected by attention. Now, we identify with our faces and with our moral character, so these two become associated with each other. Hence, when our moral character is somehow impugned, our attention is directed toward our faces and, since facial capillaries are very easily filled with blood, we blush. (see Darwin 1872:309–46)

Allegedly, attention paid to the face during a person's lifetime causes the facial capillaries to become used to filling with blood. This acquired characteristic is then passed on and strengthened through succeeding generations, accounting for its current force. Although he always maintained that natural and sexual selection played a much larger role in evolution, Darwin's Lamarckianism was pervasive. Sulloway cites a particularly informative example from the baby biography of Darwin's son William. When Darwin took William to the London Zoo, he was surprised by his son's fear of large and exotic animals. He offered the following conjecture:

May we not suspect that the vague but very real fears of child-hood, which are quite independent of experience, are the inherited effects of real dangers and abject superstitions during ancient savage times? It is quite conformable to what we know of the transmission of formerly well-developed characteristics, that they should appear at an early period of life [of descendants], and afterwards disappear. (cited in Sulloway 1979:245)

This passage invokes another important evolutionary thesis, one that was given its most explicit formulation by Freud's countryman, Ernst Haeckel. According to the biogenic law, "ontogeny is the short and rapid repetition of phylogeny" (cited in Sulloway 1979:199). Thus, in the case of humans, the development from fetus to adulthood recapitulates the history of the species. Darwin was not himself a recapitulationist, although, as this passage indicates, he thought the position was reasonable and perhaps even true. Nevertheless, recapitulationism became a central feature of the study of evolution, because it was the standard technique for reconstructing evolutionary histories. Earlier forms of animal lineages were inferred from the development of contemporary animals (Nordenskiöld 1917:36; Gould 1977:70–72). Frank Sulloway argues in great detail that Freud's acceptance of the biogenetic law is the least recognized biological influence on psychoanalysis (Sulloway 1979:199, 259). Later, we will see that his unswerving reliance on recapitulationism was also his most costly mistake in interdisciplinary reasoning.

In discussing sexual selection in humans, Darwin took up a popular nineteenth-century question: What was the origin of that most basic and universal social tie, marriage (Darwin 1874)? Sir John Lubbock, among others, had maintained that early humans lived in what he delicately called "communal marriages." Lubbock did not believe that primeval promiscuity was absolute, however; rather, he believed that men and women probably entered into temporary unions (Darwin 1874:582–84). Total promiscuity would prevent the operation of sexual selection. Darwin followed Lubbock up to a point, but then added his own contribution. Not surprisingly, he reasoned that, in hypothesizing about the hominid ancestors of contemporary humans, it was useful to consider the behaviors of contemporary great apes. These offered two models, monogamy and polygamy. Most commonly, great apes are found in living arrangements where one male dominates several females. Young males are expelled from the troop as they grow up, until finally the dominant male becomes too feeble to defend his rights and is overthrown by a victorious younger male. Had early hominids lived in such "primal hordes," they would have been forced into widespread exogamy—the men of one tribe taking wives from a different tribe—thereby adding to the fitness of the group by preventing inbreeding.

In apes, sexual jealousy was, Darwin believed, the key factor in eliminating promiscuity in favor of monogamous or polygamous unions. He inferred that the same would be true in early humans. Thus, complete promiscuity was unlikely and sexual selection could operate and so favor, he presumed, strong men and attractive women. If jealousy led early humans to monogamy, then the development of the institution of marriage would not be very surprising. However, polygamy may have been the norm and, having defended the probable influence of sexual selection, Darwin did not try to speculate about how polygamy might have led to monogamous marriage (Darwin 1874:582–86).

Psychology and Psychiatry
The prevailing outlook in psychology during the last third of the nineteenth century was hardly new and indicated little progress since Hume and Hartley. Psychology was largely associationist. For any mental accomplishment, the default assumption was that it was the result of a previous association of conscious ideas. The structure of mental processes, how one idea led to another, was explained by assuming that an association had been produced between them, either by their intrinsic similarity or contrast or, more often, by their having been experienced together (or frequently experienced together, or experienced together in the presence of pleasure or pain). Franz Joseph Gall's use of bumps on the head to determine the strength of mental powers had made faculty psychology, already in decline, unacceptable in scientific circles. Nevertheless, as Wundt observed, important work was being done on the localization of functions, and the results resembled some claims of phrenology (Wundt 1902:292–93).

To avoid the appearance of faculty psychology, Gall's terminology of "mental organs" was replaced by "centers." Thus, the discoveries of Broca and Wernicke, for example, could be described in terms of finding centers or areas (but not organs) that subserved different aspects of speech. By whatever name, associationism was accompanied by a serious effort to decompose mental activities into separable functional units. In criticizing the influence of Flourens's doctrine of functional equivalence, Wundt explained why distinguishing functions was inevitable.

> Moreover, it remains unclear what significance is supposed to inhere in the individual parts which anatomical dissections of the

hemispheres have distinguished, if these have about the same level of homogeneity in functional connection as the liver. Undoubtedly, this [problem] induces the anatomists to return to letting themselves be involved in speculating over the significance of divisions of the brain, mostly to a representation of the location of mental capacities. (Wundt 1874:234; my translation)

Writing nearly thirty years later, Wundt observed that Flourens's position had fallen into disrepute because "this principle of *functional interaction* [distinguishing the functional units so that the whole capacity might be explained in terms of their interaction] has come to be our most valuable guide in the psychophysical analysis of the cerebral functions" (Wundt 1902:293). After criticizing the new "antiphrenologists" for crude abrogation experiments, he laid out the proper means of proceeding.

> What we rather need is, evidently, an *analysis of the individual central functions*, in the light of observations of pathological defects, carefully collected and compared. Hence instead of asking: What are the consequences of the lack of a given cortical area, and what functions are accordingly to be ascribed to it? we must now raise the question: What central changes do we find, when a given function (language, the act of vision, etc.) is deranged, and what is the nature of the parallelism between the functional and anatomical disturbances? (Wundt 1902:293)

Psychiatry also encompassed several distinct and seemingly incompatible currents. Meynert, Wernicke, and many others followed Wilhelm Griesinger's dictum that mental diseases were brain diseases. Although this approach led to some solid results, it also encouraged a speculative physiologizing that came to be stigmatized as *"Hirnmythologie"* ("brain mythology") (Ellenberger 1970:284). Emil Kraepelin opposed this attitude, arguing that, in addition to anatomy and physiology, information from experimental psychology and life histories should be used in understanding mental illness (Ellenberger 1970:284–85). Further, as Pierre Janet observed, for a number of diseases, including hysteria and so-called neurasthenia, there was no evidence of neurological abnormality (Ellenberger 1970:372–75).

In his impressive study of early dynamic psychiatry—psychiatry involving unconscious forces—Henri Ellenberger captures the practice in terms of five parameters. The main approach was through hypnotism, which had been made passably respectable by the work of Hippolyte Bernheim and Jean-Martin Charcot. Somnambulism, lethargy, catalepsy, and later hysteria were the presenting clinical syndromes.

Most theories of these conditions involved a new model of the mind, one that included both conscious and unconscious elements. The pathogen was originally taken to be an unknown fluid; later it was thought to be mental energy. Standard therapies included hypnotism and suggestion and were believed to require a special rapport between therapist and patient (Ellenberger 1970:111–19).

For reasons that are still quite mysterious, hysterical symptoms, from blindness to various paralyses and amnesias, were extremely common at this time, even though they have all but disappeared today. The first systematic study of hysteria was carried out by Pierre Briquet in 1859. Briquet discovered a high degree of heritability, with 25 percent of the daughters of hysterics themselves developing the disorder. Although the classical connection between hysteria and the womb was no longer at issue, he did find that female hysterics outnumbered males by a ratio of twenty to one. He also tested the common wisdom that hysteria was a result of erotic frustration, by comparing the percentages of afflicted nuns and prostitutes. Since hysteria was more common in the latter group, he concluded, perhaps hastily, that frustration was not the cause. On balance, he took hysteria to be the effect of violent emotions upon people predisposed to the disease (Ellenberger 1970:142).

Pierre Janet, whom Ernest Jones dismissed in his official biography as a theorist "erroneously regarded" as Freud's precursor (Jones 1961:36–37), offered a more detailed hypothesis. Janet took hysterical pathogens to be subconscious fixed ideas. These were both the cause and the effect of mental weakness that led to the narrowing or splitting of consciousness characteristic of hysterics. Janet distinguished psychological force, which he regarded as a quantity that could exist in both latent and manifest states, from psychical tension (a somewhat confusing choice of terms), which he described as the capacity to use psychical energy. This capacity became greater, the greater the individual's ability to integrate mental operations and deal with reality. Although he presented these forces in psychological terms, he did not doubt that they were physiological and could someday be measured (Ellenberger 1970:361, 376, 377–82).

The psychiatry of this period was populated by famous patients, such as Marie, who was apparently cured by uncovering and removing fixed ideas acquired from earlier traumas, and Marcelle, whose mind was much clearer after crises brought on by hypnosis and "automatic" writing. Janet urged caution about hypnosis and exemplary patients: Under hypnosis, the unconscious may disclose itself, but subjects also seem to play roles to please their therapists (Ellenberger 1970:358–80).

Late nineteenth-century trends in psychology and psychiatry exercised a profound influence on the working assumptions of psychoanalysis. Like most before and after him, Freud never doubted the truth of associationism. He also assumed that the scientific approach to the mental apparatus was to see it as composed of functional units that had been added through time by evolutionary forces. Although he rejected the brain disease model of many mental illnesses, on the standard grounds of the absence of postmortem damage, he embraced the ideas of unconscious mental elements and sexual etiologies as no one else has, before or since.

Sexology

During the 1880s, 1890s, and first decades of the twentieth century, sex was a subject of serious and intense investigation.[4] Partly because sex was so important to evolution and partly because homosexuality was treated so harshly in the courts, a number of dedicated scientists tried to fathom the varieties and foundations of sexuality. In an age when these topics are often relegated to journalism, it may be hard to see how such work could be scientific, but sexologists formulated and tested reasonably clear hypotheses, devised more adequate theories to cope with richer data, and in time achieved a fair amount of consensus.

The debate centered on whether the "perversions" were innate or acquired.[5] Richard Krafft-Ebing proposed a theory of "neuropsychopathic degeneration," which took illness to result when a congenitally weak nervous system encountered the strain of civilized life. He was opposed by association psychologists who put the blame on accidental life experiences. However, early hypotheses about familial degeneration and boarding school seductions gave way to more subtle accounts. The recognition of cases of physical hermaphroditism and the bisexuality of young embryos, along with the existence of vestigial male sexual characteristics in women and vice versa, led to the view that the true origin of homosexuality lay in an underlying bisexual nature. On this account, monosexuality developed from the original bisexual state, with homosexuality resulting from a "failure" to follow normal development. Although these "failures" were largely determined by constitutional factors, life experiences could affect the form "perversions" took.

Observation of "civilized" and "primitive" children produced the complementary theory that sexual instincts were polymorphous—expressed in many different forms—in immature humans (Sulloway 1979:316–17). Havelock Ellis's extensive studies included the hypothesis that childhood sexuality was often anal or oral in character. In particular, he noted similarities between nursing infants and couples engaged in intercourse (Sulloway 1979:305–6). Polymorphous sexuality in children, perversions such as sadism and masochism, and a commitment to the biogenetic law suggested a model of "component" instincts. Since "primitive" animals sometimes mix sex and cannibalism, for example, some remnants of a cannibalistic sexuality will be present in immature "higher" animals. Again, "normal" sexuality was the result of these various components being overcome or synthesized in the course of development (Sulloway 1979:297, 298, 299–304). Albert Moll refined the two-stage account originally proposed by Max Dessoir. Dessoir's first undifferentiated (and so apparently perverse) stage should be extended back to early childhood; at puberty, these "perverse" tendencies usually faded or blended into "normal" heterosexual behavior (Sulloway 1979:303–4).

As Sulloway observes, a careful look at Freud's predecessors and contemporaries in sexology is extremely revealing. All of the sexual issues with which psychoanalysis is associated, including infantile sexuality, repression, regression, and psychosexual development, were explored in detail by others; all the concepts it used to analyze and explain those issues, such as libido, component instincts, and erotogenic zones, were introduced by others and enjoyed fairly common usage as Freud was developing his own views (Sulloway 1979:277–78).

Evolutionary Anthropology

Anthropology, in the broad sense, was the intellectual problem of the 1860s. Contemporary discoveries in prehistoric archaeology and comparative philology, the sociological and historical theorizing of Comte and Buckle, studies in comparative mythology, ethnology, and the physical types of mankind, and, most critically, the work of Darwin, "focused a whole range of developing knowledge in the biological and historical sciences on the question of the origin and antiquity of mankind and of human civilization" (Stocking 1968:74). Writing in 1891, Tylor gave the working assumption in its negative version: "To expect to look modern life in the face and comprehend it by mere inspection, is a philosophy whose weakness can easily be tested" (Tylor 1891:19). Positively, the aims were to uncover laws governing the development of culture and of the human intellect, by comparing civilization at different places and stages.

Three divisive issues will give a sense of this discipline. One major controversy concerned the stem of contemporary humans. Did all people come from a common ancestral group, as claimed by the monogenists, or were there originally several, unequal races that gave rise to the current human population (polygenism)? Second, was human history a tale of progress, with contemporary civilization naturally evolving from lower forms, or one of degeneration, as maintained by a number of prominent clerics?

Darwin's work gave comfort to the monogenists, and Buckle, Tylor, and Adolf Bastian all assumed the psychical unity of mankind (Tylor 1891:1; Stocking 1968:74–76; Boas 1940:270). Given their methodology, they had no option. For the only way to reconstruct prehistorical stages of civilization was to assume constant psychological laws across time. These men were also ardent progressivists. The current level of civilization, including religion and morality, had evolved naturally from more primitive conditions. To prove this, numerous potential genealogies of morals were advanced, ranging from Darwin's gentle story of paternal and filial affection developing into broader feelings to Nietzsche's vision of cowards and curs inflicting their own modus vivendi on their betters (Darwin 1874:95; Nietzsche 1887). Many, including Tylor, Lubbock, and Wundt, also attempted to explain how even the oddest features of religion might have arisen naturally from primitive practices.

The third controversy was slightly less grand, more a matter of epistemological than metaphysical differences. Could evolutionary anthropology inform the study of comparative mythology and, if so, how? F. Max Müller represented the old school: Comparative mythology was founded on a comparison of names and, hence, on the very solid achievements of comparative philology, which had established, for example, laws governing patterns of change in various sounds (Müller 1897:17). He believed further that mythology was grounded in the physical world and that myths were, in the first place, attempts to understand the physical world (Müller 1897:51). Given these two real anchors, he felt that comparative mythology could be a science, where scholars could resolve disagreements through further research into etymologies and physical conditions. As Müller saw it, his opponents were little better than journalists. Lacking the necessary languages to make detailed studies, Herbert Spencer, Andrew Lang, and their followers mainly studied travelers' accounts of contemporary "savages" and developed general categories, such as animism and totemism, in order to grasp the psychological underpinnings of various myths [Müller 1897:17–18]. Müller did not think mythology could be pushed this hard. Although there might be interesting psychological depths below myths, he did not see how the techniques of comparative mythology could uncover them: "When we have traced the name of Zeus back to the Sanskrit Dyaus, the bright sky . . . we have reached . . . a stratum below which there is nothing to interest the student of mythology" (Müller 1897:23). "We . . . try to trace [my-thology] back to its origin, but we never say that this origin carries us down to the beginning of the world or to the seventh day of creation" (Müller 1897:13; general discussion from 1–102, passim). Müller lost this fight. Interpretations of myths that depended on claims about the psychology of "primitive" peoples, including Freud's, largely pushed aside the earlier linguistically based tradition, although there were some attempts at integrating the two approaches.

Sociology

Like anthropology, nineteenth-century sociology—or, better, proto-sociology—was evolutionary. Its typical questions concerned how par-ticular social institutions evolved. Many followed Mill in taking social phenomena to be nothing over and above the phenomena of human thought, feeling, and action (Mill 1843:572). Further, such major think-ers as Darwin and William James took human will and reason to be a development from instincts and habits (Fletcher 1971, vol. 2:84–105; Darwin 1874:604–5). When both positions were held together, as they frequently were, it appeared possible to explain social institutions by showing how they evolved from our basic biological endowment.

A famous example was Edward Westermarck's hypothesis about incest avoidance. Besides explaining the universal taboo against sexual contact between siblings, this hypothesis also promised to explain the ancient practice of exogamy, marrying outside one's own tribe. Ac-cording to Westermarck, in the course of normal human development, people acquired a disposition against having sexual relations with those with whom they were reared. Over generations, this acquired trait was reinforced and eventually became instinctual, so that even without any direct experience of incest, people were innately repulsed by the thought of sex between individuals brought up in the same household. This innate and universal abhorrence of incest was then expressed as a social taboo (*Totem and Taboo*, 1913, S.E. XIII:122). Thus, contrary to what one might have thought, humans were not appalled by incest because there are strong social sanctions against it; there are strong social sanctions against incest, because humans are appalled by it. In the same vein, Westermarck argued that "marriage is rooted in the family rather than the family in marriage"; that is, the institution of marriage did not produce a close bond between a man, a woman, and their offspring, but was a reflection of that preexisting instinctual bond (Fletcher 1971, vol. 2:99). Freud joined the chorus of Wester-marck's critics, noting, among other points, the implausibility of be-lieving that social sanctions would be established if people were innately predisposed against incest (*Totem and Taboo*, 1913, S.E.

XIII:122–23). However, this controversy was firmly within the tradition. Freud did not doubt the soundness of Westermarck's approach, but thought that he had misinterpreted the evidence: Strong social taboos suggest, on the contrary, that people are strongly predisposed *toward* incest.

As in anthropology, the primary method of sociology was comparative. Research began by classifying different societies, by their sanctions and religious rituals, for example. Then the institutions of different societies were compared, in order to find universal practices. Once these were found, the problem was to explain why such practices were universal, by showing how they evolved from earlier stages and, possibly, from biological factors. Many accepted Mill's view that if a practice that rested on biology and psychology was also found, by comparative study, to be universal, then, by the agreement of both processes, the evidence could be raised to the level of proof and the generalization to a scientific law (Fletcher 1971, vol. 2:99; Mill 1843:594–606). During the 1890s Emile Durkheim began formulating a very different conception of sociology, which separated biology and psychology from sociology (Durkheim 1895:135 and passim). Freud referred to Durkheim's work several times, but never to his revolutionary theoretical ideas, which did not attract much international attention until the mid-teens and did not become dominant until the thirties.

Philology
I end this selective overview of the disciplines with a brief consideration of philology. Appeals to philology did not form a large part of Freud's case for any theses of psychoanalysis. Nevertheless, philology was important in the development of his ideas for two reasons. First, language is a unique human accomplishment, and it was not unreasonable to think that the history of linguistic development might furnish important clues to the development of human mentality. Further, comparative linguistics was the most obviously scientific of the social sciences (Müller 1861:15–20; Pedersen 1962 302–3; Antilla 1972:25).

Like other disciplines, philology was primarily comparative and historical. The great discovery of the kinship between Sanskrit and Greek and Latin led to a number of important studies of the precise relationship among Indo-European languages (Robins 1968:149). August Schleicher (1821–68) published a compendium of this work in which he brought the various discoveries together in a genealogical tree illustrating the relations between the parent languages and the known Indo-European languages (Robins 1968:178). This burst of philological activity also led to the adoption of important methodological principles, including "Grimm's law": If between two languages, there is agreement in forms of indispensable words, such that even rules for altering letters can be predicted one from the other, then there is a basic relationship between these languages (cited in Robins 1968:171). Since so many languages were related, historical linguistics could acquire evidence for laws governing changes of word forms and make inductive predictions about as yet unstudied cases (Antilla 1972:25).

Toward the end of the century, the Neogrammarians argued that, within the same dialect, all sound changes took place according to exceptionless laws (Robins 1968:183). Perhaps the strongest methodological principle was "Verner's law": Apparent exceptions to laws of sound change are themselves lawful (Robins 1968:184). The Neogrammarians were opposed by scholars who thought that each word had a history that was the key to its meaning. To take an example that will be comprehensible to current readers, the German word *"beten"* (to pray), and the English word "bead" are quite similar. This linguistic fact is mysterious until one recalls the historical fact that people often kept track of prayers with beads (Antilla 1972:137). Notice, however, that these positions were not really incompatible. It would be entirely reasonable to think that both approaches could be used together, universal laws governing changes in word forms augmented by histories of specific words. When these two methods were put together, the promise of this social science appeared enormous: At least in theory, it seemed possible to explain all the apparently meaningless quirks of the most unique product of human minds, by tracing their development from earlier forms and practices.

Recapitulation

The goal of this chapter has been to present important pieces of theoretical background to Freud's construction of psychoanalysis. Part of that background included metatheoretic views about the fields capable of contributing to a science of the mind and the possible relations among them. I have also discussed some of the important developments that were part of his general intellectual milieu and some of the specific results that he presupposed or explicitly credited in his own work. Given the span of years and the number of different areas, this has involved a substantial amount of diverse material. Still, I think the essential contributions can be reduced to twelve: the neuron and reflex doctrines from physiology and Fechner's hypothesis of the link between neural equilibrium and pleasure and pain, associationism and the idea of evolutionary-functional units from psychology, instincts and recapitulationism from evolutionary biology, the comparative/historical approach from anthropology and sociology, the accessibility of ancient languages from philology, the thoroughgoing historicism of the social sciences generally and—most importantly—unconscious ideas from psychiatry and the pivotal role of sex in human life, from evolutionary biology, psychiatry, sexology, and sociology.

Chapter 3

Metapsychology: How to Construct Psychoanalysis

What Is Freud's Metapsychology?

Chapter 2 highlighted various theorists' reflections about the different fields that study mental phenomena and how they fit together. In this chapter, I describe Freud's understanding of the conditions that must be met for an account of mental life to be scientifically adequate. Following this abstract account, the next two chapters present the realization of his metatheoretic vision in the construction of psychoanalysis. Chapter 4 traces the development of his major doctrines, illustrating their dependence on his metatheoretic principles and on the scientific results just canvassed. In chapter 5, I try to confirm my interpretation of Freud's approach to theory construction and its imprint on his substantive views by showing how it enables us to make sense of some quite puzzling features of *The Interpretation of Dreams*.

Freud's theoretical works contain a number of discussions of what psychological explanations should look like, but none seems clearer than this passage from his 1915 paper, "The Unconscious."

> It will not be unreasonable to give a special name to this whole way of regarding our subject-matter, for it is the consummation of psycho-analytic research. I propose that when we have succeeded in describing a psychical process in its dynamic, topographical and economic aspects, we should speak of it as a *metapsychological* presentation. We must say at once that in the present state of our knowledge there are only a few points at which we shall succeed in this. (S.E. XIV:181)

This passage makes three points: A "metapsychological presentation" is the goal, or more poetically, "consummation" of psychoanalytic research; a metapsychological presentation consists in describing psychical phenomena according to three aspects, the dynamic, the topographic, and the economic; and, so far, psychoanalysis has attained this ideal for only a few phenomena and, even there, only partially.

Despite the centrality that Freud assigned metapsychology in this passage, his heirs try to disown it. *The Language of Psycho-Analysis*, published by the London Institute of Psycho-Analysis, offers the following definition:

> Metapsychology constructs an ensemble of conceptual models which are more or less far removed from empirical reality. Examples are the fiction of a psychical apparatus divided up into agencies, the theory of instincts, the hypothetical process of repression, and so on. (Laplanche and Pontalis 1973:249–50)

Not content with linking metapsychology with fictions and hypothetical processes, more or less far removed from reality, the authors continue by making an analogy between metapsychology and metaphysics. According to this official portrait, metapsychology includes the neurophysiological, biological, and, more generally, speculative parts of psychoanalysis that rest on discredited nineteenth-century science—that is, most of the parts contemporary analysts feel uncomfortable defending.

A number of contemporary Freudians have adopted what amounts to a two-pronged strategy for dealing with this material. First, relegate it to metapsychology and, then, sharply distinguish metapsychology from psychoanalysis proper: the "clinical" theory. George Klein, who was a pioneer in the effort to save the clinical theory from metapsychology, characterizes the latter as follows:

> This energic conception [the drive-discharge theory] is connected with Freud's fundamental belief upon which his entire metapsychology was constructed: that the source of all activity in the organism, perhaps even characterizing it as "living" altogether, is its tendency to deal with the energic influxes of "stimuli," to discharge them, to reduce the tensions produced by their energic quantity. This was the all-embracing precept that included the special theory of sexuality. It was designed to serve Freud's conception of his own scientific objectives of "explanation," which have become the conventions of psychoanalytic metapsychological theorizing. Through the concepts of metapsychology, developed from this basic precept, he sought to create interfaces with other disciplines, particularly with physiology, and to relate his conceptions of human psychology to the theory of evolution. (Klein 1976:15–16)

I agree with Klein on two points: Metapsychology reflected Freud's conception of how to construct a science of the mind, and this involved relating psychology to at least physiology and evolutionary biology.

His objection is that, for dubious reasons having little to do with psychoanalysis itself, Freud appended an implausible, theoretical superstructure to the basic claims of psychoanalysis. This evaluation is, I will argue, wrong on two crucial counts. First, Klein assumes, more or less without argument, that Freud's principles for theory construction were mistaken. In stark contrast, I will argue that, when we take a careful look at these principles, they turn out to be eminently defensible and very like the canons guiding contemporary interdisciplinary research in cognitive science. Further, Klein's criticism reflects the hope that the metapsychology is reasonably separable from the clinical theory. As already noted, however, metapsychology was supposed to be the culmination of psychoanalysis and, as Klein himself observes, Freud never separated metapsychology and the clinical theory (Klein 1976:16). Although it is possible to tease some of Freud's claims apart from others, here and in the next two chapters, I will offer an extended argument for the view that metapsychology was so influential in shaping the development and details of psychoanalysis that trying to isolate it both distorts the historical record and leaves the clinical theory without an adequate theoretical foundation. For the most distinctive feature of Freud's work was its grand sweep, its attempt to draw on all the relevant sciences to construct a complete theory of mental life, including its primeval origins, organic foundation, and proximate psychical causes.

Although Grünbaum is generally critical of efforts to divorce Freud's work from its "scientistic" methodological principles, he accepts the official account of metapsychology. Grünbaum concedes that Freud's early neurobiological theories of mental functioning played a "heuristic" role in the development of psychoanalysis. He maintains that by 1896, however, "Freud had despaired of foreseeably *reducing* the clinical theory *globally* to neurobiology" (Grünbaum 1984:3). He continues by citing Freud's description of metapsychology as a "speculative superstructure . . . that can be abandoned or changed without loss" in order to deny the suggestion that Freud regarded metapsychology as making any essential contribution to the support of his mature clinical theories (Grünbaum 1984:4–5). In Grünbaum's history, metapsychology offered early inspiration, but Freud did not see his clinical doctrines as deriving support from above, from theoretical considerations, but believed instead that they rested on "the evidence of the couch."

If the official story is right and metapsychology was a speculative appendage that either was or could have been discarded, then Grünbaum's critique of Freud is incredibly direct and devastating. Freud attempted to defend an elaborate theory of mental functioning solely on the basis of clinical evidence: If a theory was used in an analysis that (apparently) cured the patient, then that confirmed the theory. With impeccable logic, Grünbaum argues that real or putative cures cannot be used as evidence in the absence of some means of ruling out suggestion or the placebo effect as agents of the cure. Thus, there is not now—and there never has been—any real evidence for Freud's claims.

Grünbaum does not adopt this view of metapsychology merely because if furthers his project, however. He cites texts that appear to provide unequivocal evidence for the contention that Freud did not regard metapsychology as essential to psychoanalysis.

> Such ideas as these are part of a speculative superstructure of psycho-analysis, any portion of which can be abandoned or changed without loss or regret the moment its inadequacy has been proved. But there is still plenty to be described that lies closer to actual experience. (*An Autobiographical Study*, 1925, S.E. XX:32–33; see also "Psycho-Analysis," 1926, XX:266)

On the other hand, there are texts that run exactly counter to this interpretation, including the passage already cited from "The Unconscious" (1915) and the following:

> In the theory of psycho-analysis we have no hesitation in assuming that the course taken by mental events is automatically regulated by the pleasure principle . . . that is . . . that the course of those events is invariably set in motion by an unpleasurable tension. . . . [Thus] we are introducing an 'economic' factor in addition to the 'topographical' and 'dynamic' ones. . . . (*Beyond the Pleasure Principle*, 1920, S.E. XVIII:7)

In determined opposition to the official view, Frank Sulloway argues that the biological assumptions embedded in Freud's metapsychological claims exerted a constant pressure on the development of psychoanalysis. However, he claims that the influence was thoroughly baneful. Unwilling to give up any claims to originality, Freud denied the biological underpinnings of his theories, thus turning himself into a "crypto-biologist" (Sulloway 1979:esp. 3–5). He constantly made use of biological theories, for both inspiration and collateral support for psychoanalytic claims. This fact was hidden from his students, however, in part because he shredded (as we would now put it) all his notes, manuscripts, diaries, and correspondence, twice—once in 1885 and again in 1907 (Sulloway 1979:7). Freud's intellectual heirs have continued the denial of biological foundations, now with two motivations. Besides the wish to enhance the creative genius of their hero, they are understandably reluctant to take seriously the idea that much of Freudian theory stands—or falls—with nineteenth-century biology.

Sulloway characterizes metapsychology in terms of a number of "fundamental psychophysical hypotheses." First, there is the economic theory (first) offered by Breuer and Freud, a theory that describes hysterical symptoms as having a quota of affect (excitation) that is "converted" into inappropriate somatic channels. Then there is the dynamic theory, which "aims to explain how a pathological 'damming up' of affect can occur within a portion of a mind that is inaccessible to consciousness." Finally, there is a topographic claim, which amounts to the positing of an unconscious portion of the mind (Sulloway 1979:62–64; citation from 63). Like his opponents, Sulloway identifies metapsychology with a collection of outdated quasi-physiological speculations. He differs in maintaining that these assumptions guided Freud throughout his struggle to construct psychoanalytic theory.

Recent interpreters disagree on the extent and the duration of metapsychology's influence on psychoanalysis, but agree on its content. Metapsychology comprises a group of speculative hypotheses grounded in nineteenth-century science. What I will argue is that when the duration dispute is firmly resolved—as it can be—the resolution casts some doubt on the point on which Klein, Grünbaum, and Sulloway all agree: Metapsychology is to be identified with particular theses inspired by then contemporary science.

If, as is obvious from the text, metapsychology amounted to examining mental phenomena in their dynamic, topographic, and economic aspects, then a simple chronological review reveals that Freud never gave up metapsychology. He gave his inchoate psychoanalytic theory an economic, dynamic, and topographic foundation in the *Project for a Scientific Psychology* (1895, S.E. I:283–387); this view was repeated with some alterations in the seventh chapter of *The Interpretation of Dreams* (1900–30, S.E. V:509ff.); he published five papers on metapsychology (1915–17, S.E. XIV); *The Ego and the Id* offered a substantially revised metapsychology (1923, S.E. XIX:19ff.); in an article for the *Encyclopaedia Britannica*, he presented his "depth-psychology" in terms of dynamic, economic, and topographic studies (1926, S.E. XX:264–69); in the final major piece in the *Standard Edition, An Outline of Psycho-Analysis*, he again approached his material from the dynamic, economic, and topographic points of view (1938, S.E. XXIII:144ff.).

If Freud never forswore metapsychology, then how can we make sense of the fact that he announced that it could be abandoned without loss? Further, he actually changed several metapsychological doctrines: The mental topography of "The Unconscious," which posited conscious, unconscious, and preconscious systems of the mind, was supplemented by that of *The Ego and the Id* (1923), with its ego, id, and superego (as *An Outline of Psycho-Analysis*, 1938, S.E. XXIII:157ff.); in *Beyond the Pleasure Principle*, the long-dominant economic principle, the pleasure principle, was suddenly joined by an equally important biological force, the death instinct (1920, S.E. XVIII:34ff.).

We can reconcile these shifts and the texts cited to show that Freud abandoned or put little stock in metapsychology with the endorsements of metapsychology that span more than forty years by a reasonably straightforward interpretive hypothesis: He used "metapsychology" ambiguously to indicate both substantive doctrines and metatheoretic directives for the construction of psychoanalysis. The distinction between doctrine and directive can be seen fairly clearly in other scientific programs. In Newtonian mechanics, for example, substantive claims such as the laws of motion emerged from a program guided by the metatheoretic principle that the behavior of any physical object should be explained by determining the forces operating on it. Evolutionary biology tries to explain the characteristics of organisms on the assumption that all such accounts must involve the modification of features found in ancestral populations.[1] Applying the distinction to the puzzle about metapsychology, what Freud continued to support were the metatheoretic directives embodied in his metapsychology. The ideal of psychoanalysis was always to construct complete theories of mental phenomena that captured their dynamic, economic, and topographic dimensions. By contrast, Freud was willing—at least in theory—to modify or cast aside substantive metapsychological claims such as the pleasure principle and the theory of instincts. Besides resolving textual inconsistencies, this interpretation has a further advantage. It allows us to separate Freud's metatheoretic directives from his substantive theories and so achieve a better understanding of the relation between the two.

The crucial passage from "The Unconscious" where Freud introduced "metapsychology" confirms that he sometimes viewed it as an approach, as a "way of regarding our subject-matter." However, the strongest textual support for this interpretation occurs in *An Autobiographical Study*, in a discussion that also appears to limit the significance of metapsychology.

> Later on I made an attempt to produce a 'Metapsychology'. By this I meant a method of approach according to which every mental process is considered in relation to three co-ordinates, which I described as *dynamic*, *topographical*, and *economic* respectively; and this seemed to me to represent the furthest goal that

psychology could attain. The attempt remained no more than a torso; after writing two or three papers . . . I broke off, wisely perhaps, since the time for theoretical predications of this kind had not yet come. In my latest speculative works I have set about the task of dissecting our mental apparatus on the basis of the analytic view of pathological facts and have divided it into an *ego*, an *id*, and a *super-ego*. (1925, S.E. XX:59; my underscoring)

Given this passage and those already cited to show that Freud never gave up metapsychology, the controversy over duration is hardly surprising. Here, however, Freud's self-reporting was clearly inaccurate. He did not write two or three metapsychological papers, but twelve, according to Ernest Jones (Jones 1961:344). By 1924, when he was composing this essay (Jones 1961:450), five had appeared in print! More importantly, he did not change his approach in *The Ego and the Id*. This work is replete with references to dynamic and economic factors, and to topography—mental systems that are differentiated by principles of functioning, antiquity, and perhaps location (e.g., 1923, S.E. XIX:14, 17, 19, 21–22, etc.). What was new was the proposal of a distinctive mental topography. As noted, the theory of the ego, id, and superego enriched the conscious, unconscious, and preconscious systems. In this passage, Freud may have been (in part) a victim of his own ambiguous terminology. He wanted to emphasize that he had changed his doctrines on the basis of insights gained through analyses. Since some of his old substantive metapsychological doctrines had been altered and he was endorsing the method of analytic observation, he failed to appreciate that his basic metapsychological approach to theorizing about the mental had changed not at all.

At least in theory, Freud's substantive metapsychological doctrines were all dispensable. The position he clung to throughout his long career was metapsychology as a set of directives for constructing a scientific psychology. Because metapsychology has been identified only with specific theses, little effort has been made to understand the approach itself, beyond vague suggestions that it was mechanistic or reductionistic. In particular, interpreters have not adequately considered what Freud meant by the three dimensions. What were these dimensions, and why did he set them up as criteria of adequacy for psychoanalytic explanations?[2]

The Dynamic Dimension

All of Freud's theorizing will be clearer if we note that he restricted the realm of psychoanalytic explanation. Not all facets of mental life could be understood by psychoanalytic means. Psychoanalysis had nothing to say about cognition and almost nothing to contribute to an understanding of perception. The focus of psychoanalytic explanation was behavioral motivation. However, not all behavior, not even all neurotic behavior, was susceptible to distinctively psychoanalytic explanation or remediation. From early in his career, Freud recognized a difference between the psychoneuroses, which he believed he could alleviate, and the "actual neuroses," such as anxiety neurosis. Although anxiety neurosis had a sexual origin, it did not derive from sexual ideas: "[I]t has no psychical mechanism. Its specific cause is the accumulation of sexual tensions, produced by abstinence or by unconsummated sexual excitation" ("Obsessions and Phobias," 1895, S.E. III:81). Thus, even in a case of sexually induced neurotic behavior, there might be no role for psychoanalytic explanation.

Freud seemed to suggest, by contrast, that psychoanalytic explanation was in order when the cause of behavior was an idea. However, this characterization is still too broad. If friends had set out for the Vienna *Staatsoper* because they knowingly enjoyed opera, then it would be unnecessary to appeal to psychoanalysis to explain their actions. The actors themselves were witness to both their behavior and its cause (*An Outline of Psycho-Analysis*, 1938, S.E. XXIII:144). Psychoanalytic explanation was called for only when the determinants of an action were both psychical and unobserved. In terminology that is now familiar, the distinctive and, indeed, definitive range of psychoanalysis was behavior produced through unconscious motivation.

The methodological directive embodied in the dynamic dimension of metapsychology was to find general descriptions of the unobserved, psychical causes of behavior. These would include both ideas and the forces that acted on ideas, such as repression, sublimation, and reaction-formation (the strengthening of an opposing idea). Sometimes these forces were nearly contemporaneous with the event; more often they operated over long stretches of the individual's life. Psychoanalysis, in its dynamic approach, was to provide qualitative accounts of the unconscious determinants of conscious mental life and behavior that would replace inadequate medical or commonsense explanations.

Since this interpretation differs sharply from the standard view, which lumps the dynamic aspect together with the rest of metapsychology as some type of quasi-physiological thesis, I offer considerable textual support. In *The Ego and the Id*, Freud wrote:

> But we have arrived at the term or concept unconscious along another path, by considering certain experience in which mental *dynamics* play a part. We have found—that is we have been obliged

to assume—that very powerful mental processes or ideas exist (and here a quantitative or *economic* factor comes into question for the first time) which can produce all the effects in mental life that ordinary ideas do . . . though they do not themselves become conscious. (1923, S.E. XIX:14)

That is, the subject matter of mental dynamics were unconscious ideas and processes that have effects on human action. The relation between dynamics and the economic factor alluded to was clarified in the *Introductory Lectures on Psycho-Analysis.*

I have introduced a fresh factor into the structure of the aetiological chain—namely the quantity, the magnitude, of the energies concerned. We have still to take this factor into account everywhere. A purely qualitative analysis of the aetiological determinants is not good enough. Or, to put it another way, a merely *dynamic* view of these mental processes is insufficient; an *economic* line of approach is also needed. (1917, S.E. XVI:374)

That is, the dynamic dimension was qualitative as opposed to quantitative. Passages from *The Question of Lay Analysis* and *Psycho-Analysis* clarify the need for these forces and give some indications of their nature.

[F]or that purpose we must study our ego and our id from a fresh angle, from the *dynamic* one—that is to say, having regard to the forces at work in them and between them. Hitherto we have been content with a *description* of the mental apparatus. (1926, S.E. XX:200)

From the first of these standpoints the *dynamic* one, psycho-analysis derives all mental processes . . . from the interplay of forces, which assist or inhibit one another, combine with one another, enter into comprises with one another, etc. All of these forces are originally in the nature of *instincts;* thus they have an organic origin. (1925, S.E. XX:265)

Dynamics concerned the forces that operated within and between systems of the mind, and these forces derived from instincts. Again, the dynamic point of view was concerned with mental forces. Freud's further characterization embodied two substantive hypotheses: Since there were different systems of the mind, there must be two kinds of forces, those that operated within systems and those that operated between them, and all mental forces originated in biological instincts.

Two key points emerge from these explicit discussions of mental dynamics. First, this aspect was intimately connected with the other two. The dynamic point of view provided a qualitative description of mental forces, but forces are measurable, so there must be some quantitative or economic aspect to them. Given a mental topography that posited distinct mental systems, dynamics must include a description of intersystemic forces. Freud's second point was that, despite these connections, the three aspects were different. In the citation from the *Introductory Lectures*, he clarified the dynamic and economic aspects by contrasting them. Similarly, the passage from *Lay Analysis* introduced the dynamic aspect by contrast with the topographic, which described the different subsystems within the mental apparatus.[3]

Since the official view is so widely held, I offer two further, systematic textual points in support of interpreting the dynamic dimension as seeking general but qualitative descriptions of the unconscious ideas and forces that determine mental life. This reading is strongly confirmed by the fact that Freud characterized the psychoanalytic conception of the unconscious as "dynamic," in contrast to the usual "descriptive" sense of the term. As a description, to say that an idea was "unconscious" was simply to say that it was not (presently) an item of conscious awareness. By contrast, the dynamic, psychoanalytic sense of "unconscious" signified both that an idea was not present to awareness, because it was actively repressed (by some force or other), and that it was nevertheless an active force in the determination of behavior ("A Note on the Unconscious in Psycho-Analysis," 1912, S.E. XII:261; "The Unconscious," 1915, XIV:173; *Beyond the Pleasure Principle*, 1920, XVIII:19–20; *The Ego and the Id*, 1923, XIX:13–15). Presumably Freud used the same word—"dynamic"—to describe his most important theoretical posit, the unconscious, and a central goal of psychoanalytic theorizing, because he saw an intimate relation between the two.

My second global textual point is that Freud did not always make explicit reference to the dynamic approach. Rather, he would present a prototypical Freudian account of the forces involved in, for example, melancholia (such as regression, identification, and sadism) and then note that he had not yet offered anything in terms of an economic or topographic account ("Mourning and Melancholia," 1917, S.E. XIV:255 and 255, n. 1; see also "The Unconscious," 1915, XIV:166–73). Given this practice, it seems reasonable to assume that he regarded his discussion of the forces acting on unconscious ideas as already providing the dynamic account.

On my reading, the dynamic dimension of metapsychology and the dynamic unconscious were intimately related: The ideal of dynamic metapsychology was to provide general, qualitative descriptions of the ideas and forces that constituted the dynamic unconscious. These descriptions were the potentially modifiable doctrines of substantive dynamic metapsychology. Although Freud was a master of the telling anecdote, even the case histories were not merely anecdotal. They were potential contributions to mental science, because beyond specific etiologies for specific symptoms, they offered general descriptions of the unconscious determinants of neurotic behavior and of their development.

Where did the metapsychological theorizing begin? With the force of repression, the system Unconscious, the claim that repressed ideas were sexual, the theory that the strongest determinants of neuroses were repressed *childhood* sexual ideas, or the hypothesis that all dynamic forces were instinctual? Although these claims may have been increasingly speculative, all were inspired by the same metatheoretic directive, and there is no obvious place to draw a line. Freud's own discussions reveal that clinical relevance provided no line of demarcation. In presenting clinical material, he constantly adverted to repression, reaction-formation, and the like, and even to quantitative factors to explain the causes of illness and the outcome of treatment. Freudians have tried to dismiss dynamic metapsychology because of its association with the unpopular topographic and economic dimensions. But this cannot be done. Far from being dispensable to the therapist, Freud's many dynamic hypotheses provided the basic psychoanalytic explanation of symptoms. Further, although particular dynamic hypotheses might be altered, the dynamic approach could be relinquished only at the price of giving up the science of psychoanalysis. Unconscious ideas were the raison d'être for psychoanalysis, and both science and therapy required general, qualitative descriptions of the forces that shaped them.

Mental Topography

My interpretations of the topographic and the economic parts of metapsychology are far less controversial, so I offer less textual defense. In writings separated by a quarter of a century, Freud presented the topographic approach through the same simile, that of a "psychical locality."

> I shall entirely disregard the fact that the mental apparatus with which we are here concerned is also known to us in the form of an anatomical preparation, and I shall carefully avoid the temptation to determine psychical locality in any anatomical fashion. I shall remain on psychological ground, and I propose simply to

follow the suggestion that we should picture the instrument which carries out our mental functions as resembling a compound microscope . . . or something of the kind. On that basis, psychical locality will correspond to a point inside the apparatus at which one of the preliminary states of an image comes into being. . . . [Thus we] attempt to make the complications of mental function-ing intelligible by dissecting the function and assigning its differ-ent constituents to different component parts of the apparatus. (*The Interpretation of Dreams*, 1900 S.E. V:536; see also "Psycho-Analysis," 1926, XX:266; my underscoring)

Even without the analogy, Freud's message should be particularly clear to current readers. In proposing topographic divisions of the mind, he was endorsing the strategy of functional decomposition in psychology, a strategy that is widely used today (Cummings 1975). He hoped to introduce order into the apparent chaos of mental life, by determining whether some of the operations carried out in various processes were sufficiently similar that they could usefully be assigned to identifiable functional units. A functional unit counted as a unit if there were important similarities among the functions it performed. So, in the central case of the unconscious, for example, Freud argued that it must be regarded as a system, a unit—as an Unconscious—because the processes he assigned to it were all carried out according to the same set of principles: timelessness, exemption from mutual contradiction, and so forth ("The Unconscious," 1915, S.E. XIV:186–89).

Not only should Freud's topographic approach be readily compre-hensible to the modern reader, it should also be completely congenial. Psychology books and journals are filled with attempts to sort the mental tasks humans perform into gross functional divisions. In recent years, for example, there have been hypotheses about episodic versus semantic memory systems, various attentional systems, imagery sys-tems, and the like. Further, proponents of these systems sometimes try to correlate the gross functional units with known regions of the brain, a temptation that Freud acknowledged in the citation and suc-cumbed to in many of his highly theoretical writings.

Despite the similarity with present research goals, this reading of Freudian topography is not anachronistic. In believing that a com-pleted psychoanalytic theory should contain a topographic portion, Freud was explicitly adopting one of the acceptable modes of theory construction of the 1890s. As noted in chapter 2, Wundt regarded the division of central processes into separate, interacting functional units to be the most valuable guide to psychophysics. Further, we can see this approach in action in the work of John Hughlings Jackson.

I presented a brief outline of Jackson's theory in chapter 2. The nervous system was composed of different, increasingly complex units representing different stages of evolutionary development. In mental illness, thinking was taken over by more primitive thought processes, because higher systems were not functioning properly (Jackson 1873ff.:3–118, passim). For Jackson, the critical explanatory level lay between neurons and behavior and divided the mental apparatus into functional, evolutionary units.[4] These units mapped only crudely into cerebral locations (Jackson, "Localisation and Convulsion," 1873ff.:89). At an abstract level, Freud's endorsement of topography simply repeated Wundt's methodological advice to look for functional units. In its details, Freud's topographic approach was remarkably like Jackson's: Look for functional divisions within the mind that were supported by plausible scenarios about the evolution of such systems.

If we consider what Freud was trying to do—topography as an approach rather than as a set of substantive theories—then it is a reasonable strategy for theory construction both by current standards and by the standards of his time. His heirs try to disown this aspect of metapsychology in part because they wish to revise his divisions of the mind. However, this is no reason to criticize the topographic *dimension*. As in the case of dynamics, Freud sometimes had to modify particular theories about mental topography himself. Still, he wisely remained loyal to the goal of trying to understand the mind in terms of its gross evolutionary and functional divisions.

Just as the dynamic dimension cannot be abandoned by anyone who wishes to explain mental life in terms of the dynamic unconscious, so the topographic aspect cannot be given up for the same reason. To believe in a Freudian Unconscious at all is to believe that there is a system in the mind whose principles of operation are significantly different from those that govern the system to which we have access through consciousness. As Sulloway observes, the topographic aspect "inheres in the hypothesis of an 'unconscious' portion of the mind" (Sulloway 1979:64). Freud did not accept the idea of an Unconscious and then engage in unnecessary speculation about topographic divisions in order to meet the requirements of a misguided scientific method. Rather, he realized that in proposing an Unconscious system, he had entered the scientifically respectable field of mental topography ("The Unconscious, 1915, S.E. XIV:166–76). To develop psychoanalytic theory, the topographic dimension had to be pursued. Divisions within the mind had to be clarified, particularly with respect to their relation to consciousness, and mental operations had to be assigned psychic locations within these divisions.

The Economic Point of View

Given the results so far, if metapsychology was either a pernicious or an irrelevant appendage to psychoanalysis, then it must have been by virtue of its economic aspect. In fact, it is Freud's substantive economic theories, with their appeals to mechanisms such as "cathexis," "anti-cathexis," and "side-cathexis," and to such quasi-quantitative notions as "quotas of affect," "hypercathexis," and the "constancy or pleasure principle" that have been the targets of most of the antimetapsychological rhetoric. In the next chapter, I argue that, given available knowledge, many of Freud's central economic theories were quite reasonable. Here I consider only the rationale for the economic approach.

Freud presented his goal clearly in a classic statement in the *Project for a Scientific Psychology.*

> The intention is to furnish a psychology that shall be a natural science: that is, to represent psychical processes as quantitatively determinate states of specifiable material particles, thus making those processes perspicuous and free from contradiction. Two principal ideas are involved: (1) What distinguishes activity from rest is to be regarded as Q [quantities of neural energy that are subject to general laws of motion and that pass through or fill neurons]. (2) The neurones are to be taken as the material particles.[5] (1895, S.E. I:295)

Freud's theoretical strategy should again be familiar to present readers. His hope was that by tying his account of psychological processes to specific physical realizations of those processes, he could discover any hidden contradictions in his explanatory schemas. Similarly, for the last twenty years, cognitive scientists have been telling themselves that one of the great advantages of computer simulations is that by running a program that simulates a mental operation, it is possible to tell whether an analysis of how the process could happen is both consistent and nonmiraculous. Had he brought it off, Freud's demonstration would have been much better. For the brain is not just a model, but *the* model, for it is what does the thinking. If psychical processes could have been represented in terms of energy transfers among the items that constitute the brain, the neurons, that would have greatly enhanced their scientific status—to say the least.

This citation is from the never published *Project*, and most interpreters believe that Freud abandoned its goals as well as its speculative neurophysiology in his later works. Presumably he left the *Project* unpublished either because he could not complete it, or because he came to regard it as too speculative, or because he did not want to tie his theories so closely to neurophysiology, or for some combination of these factors. However, none of these considerations provides a reason for rejecting its goals, and many later passages underscore Freud's commitment to the fact that, ultimately, psychoanalytic theories had to be grounded in the biology of the brain: "[W]e must recollect that all our provisional ideas in psychology will presumably some day be based on an organic substructure" ("On Narcissism," 1914, S.E. XIV:78); "Our psychical topography has *for the present* nothing to do with anatomy . . ." ("The Unconscious," 1915, S.E. XIV:175); "The theoretical structure of psychoanalysis that we have created is in truth a superstructure, which will one day have to be set upon its organic foundation. But we are still ignorant of this" (*Introductory Lectures on Psycho-Analysis*, 1917, S.E. XVI:389).

The changes from the *Project* were matters of timing and specificity. Given the state of neurophysiology, psychical hypotheses could not be tied to specific neurological features for the foreseeable future. As we have seen, however, Freud continued to believe that psychoanalysis required a quantitative or economic dimension for the rest of his career. So, for example, in "The Unconscious" he introduced the economic point of view with the following helpful explication: "[I]t endeavours to follow out the vicissitudes of amounts of excitation and to arrive at least at some *relative* estimate of their magnitude" (1915, S.E. XIV:181). Further, all his theoretical works avert to "cathexes." "Cathexis" is the English rendering that his disciples provided for "*Besetzung*," literally an "occupation" or "filling." Although "cathexis" is a technical term, where "*Besetzung*" is a common one, this translation has the advantage of making a metaphorical link to electrical charge (as in "cathode"). In the nineteenth century, it was widely assumed that brain processes were either chemical or electrical (Wundt 1874:235–36). Even if specific claims about the neural realization of psychical processes had to be postponed, Freud believed that psychoanalysis had to have an economic dimension, because the brain was the organ of the mind and the brain involved quantifiable chemical or electrical processes. Thus, in formulating psychoanalytic explanations, it was necessary to consider how the qualitative descriptions might eventually be tied down to underlying quantitative processes. In the last section I noted that Freud's description of mental dynamics as "forces" implied that they could be measured. However, he did not believe in the necessity of a quantitative approach because he described the determinants of unconscious motivation by such terms as "force," "energy," and "intensity." On the contrary, he used this terminology because he believed that psychoanalysis must have a quantitative dimension.

Despite the clear textual evidence that Freud regarded the mind as the brain, Sulloway maintains that he was in fact a dualist (Sulloway 1979:48, 50–51). Were this true, his commitment to the economic standpoint would rest on nothing more than a belief that any science must be quantitative, and Klein's critique of an overly narrow perspective would be justified. Some texts do imply a metaphysical dualism, for example: "[T]here are both psychical and physiological phenomena in hypnotism, and hypnosis itself can be brought about in the one manner or the other" ("Preface to Bernheim," 1888, S.E. I:81). Still I think there is a straightforward, if philosophically embarrassing, explanation for Freud's apparent inconsistency in this matter.

As Sulloway points out, Freud's views on the mind-body problem were borrowed explicitly from Jackson (Sulloway 1979:50; *On Aphasia*, 1891, S.E. XIV:206–8). Here is Jackson's considered opinion on the matter:

> I do not concern myself with mental states at all, except indirectly in seeking their anatomical substrata. I do not trouble myself about the mode of connection between mind and matter. It is enough to assume a parallelism. That along with excitations or discharges of nervous arrangements in the cerebrum, mental states occur, I, of course, admit; but how this is I do not inquire; indeed, so far as clinical medicine is concerned, I do not care. If anyone feels warranted in assuming that physical states in the highest nervous centers and mental states are one and the same thing, he is just as much bound as anyone else to seek the anatomical nature of the nervous arrangements in which the psychico-physical states occur. *To give a materialistic explanation of mental states is not to give an anatomical one.* (Jackson "Localisation of Movement," 1873ff.:52)

That is, from the point of view of scientific practice, there was no difference between believing that the mental runs parallel to, is a "dependent concomitant" of, physical processes, and simply identifying them. Whether one was a materialist or a parallelist, one still had to find the underlying physical structures that subserved mental functions. The only difference between the positions was philosophical—whether one preferred to explain the enigma of why the mind and the brain happened to run in parallel or the paradoxical identification of two apparently very different entities. Neither Jackson nor Freud had the slightest interest in either philosophical conundrum. At one point Freud remarked, with obvious sarcasm, that he had a constitutional incapacity for philosophy (*An Autobiographical Study*, 1925, S.E. XX:59). So both Freud and Jackson adopted the pragmatic solution of treating the mind as if it were the brain, without choosing between the philosophical positions of dualism and materialism, which they took to be irrelevant to the real work of understanding the functional divisions within the mind and their organic substrata.

The *Project* provides a clear statement of Freud's purpose in adopting the economic standpoint: to make psychoanalytic theorizing internally consistent and biologically plausible. Published texts demonstrate that he adhered to these principles in constructing his theories. In discussing in manic phase the melancholia, for example, Freud offered the hypothesis that, in melancholia, the ego finally gets over the loss of its love object, at which point the energy it had been using to repress unpleasurable thoughts of that object is released, bringing on the manic phase. But he continued:

> This explanation certainly sounds plausible, but in the first place it is too indefinite, and secondly, it gives rise to more new problems. . . . In the first place, normal mourning, too, overcomes the loss of the object, and it, too, while it lasts, absorbs all the energies of the ego. Why, then, after it has run its course, is there no hint in its case of the economic condition for a phase of triumph? I find it impossible to answer this objection straight away. It also draws our attention to the fact that we do not even know the economic means by which mourning carries out its task. ("Mourning and Melancholia," 1917, S.E. XIV:255)

Freud's problem was that, when he thought about his explanation for melancholic mania in terms of the economic model he had provisionally adopted, including the damming up and release of energy, he was struck by the fact that there should be no difference in discharge between melancholia and normal mourning, so somewhere his theory was inadequate.

Psychoanalysis had to have an economic part, because the mind had to be regarded as the brain in scientific work. Freud also thought that economic factors were very important in therapy. One of his last papers, "Analysis Terminable and Interminable," offered a lengthy discussion and defense of this point. After asking whether it is possible to tame instincts, he answered, "Formulated in these terms, the question makes no mention at all of the strength of the instinct; but it is precisely on this that the outcome depends" (1937, S.E. XXIII:225).

Somewhat later, after noting that various accidents, such as traumas and frustrations, could reinforce instincts (just like the physiological reinforcement provided by puberty), he concluded, "The result is always the same, and it underlines the irresistible power of the quantitative factor in the causation of illness" (226).

Once again, the economic approach should strike current philosophers of psychology as both familiar and correct. Since the mind is the brain and neural processes involve electrical and chemical changes, any psychological account must be able to be related—eventually—to underlying quantifiable factors. Further, like current theorists, Freud was determined to be consistent with the few facts that were known about neural or biological forces. So, for example, in considering the relation between the strength of the feeling of pleasure or pain and the quantity of energy present, he rejected one possibility on the basis of psychophysical discoveries.

> What we are implying . . . is not a simple relation between the strength of feelings of pleasure . . . and the corresponding modifications in the quantity of excitation; least of all—in view of all we have been taught by psychophysiology—are we suggesting any directly proportional ratio. . . . (*Beyond the Pleasure Principle*, 1920, S.E., XVIII:8)

Although the rationale behind the economic dimension was fundamentally sound, Freud differed from most present-day cognitive scientists in a crucial respect. He recognized that he was largely ignorant of any facts that could contribute to economic accounts, but he still tried to assign at least relative magnitudes to different qualitative processes.

Metapsychology, Reduction, and the Other Sciences

Freud's commitment to metapsychology committed him to relating psychoanalysis to other disciplines. This is most obvious in the economic point of view. Insofar as psychoanalysis strove to offer theories that were compatible with the neural activities underlying mental processes, it had to be guided and constrained by anatomy and physiology. Freud also recognized that mental topography needed to take account of findings in anatomy and evolutionary biology. As we will see in chapter 4, his reluctance to commit himself to anatomical claims for his topographies rested on anatomical discoveries.

The search for forces governing the Unconscious also led to other disciplines. If the mind was the brain, then the forces involved in mental dynamics had to be biological forces or had to have developed from the interaction of biological forces with physical and/or social environments. So the dynamic part of psychoanalysis also had to be guided and constrained by biology. In *An Autobiographical Study*, Freud explained an important development in psychoanalysis by noting that "biological considerations seemed to make it impossible to remain content with assuming the existence of only a single class of instincts" (1925, S.E. XX:57). More dramatically, in *Beyond the Pleasure Principle*, he expressed great concern that our biological knowledge gave the lie to his hypothesis of the death instinct. Oddly enough, the apparently troubling cases were protozoa, animalcules that appeared to some to be immortal. After a four-page discussion of the protozoa problem, Freud concluded with relief:

> Thus our expectation that biology would flatly contradict the recognition of death instincts has not been fulfilled. We are at liberty to continue concerning ourselves with their possibility, if we have other reasons for doing so. (1920, S.E. XVIII:49)

Given some of Freud's substantive assumptions, metapsychology also forged connections with other disciplines in the search for general dynamic principles. So, for example (as we will see in chapter 4), because he was a recapitulationist, he expected that the study of primitive peoples and myths would reveal the origins of forces currently governing unconscious ideas. Klein is right that Freud's metapsychology entangled psychoanalysis with other disciplines. But this was no vice. The metatheoretic directives of Freud's metapsychology were fundamentally sound.

The official view also errs in suggesting that Freud renounced metapsychology or regarded it as dispensable to psychoanalysis, or at least to clinical work. At the age of 81, while reflecting on the difficulties of psychoanalytic treatment, he made the following observations about cures and failures:

> If we are asked by what methods and means this result [the instinct being brought into harmony with the ego, i.e., a cure] is achieved, it is not easy to find an answer. We can only say: "So muß denn doch die Hexe dran!—the Witch Metapsychology.[6] Without metapsychological speculation and theorizing—I had almost said 'phantasyzing'—we shall not get another step forward. ("Analysis Terminable and Interminable," 1937, S.E. XXIII:225)

> [So too with failures.] [W]e have had occasion to recognize the paramount importance of the quantitative factor and to stress the claim of the metapsychological line of approach to be taken into account in any attempt at explanation. (234)

I conclude my defense of Freud's general approach to theory construction by parrying two further, likely objections: Metapsychology was reductionistic; Freud was naive in allowing his theorizing to be guided by nineteenth-century biology and physiology, given their primitive states of development. As already noted, "reductionism" is more often a term of abuse than information. So, before beginning a defense, I will try to clarify the objection.

As "reduction" has been used in twentieth-century philosophy of science, the heart of the claim that one science reduces to another is that the laws or principles of the reducing science explain why the laws of the reduced science are true, to the extent that they are (Kemeny and Oppenheim 1956; Nagel 1961; Feyerabend 1962; Schaffner 1967). That is why the reducing science is considered more basic. When hurled as an objection, "reductionism" is often taken to imply that the reducing science is supposed to replace the reduced science or make it otiose. When combined, the idea is that a science such as physiology will replace psychology because it is more basic.

Even early in his career, Freud's approach was not reductionistic in either of the central descriptive or the central pejorative senses just indicated. In his monograph *On Aphasia*, published in 1891, he objected to attempts to localize basic psychical elements in nerve cells. First he pointed out the folly of trying to identify a complex mental concept or activity with locally bounded neural activity. Then he noted that there was no reason to believe that elements that were simple from a psychical point of view were also physiologically simple. Why couldn't a simple psychical element correspond to a very complicated state of affairs in the physiological world? He conjectured that the physiological correlate of even a simple psychical presentation was a process that started at a certain point in the cortex and either spread over the entire cortex or followed certain tracts (S.E. XIV:206–8). Given so complex a correspondence between the psychical and the physiological, the prospects for reduction would not be auspicious, although it was not completely ruled out.

Nor was the *Project* written with a view to ceding psychology to physiology. On the contrary, Freud presented psychopathology as informing physiology about the overload of Q and also appealed to dream interpretation and to evolution to fill in details about the workings of the system (1895, S.E. I:295–96, 302, 341ff.). The aim of the *Project*, as he explained to his friend Wilhelm Fliess, was to furnish "a psychology for neurologists" (283). Neurology was to benefit from the results of psychotherapy, and general theories of mental functioning were to be tested by comparing their implications about the flow of energy through the system with the discoveries of neurology (283–84).

One passage in the *Project* makes it especially clear why Freud was not a reductionist.

> I find it hard to give a mechanical (automatic) explanation of its [psychical attention's] origin. For that reason I believe that it is biologically determined—that is, that it has been left over in the course of psychical evolution because any other behaviour by ψ [one of the systems of the mind] has been excluded owing to the generation of unpleasure. (1895, S.E. I:361)

That is, when dealing with psychological processes, sometimes they can be explained by appeal to the underlying hardware, but at other times it is necessary to consider the history of their development. Freud did not regard physiology as more basic than psychology in the sense that it could explain why the latter was true, because he believed that it was often necessary to appeal to the psychical history of the race to explain both its current psychology and its current physiology. The generation of unpleasure (a psychical event underlain by a complex physiology) led to modifications in psychology and the underlying physiology.

In another passage in the *Project*, he elaborated on his purposes in appealing to other sciences.

> Anyone, however, who is engaged scientifically in the construction of hypotheses will only begin to take his theories seriously if they can be fitted into our knowledge from more than one direction and if the arbitrariness of a *constructio ad hoc* can be mitigated in relation to them. (1895, S.E. I:302)

Finally, there is no suggestion early or late in the Freudian corpus that he expected that psychoanalysis, with its rich sources of insight into individual histories and that of the race, would ever be replaced by a purely physiological science.[7]

The charge of reductionism reflects the poverty of our vocabulary for describing relations between theories more than Freud's practice. His view of the relations among the disciplines can be clarified by appealing to the threefold classification used in chapter 2. Because he was a materialist, Freud believed that psychoanalysis was ontologically dependent on physiology. The forces and systems it described were realized in neural matter, the proper subject of brain anatomy and physiology. Hence, like Wundt, he believed that all his hypothesizing was constrained by known properties of the nervous system. If psychoanalysis failed to be consistent with basic principles of neurophysiology, then it had to be wrong. Further, given that the mind was the brain, eventually the qualitative descriptions of forces supplied by the dynamic dimension had to be supplemented or extended by quantitative (economic) accounts of these forces. The crucial point to recognize, however, is that these quantitative accounts were intended, not to supplant qualitative accounts, but simply to extend them.[8] So, for example, the longed-for discovery of the somatic sources and chemical composition of instinctual sexual energy (libido) would not make libido otiose as an explanatory construct. Rather, it would clarify the nature of libido and make it amenable to more precise quantitative description.

Freud wanted to write a "psychology for neurologists," because he believed that neurophysiology was de facto, though not in principle, partly epistemologically dependent on psychopathology and so on psychoanalysis. However, he saw this as a two-way street. Psychoanalysis and psychology more generally had much to learn from neurophysiology about the basic functioning of the nervous system, whether, for example, it involved one or two fundamentally different forms of energy (*Project for a Scientific Psychology*, 1895, S.E. I:369; *An Outline of Psycho-Analysis*, 1937, S.E. XXIII:164). Chapters 4 and 5 will show that he also took psychoanalysis to be epistemologically dependent on prehistoric anthropology and linguistics. Further, it needed anthropology and linguistics to extend its explanations. In the former case, for example, psychoanalysis needed to learn from anthropology about the conditions during which our various mental systems evolved. Psychoanalysis might explain a particular adult behavior by appealing to primitive forces in the Unconscious mind; primitive anthropology would extend that explanation by explaining how those forces came to be.

Relations of ontological dependence and epistemological interdependence between psychoanalysis and physiology do not justify the charge of reductionism. That would require explanatory dependence, the view that the phenomena of psychoanalysis were explained directly by laws of physiology or that they were explained by laws of psychoanalysis, which were in turn explained by laws of physiology. But Freud did not subscribe to either claim. This aspect of his thinking can be brought into sharp relief, by appealing to Tinbergen's famous four questions of biology:

1. In what ways does this phenomenon (behavior) influence the survival, the success of the animal?
2. What makes the behavior happen at any given moment? How does its "machinery" work?

3. How does the behavior machinery develop as the individual grows up?
4. How have the behavior systems of each species evolved until they became what they are now? (Tinbergen 1968:79)

As the citation about attention above illustrates, Freud did not always answer the question of why a psychological phenomenon occurred by giving a mechanical explanation (2). To explain attention, he felt it was necessary to consider the evolution of the system (4). Many, many of his explanations were functional (1), developmental (3), or historical (4). One great difference between nineteenth-century and twentieth-century science is our preference for synchronic explanations, that is, explanations that appeal to contemporaneous as opposed to historical factors. Hence, when current scholars see that Freud tried to explain human behavior and that he was very concerned to make his theory comport with neurophysiology, they assume that he was primarily interested in mechanical explanations. So the specter of reductionism arises. But Freud was a child of nineteenth-century science and gave equal importance to functional, developmental, and historical explanations. Prehistory anthropology, developmental psychology, evolutionary biology, or neurophysiology might offer further insights into why the laws of psychoanalysis were true. However, no one science could perform this task and no one science could begin to take over the explanatory work of psychoanalysis. Although I will provide a more complete picture of Freud's understanding of the relations of the disciplines at the end of chapter 4, figure 3.1 offers a preliminary distillation of his views about the complex relations of ontological dependence, weak epistemological dependence, and explanatory extension among the disciplines.

Through the influence of his basic metapsychology and some substantive doctrines, Freud's theory construction became highly dependent on other disciplines. Even if the approach was sound in principle, it is easy to see it as naive in practice. Very little was known about the functioning or evolution of the brain. In appealing to contemporary biology and physiology to construct a general theory of mental functioning, Freud was building on impermanent foundations. The objection is that he should have known and desisted.

Freud had no choice but to work with other disciplines as he found them. Further, it is better to allow theory construction to be informed by current research in related fields than to ignore this work. The critical question is whether Freud's attitude was appropriately circumspect. This issue will recur for particular disciplines and particular

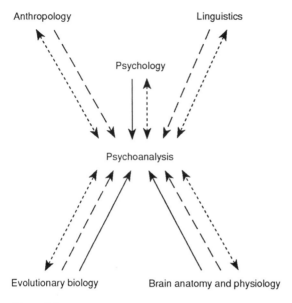

Figure 3.1
Freud's view (preliminary version). The bottom-to-top layout indicates ontological priority. Solid arrows indicate relations of constraint and guidance and run from the constraining to the constrained disciplines. Dotted arrows indicate the weaker epistemological relations of support and inspiration, running from the supporting to the supported disciplines. Finally, dashed arrows represent relations of explanatory extension and run from the extending to the extended disciplines.

results throughout the book. At least at the rhetorical level, however, the charge of naiveté cannot be sustained.

Freud saw the dangers of tying his theories to current physiology and biology and tried mightily to avoid them. Thus, in a passage often cited to show that his theories were independent of dated biological assumptions, he explained that "I try in general to keep psychology clear from everything that is different in nature from it, even biological lines of thought" ("On Narcissism," 1914, S.E. XIV:79). In *Jokes and the Unconscious*, he suggested that even though his psychical theories had someday to be tied to an organic foundation, he was not yoked to *current* physiology.

> To avoid misunderstanding, I must add that I am making no attempt to proclaim that the cells and nerve fibres, or the systems of neurones which are taking their place to-day, are these psychical paths, even though it would have to be possible in some

manner which cannot yet be indicated to represent such paths by organic elements of the nervous system. (1905, S.E. VIII:148)

Despite such efforts to draw back, Freud recognized that—like it or not—he was dependent upon current biology: "In spite of all our efforts to prevent biological terminology and considerations from dominating psycho-analytic work, we cannot avoid using them even in our descriptions of the phenomena we study" ("The Claims of Psycho-Analysis to Scientific Interest," 1913, S.E. XIII:182). If psycho-analytic theory construction was going to be constrained and inspired by work in biology and other disciplines, then it had to have some share in their fates. Freud was not completely naive on this point.

On the other hand it should be made quite clear that the uncertainty of our speculation has been greatly increased by the necessity for borrowing from the science of biology. Biology is truly a land of unlimited possibilities. We may expect it to give us the most surprising information and we cannot guess what answers it will return in a few dozen years to the questions we have put to it. They may be of a kind which will blow away the whole of our artificial structure of hypotheses. (*Beyond the Pleasure Principle*, 1920, S.E. XVIII:60)

At least in reflective moments, he saw his position as a theorist with painful clarity: Whatever its virtues, his interdisciplinary approach made his theories hostage to unfavorable developments in other fields.

Chapter 4

Freud's Theory of Mental Life

Metapsychology and the Construction of Psychoanalysis

The results of the last chapter can be summed up in four interrelated claims. In espousing metapsychology, Freud committed himself to an ideal of how psychological theories should be constructed as well as to specific doctrines. When understood as a set of directives for theorizing about the mind, there was nothing objectionable about metapsychology, despite all the criticisms that have been aimed at it. Freud never gave up this approach, although he expressed serious misgivings about any of his substantive results being permanent. In pursuing metapsychology, he committed himself to an interdisciplinary approach to theory construction.

This chapter will show how the directives shaped the theory, how the search for dynamic forces, broad topographic divisions, and economic principles that reflected the quantitative character of brain processes led to the distinctive doctrines of psychoanalysis. In tracing the construction of psychoanalytic theory, I will return to the central question raised in the last chapter. Even if the directives embodied in his metapsychology were sound in principle, did Freud err in allowing himself to speculate far beyond what was reasonable, given the state of the social and biological sciences in the nineteenth century?

Nothing is wrong with speculation per se. Freud proudly described himself as a bold speculator, and if the history of science proves anything, it is that faint heart never won fair theory. So the critical question must be divided into several, more precise questions. Did he err in adopting speculative, poorly supported social and biological theories? Even if he used theories that were reasonable by the standards of his time, did he put more weight on them than they could bear, either by extending them too far or by having too much faith in their ultimate correctness? Despite the common charge of wild speculation, the picture that emerges is one of reasonably sober theorizing. For most cases, at least the first question will be given a negative answer. In working out the core principles of psychoanalysis—those he took to be fundamental and not at all speculative—Freud drew upon some of the most spectacular and apparently solid results of nineteenth-century science.

Since there is a large territory to cover, the chapter is rather long. Three prefatory observations may make it easier to fit the details to come into a coherent picture. First, I will disagree with the standard view that Freud's theory changed in important ways over time. Allegedly, in the late 1890s, when his father died and he underwent self-analysis, he abandoned his physiological foundations and turned to pure psychology or, in some versions, changed from regarding psychoanalysis as a *Naturwissenschaft* to seeing it as one of the *Geisteswissenschaften*.[1] Without digressing to consider particular accounts of these supposed changes, I will present a great deal of evidence to demonstrate the amazing constancy of his position. Far from undergoing revolutionary change, psychoanalytic theory was gradually elaborated and extended, as new theses were added and, very rarely, old theses partially abandoned. The underlying blueprint was unaltered by time or events.

My second and third observations concern background assumptions of nineteenth-century science. Freud was explicit about one. In lectures delivered at Clark University in 1909, he explained that he had long operated under the sway of a "prejudice," the prejudice that mental processes were strictly determined (S.E. XI:29). He did not mean that all mental processes were psychically determined. As noted, he took the actual neuroses to be caused by purely somatic factors, and he believed that biologically based economic factors could be decisive in illness. What he meant was that every aspect of a symptom, its strength, time of onset, and the "choice of neurosis" itself, could be explained by reference to causes. Anyone who pursues a science of mental life must assume that there are some statistical or deterministic regularities to be found in it, whether the causes are social, psychological, neurological, somatic, or all of these. Freud's assumption was much stronger. Like many nineteenth-century scientists, he assumed that all laws were exceptionless and that all phenomena could be explained by law.

The second background assumption will seem considerably stranger. Nineteenth-century social and biological explanations were largely historical. A present phenomenon was explained by offering an account of its development, or evolution, from earlier conditions. Special creations and leaps of nature had no place in serious science. When these trends were combined, they produced a style of explanation that may be labeled "evolutionary naturalism." For any mental, social, or generally "higher" human achievement, the default assumption (as we say) was that the explanation should describe how it evolved or could have evolved from earlier, unproblematically natural phenomena, paradigmatically, from conditions shared with animals.

Besides his metapsychological directives, Freud constructed psychoanalysis under the sway of strict determinism and evolutionary naturalism. The theoretical core of psychoanalysis came into being when discoveries from relevant disciplines were seen in the light of these metatheoretic principles. Although I do not believe that Freud's theory underwent radical change, I present its elaboration more or less chronologically, beginning with the economic assumptions of the *Project*. The one exception is *The Interpretation of Dreams*, which will not be discussed until chapter 5.

Two Principles of Mental Functioning

Freud did not publish "Formulations on the Two Principles of Mental Functioning" until 1911, but he developed the theory fully—much more fully than in the later version—in the *Project*. The two principles were the pleasure principle and the reality principle. Although the *Project* remained unpublished, it provides a very clear picture of Freud's motivation for adopting these principles and of their dependence on results from other sciences, specifically, histology, psychology, anatomy, and physiology. After using this rich source of material to present the details of the theory, I will consider differences between the *Project* and published discussions of these principles.

If psychical processes were realized in the brain, then at some level, they had to be describable in terms of transfers of energy among neurons or groups of neurons. In the *Project*, Freud appealed to the important histological result that neural matter was made up of distinct neurons that "have contact with one another through the medium of a foreign substance" (1895, S.E. I:298) to develop his two principles of functioning. He took a single neuron, which could be filled with and then discharge neural energy, as the model for the system. This suggested that the mental apparatus as a whole acquired and discharged mental energy. In *Beyond the Pleasure Principle* (1920), he noted that Gustav Fechner believed that when energy was discharged, it was accompanied by subjective feelings of pleasure; by contrast, if the energy level became too high, the individual had the subjective sensation of pain. It is not clear when Freud became aware of Fechner's views. In any case, he sometimes referred to this basic principle of neural functioning as the "pleasure principle," sometimes as the "constancy principle," and, in the *Project*, as the "inertia principle."[2]

Freud saw the pleasure principle as furnishing an explanation for the widely recognized phenomenon of reflex movement. Energy came into the system through sensory neurons and was given off through motor neurons—hence the need for the two structural types of neuron discovered in the spinal cord. As noted in chapter 2, the early idea of spinal reflexes had been extended by a number of German physiologists to include cerebral reflexes as well. The pleasure principle combined the latest discoveries of histology with the increasingly popular assumption that all neural activity was reflexive. Although Freud's conception of the nervous system had reflexes as basic, he introduced an important complication. He recognized endogenous stimuli that could not be dealt with effectively by a simple motor reflex. This problem required a second type of mental functioning.

Freud reasoned that endogenous stimuli, generated by hunger or sexual desire for example, would keep pouring into the system until these needs were met. Hence, these stimuli necessitated what he called "specific actions." But specific action—performing the appropriate action on the appropriate object in order to satisfy a biological demand and so stop the flow of endogenous stimuli—required considerable stage setting. He offered a hypothesis about how such actions could have come into being. At first, when an infant was hungry, for example, the source of food was simply placed in the child's mouth by turning its head. The food satisfied the biological need and the endogenous stimuli ceased, causing a reduction of energy and a feeling of pleasure. Following a psychological tradition that goes back at least to Hobbes, Freud assumed that mental states that were experienced together and accompanied by pleasure became especially closely associated with each other. Thus, the sensation of sucking, the visual appearance of the mother's breast, the kinesthetic sensation of moving the head, and perhaps many other sensations would become tightly associated. How could this experience help the child perform a specific action on future occasions?

Some kind of memory was needed. Freud's suggestion was straightforward. Neurons were distinct and uniformly constructed elements of the nervous system. Hence, they were only connected together functionally, by the flow of energy among them. How could anything be preserved in this type of neural arrangement? Seemingly the only possible mechanism would be some alteration in the connections among the neurons. Freud thought of these connections in terms of barriers between the contact points of adjacent neurons, but it makes no functional difference that they are gaps rather than barriers. Either would impede connections. Following explicitly in the associationist tradition, he assumed that the strength of association between two mental states depended on the frequency and magnitude (amount of pleasure) of their past associations (*Project for a Scientific Psychology,* 1895, S.E. I:300). Applying this to the neuron theory, he envisioned previous flows of energy from one neuron to another as breaking down the contact barrier and so differentially facilitating that connection (300). As a result, when the complex system of neurons that represented one of these mental states was again filled with energy, that energy would be more easily passed to the complex system of neurons representing its associated states than to other neurons.[3]

This was still insufficient to explain specific action. Reviving an earlier perception would be like merely wishing. The baby might imagine what it wanted, but sucking and swallowing at that point would bring no relief. As Freud observed, a system that followed only the pleasure principle would be biologically detrimental; it could not survive and reproduce (*Project for a Scientific Psychology,* 1895, S.E. I:325; cf. 317–18). Somehow, the baby had to compare the remembered state with its present perceptual state and act only if the two matched. This activity required two further complications. First, the neural tissue had to be capable of perceiving as well as remembering. Freud believed that perception required neurons that were unaltered by the passage of energy among them, that is, that retained no "memories." Presumably this was to allow for the possibility of objective perception. So two kinds of neurons were needed. At this point, his speculation ran into problems from histology, which found no morphological differences among neurons. He offered a conjecture: All neural tissue began with high contact barriers (or large gaps) between individual neurons. Because of the location of some gray matter, however, it was so pummeled by stimuli that all its barriers (gaps) were effectively removed. Other gray matter, deeper in the brain, was protected from massive stimulation and retained its capacity for memory. Although the neural elements were all basically uniform, because of differing locations, some assumed different functional properties. Thus, Freud resolved the potential conflict with histology by invoking the sort of anatomical considerations Wundt had used to address similar difficulties.

The second complication was required to block action in the absence of matches. Freud envisioned the apparatus as having a store of mental energy that could be deployed to prevent inappropriate motor discharge. He referred to the system of neurons within which this energy was stored as the "ego" and imagined that it deflected energy from facilitated paths by attracting it to itself. However, the mechanism of diversion is not particularly important. The crucial points were two: Given the need for specific action, the system had to have some mechanical means of preserving its past experiences; it had to have some mechanical means of preventing the discharge of all its energy in motor responses before they could be efficacious.

Hence the two principles: the pleasure principle, which referred to the tendency of individual neurons and the entire system to divest themselves of energy; and the reality principle, which referred to the opposing capacity to resist motor discharge except under appropriate circumstances. How speculative were these principles? They rested on four key assumptions, the most basic being the reflex nature of neural matter. By the time Freud was writing, the anatomy and physiology of reflexes was fairly well understood, including the relation between the intensity of the stimulus and the magnitude of the response (Brazier 1988:40–41; Herrnstein and Boring 1965:265). Wundt had remarked on the peculiar ratio of irritability of the gray matter, noting that it seemed to respond only to stimulations of particular strength and duration (Wundt 1874:174). Neural material from the spinal cord had been separated into sensory and motor nerves, suggesting that the spinal nervous system was just a collection of reflex arcs. As noted in chapter 2, the disputed question was not whether neural reflexes existed, but whether all psychical acts could be understood as a combination of reflex acts (Herrnstein and Boring 1965: 265ff.; Brazier 1988:215). In adopting the principle of inertia, Freud observed that it would explain the existence of reflexes and the general division of neural matter into sensory and motor nerves. He added that the neural system had evolved from protoplasm, which seemed in general to be irritable, as evidence by the tendency of organisms to withdraw from surface stimulation (*Project for a Scientific Psychology*, 1895, S.E. I:296).

A second major assumption was associationism from psychology. The forming of deep, but unintended, associations through pleasure and, especially, pain was crucial to Freud's accounts of mental illness. Associationism was a dominant trend in nineteenth-century psychology. Presumably, the discovery of discrete neurons enhanced its plausibility, since it is somewhat difficult to envision how specific associations could be represented in an undifferentiated medium. Freud's suggestion about the mechanism of association was a speculative but nonetheless elegant and plausible way of combining two of the leading ideas of psychology and physiology. In any case, all he needed was that recent work in histology not contradict associationism. For, like reflexology, although associationism had its critics, the point at issue was not whether some mental processes were associative, but whether they all were (Herrnstein and Boring 1965:326ff.).

Freud's third assumption was less firmly entrenched in nineteenth-century science, but nonetheless quite plausible. According to the reality principle, the nervous system was capable not only of automatically discharging energy, but also of retaining it until conditions in the real world made action appropriate. Part of this seems obvious. People do not generally start chewing before they have started a meal. Presumably, the hard part was to explain how rational action was possible, how motor activity could be delayed and not aimlessly discharged in reflex action. Again, Freud took the individual neuron as a model for the system (*Project for a Scientific Psychology*, 1895, S.E. I:297). Because there were barriers (actually gaps) between them, a neuron might be unable to discharge its energy by transmitting it to an adjacent neuron. Given the histological picture, a neuron could remain filled, or cathected, with energy. Freud reasoned that the same fate could befall the whole system, if filled neurons were somehow cut off from neurons capable of motor discharge. Since the reflex was the norm, this force or tendency would have to be opposed by some other force or tendency. Wundt had reported experiments showing that stimulating certain parts of the brain could delay or even prevent reflex action (Wundt 1874:174). He also noted that higher cortical processes appeared to be capable of inhibiting reflexes (Wundt 1874:174). Freud reasoned that the system was capable of specific action, because it was able to inhibit inappropriate reflexive discharge by drawing on stored energy within it. Apparently energy could be stored only in neurons, so he assumed the presence of a group of filled neurons, which he called the "ego." Although this account was somewhat speculative, it rested on four solid points: Some actions were not reflexive, but appropriately delayed; the neural system had the tendency to be reflexive; there was some evidence that this reflexive tendency could be opposed by inhibitory forces; energy to bring about inhibition had to be stored somewhere. Later, Freud elaborated what was only implicit in the *Project's* account. Whatever controlled the energy restraining reflexive discharge had to be in contact with reality.

In all his subsequent work, Freud assumed that the two principles operated side by side in governing mental life. This last assumption is most in need of defense. Why didn't he reason, instead, that rational action implied that neural matter was not invariably reflexive? Or that, with development, the automatic and irrational pleasure principle simply gave way to the reality principle? Freud had a ready answer to these questions: Our nightly dreams and the symptoms of neuropathology, which he viewed as remarkably similar to dreams, were important facts testifying to the continued presence of primary (reflexive) processes governed by the pleasure principle (*Project for a Scientific Psychology*, 1895, S.E. I:336). Notice, however, that the evidence of the couch provided very loose support for the hypothesis. Dreams and symptoms showed only that mental life was not always anchored in reality; they did not imply that the system was trying to discharge energy or that paths of discharge were determined by past associations.

Presumably, Freud felt justified in maintaining this stronger claim on additional grounds. A number of evolutionary theories, including Jackson's, had suggested that primitive structures often survived alongside the sophisticated mechanisms they made possible. This was clearly Freud's conception of the relations between the two principles: "[T]hese processes [are] the older, primary processes, *the residues of a phase of development in which they were the only kind of mental processes*" ("Formulations on the Two Principles of Mental Functioning," 1911, S.E. XII:219; my emphasis). Further, numerous experiments with so-called spinal (that is, decerebrated) animals demonstrated the continuing presence of reflexes in sophisticated creatures, as did uncontroversial reflexes in humans. Further still, many arguments and experiments testified to the power of accidental association. Against the background of strict determinism and the independent plausibility of associations, reflex hypotheses, and survivals of primitive forms, Freud must have seen something like the following reasoning as compelling: Certain nonrational processes, reflexes and accidental associations, were part of mental life; dreams and psychopathologies did not obey rational principles; thus, it was plausible to think they were governed, not by the reality principle, but by nonrational reflexive primary processes. Although the argument is not logically tight, it is hardly frivolous.

Freud never abandoned these two principles (although he later tried to derive the pleasure principle from a more basic tendency of living matter to return to a previous state [*Beyond the Pleasure Principle*, 1920, S.E. XVIII:34ff.]). Apart from the seventh chapter of *The Interpretation of Dreams*, his most explicit, published account of them occurred in "Formulations of the Two Principles of Mental Functioning." This discussion was considerably more cryptic than that of the *Project* and emphasized evolutionary rather than neurological considerations (1911, S.E. XII:219). In *Beyond the Pleasure Principle*, he returned to a more physiological account. The gray matter of the cortex was susceptible to stimulation (and hence reflex action), because it originated from the ectoderm; the location of some gray matter meant that it was so thoroughly battered by stimuli that it could no longer be changed by it (no effective contact barriers); whereas gray matter deeper in the apparatus was still modifiable, in that connections might be facilitated by previous flows of excitation (1920, S.E. XVIII:26). In his last major piece, *An Outline of Psycho-Analysis,* Freud again described the tensions produced by stimuli as leading to unpleasure and the ego as needing to suppress excitations until favorable conditions were indicated in reality (1938, S.E. XXIII:146). Finally, I should add that many of Freud's specific accounts of neurotic symptoms, most obviously those involving motor paralysis and tics, acquired needed theoretical backing from his account of primary processes.

I have argued for three claims: Freud always supported and drew on these two principles; we can only understand the principles and his support for them in the light of work in other disciplines; and, given the place of reflexes in physiology and psychology, associations in psychology, and the recent histological discoveries about the neuron, as he developed the principles, they were speculative, but not wildly so. Whether they were too speculative depends on the uses for which they were intended. Here, Freud appeared to follow Wundt's guidelines, noted in chapter 2. He had no illusions about making serious contributions to theoretical neurophysiology. Rather, since the brain was the organ of thought, he wanted psychoanalysis to be constrained and guided by an understanding of the general principles of brain anatomy and physiology. The rub is: How do you follow Wundt's seemingly excellent advice without running the risk that your theory will collapse if work in related fields proves impermanent?

Freud seemed to appreciate the seriousness of this threat. He did not publish the *Project,* which tied the two principles very closely to specific mechanisms such as neurons and contact barriers, and published discussions of the two principles appear to be a compromise. For sound reasons embodied in his metapsychology, he believed that psychoanalysis needed to be informed by physiology. However, he tried to be cautious: Only assume what was fairly uncontroversial and, even then, only assume that something like present accounts will be correct. The latter precaution may account for the charges that his metapsychology was "quasi-mechanistic" or "quasi-physiological." His substantive economic principles were blatantly inspecific. In 1911, he explained that the pleasure principle operated simply by "unburdening the mental apparatus of accretions of stimuli through motor innervations," the reality principle by allowing "discharge" to be "postponed" ("Formulations on the Two Principles of Mental Functioning," S.E. XII:221). Presumably, the aim was not to be "quasi-" or "pseudo-" mechanistic, however, but to be as noncommittal as possible, given his metapsychological principles. The link between discharge and pleasure was speculative, even if it had been suggested by the great Fechner and had an obvious analogue in (male) sexual consummation. But the rest of his assumptions were very minimal. All he committed himself to were the ability of the apparatus to act in accordance with indications of reality (which seems reasonable enough), the fact that it could maintain enough energy to do so, and an account of the reflexive and associative character of some of its processes that was compatible with recent histological discoveries. It is hard to see how he could have assumed any *less* and still taken psychoanalysis to be guided and constrained by the best current understanding of the mental apparatus available from histology, physiology, and psychology.

Chapter 3 laid great stress on the distinction between metapsychology as an approach and substantive metapsychological principles. One reason for sharply separating these two aspects of metapsychology is that it permits a clearer view of the relation between them. Freud's two principles illustrate a deeply problematic aspect of that relation. The approach required only that psychoanalysis be informed by whatever was known about brain anatomy and physiology. Unless the directive was completely idle, in practice, it committed him to at least temporary allegiance to inspecific, or generic, versions of then current anatomical and physiological theories. Since those assumptions were built into the theoretical foundations of psychoanalysis and he dissuaded his followers from further biological investigations (chap. 6, p. 162), the allegiances endured. Any metatheoretic principles carry some substantive commitments, most obviously, about the division of some range of phenomena into natural kinds, the reliability or appropriateness of experimental paradigms or instruments, and the tractability of certain questions. But the commitments of Freud's metapsychology were much heftier. Failing to see that these were the raw materials out of which psychoanalysis was built, his later disciples chafe under what they view as his inexplicable willingness to bind psychoanalysis to generic principles borrowed from anatomy, histology, and physiology. From the perspective of contemporary interdisciplinary wisdom, we can appreciate what he was trying to do and why it was reasonable for him to try. When we see where these principles led him (chapter 6), however, we may be equally appalled by the outcome.

Three Mental Systems

Of necessity, I present the different components of psychoanalysis sequentially, even though the theory enjoyed considerable organic unity. The doctrine of the two principles supported and was supported by the account of different mental systems. As with his substantive economic principles, much of Freud's mental topography was worked out before its formal presentation in "The Unconscious" (1915). Freud was explicit that psychoanalysis lay between biology and psychology in the order of the sciences (e.g., "The Claims of Psycho-Analysis to Scientific Interest," 1913, S.E. XIII:182). He was also quite clear that it should take over the work that medical psychiatry had tried—and failed—to accomplish (e.g., *Introductory Lectures on Psycho-Analysis*, 1916–17, S.E. XV:20–21). Chapter 2 supplied three further, critical pieces of background to Freudian topography. As Ellenberger reports, many psychiatric models of hysteria appealed to unconscious elements within the mind, most dramatically, Pierre Janet's hypothesis that hysteria was caused by unconscious fixed ideas. Wundt observed that, within psychology, an important effort was directed toward dividing cerebral activities into functional units. Finally, evolutionary biology suggested that it might be possible to decompose the mind into systems along evolutionary lines.

Given the directive from psychology and biology to look for functional/evolutionary divisions within the mind and the prevalence of appeals to unconscious elements in psychiatry, the hypothesis of an unconscious mental system acquired prima facie plausibility. I do not mean to suggest that Freud mechanically applied current approaches in theory construction to psychiatric results or that he hit upon the unconscious in a general search for topographic divisions. These trends probably reinforced each other. Psychiatry and experiments with hypnosis seemed to be turning up evidence for unconscious mental states; these results could be understood within one of the few available frameworks for grappling with "higher" functions—assign them to an evolutionarily and functionally distinct area or system within the mind.

In the "Preliminary Communication" (1893) to *Studies on Hysteria*, Freud and his coauthor Joseph Breuer offered several hypotheses about the mechanisms involved. Given the preceding discussion of the two principles, one mechanism will look familiar.

> *It may therefore be said that the ideas which have become pathological have persisted with such freshness and affective strength because they have been denied the normal wearing-away process by means of abreaction and reproduction in states of uninhibited association.* (S.E. II:11)

Although presented as if based on clinical observation alone, this claim obviously depended on several theoretical assumptions. First, it assumed a psychological version of the principle of inertia, that mental states tended to divest themselves of energy.[4] It also assumed that ideas were normally connected by association and that mental states could somehow be prevented from divesting themselves of their energy. Finally, Freud and Breuer suggested that when this occurred, the result could be pathological.

Although *Studies on Hysteria* referred only occasionally to ideas being "in the unconscious" (1893–95, S.E. II:45, 123), crucial components of the systematic conception were already present in rudimentary form. The "Preliminary Communication" closed by trying to explain the apparent efficacy of Breuer's famous "talking cure." When unconscious ideas were expressed in speech, bottled-up energy was somehow released (17). Speech was a motor activity and hence a candidate for the response phase of a reflex. In the *Project*, written two years later, Freud drew a more elaborate connection between words and the unconscious.

What is the difference between an idea that can become conscious and one that cannot? Freud took the perennially popular line that consciousness involved awareness of qualities (*Project for a Scientific Psychology*, 1895, S.E. I:308). Since sensations have quality, people could be conscious of them; ideas were more problematic. Here Freud adapted a fairly standard nineteenth-century assumption to his own purposes. Many theorists assumed that (conscious) thought was possible only by virtue of language and speech. Speech had auditory qualities, however, so that when ideas became attached to what he called "word-representations" (systems of neurons that represented the sensible qualities of words),[5] they could attract consciousness to themselves through the associated sounds (365). Further, since speech was a motor activity, energy from the associated filled idea could be discharged through it. Were this picture correct, then an idea would be incapable of being conscious if it lost or never had a word associated with it.

In all his work Freud assumed that higher creatures were capable of "biological learning," that is, of learning with greater or lesser success how to avoid pain and seek pleasure. Given the apparent clinical evidence that hysteria involved unconscious ideas that the subject would find painful if remembered, Freud reasoned as follows. When these ideas were conscious, they caused pain and so the subject learned biologically to avoid their coming to consciousness. Although this effort might originally have been intentional (Sketches for "Preliminary Communication," 1892, S.E. I:153), subjects gave no indications of continuing conscious efforts on their parts. This suggested an unconscious and irrational mechanism for keeping ideas out of consciousness. It was plausible to believe that an idea remained unconscious if it lacked or had been cut off from any word-representation that could have resulted in motor discharge and attracted consciousness. The necessity of endogenous stimuli producing appropriate, and so delayed, action already implied the presence of some internal means of preventing normal reflexive discharge through associative pathways. So Freud assumed that a similar mechanism was available to defend against recurrences of pain, by preventing ideas from leading to speech and so becoming conscious.

Although this account had speculative links, it had the great virtue of providing a functional account of hysteria, an account that appealed only to temporary differences in the connections among neurons and not to permanent morphological changes. This was critical, for, as Freud observed in "Some Points for a Comparative Study of Organic and Hysterical Motor Paralyses" (1893), the firm negative touchstone for theories of hysteria was the lack of tissue damage found postmortem (S.E. I:168). In this paper, he criticized Charcot's suggestion of "dynamic lesions." Whatever these lesions were supposed to be, they were still organic, in which case hysterical paralysis would behave like organic paralysis. As Freud observed in an oft-quoted phrase, however: "[H]ysteria behaves as though anatomy did not exist or as though it had no knowledge of it" (169). On the contrary, as Janet noted, hysterical symptoms affected parts of the body that were linked only by our ideas of them (cited in Ellenberger 1970:362–64).

Putting these strands together, Freud's early writings offered the following account of psychopathology and the unconscious. Within the mind there were ideas that influenced motor activity, but were kept out of consciousness. Hysterical symptoms, such as motor paralysis and tics, were evidence of their influence. Apparently, these ideas had once been conscious, but were no longer so, because they were painful to the subject. A possible explanation was that they had been dissociated from their word-representation, which would have led to motor discharge in speech and attracted consciousness. When ideas were cut off from their word-representations, they lacked a normal means of unburdening themselves of energy through motor discharge. Instead, their energy appeared to flow to other motor actions that had been associated with these ideas. So, for example, in a classic case described by Breuer, Anna O. had once had a hallucination of snakes coming toward her ill father. She was so frightened that she was unable to speak. At the same time, she tried to move her right arm, but could not, because it had been resting over the back of a chair and had become numb. Thereafter, when she was reminded of snakes, her right arm became paralyzed (*Studies on Hysteria*, 1893–95, S.E. II:38–39).

Before tracing the development of this account through later writings, I will pause to consider its source of support and speculative character. Two general and, by now, familiar background assumptions were clearly involved, reflexology and associationism. Another general, but highly plausible, assumption also played a key role: the ability of organisms to learn through experiences of pleasure and pain. The account also relied on four more local, but still quite reasonable assumptions. The safest was the constraint from anatomy that hysteria did not result from appreciable organic damage.

A second local assumption rested on clinical and experimental evidence. As noted, many psychiatrists took hysteria to be caused by ideas that were not present to normal consciousness. Freud argued that Charcot's demonstrations offered dramatic experimental confirmation of this view ("Charcot," 1893, S.E. III:22–23). Charcot induced symptoms similar to those found in hysteria by placing subjects under hypnosis and telling them, for example, that they could not move a limb. Both hypnotism and hysteria had been regarded with suspicion. With the interest of individuals like Bernheim and Charcot, Janet and Breuer, they acquired some scientific respectability. When their results converged on the hypothesis of active ideas not present to consciousness, it was not unreasonable to believe that something had been discovered. Further, Freud went to great lengths to gather additional evidence for active unconscious ideas through his studies of jokes and bungled actions (or parapraxes).

Freud's early work on aphasia supplied the third crucial local assumption. Clinical and pathological evidence had suggested that the representation of a word in the brain was composed of auditory, visual, and kinesthetic elements, in particular its "sound-image," "visual letter-image," "motor speech-image," and "motor writing-image" (On Aphasia, 1891, S.E. XIV:212). Of these, the most critical was the sound-image, since that was required by speech, reading, spelling, and writing. Freud followed Mill in assuming that beyond these elements, a word acquired meaning by being connected with an "object-representation," a complex of associations constituted by visual, acoustic, tactile, kinesthetic, and other representations (213). Even if this were not the entire story, pathology implied that different parts of word-representations could become dissociated. In particular, patients might suffer from "verbal aphasia" in which only the associations between different parts of the word-representation were disturbed, "asymbolic aphasia" in which the association between the word-representation and the object-representation was disturbed, and what Freud proposed to call "agnosias," disturbances in recognition of objects (that is, which had to do not with word-, but with object-representations) (214–15; cf. Wundt 1902:302–15). Given these clinical and anatomical results, it seemed clearly possible for ideas, or object-representations, to become detached from their normally associated word-representations.

Although Freud wrote metaphorically and speculatively about word-representations "attracting" consciousness, this claim rested on a fourth local assumption: Language was the necessary vehicle for conscious thought. If this were true—and many nineteenth- and twentieth-century theorists have regarded conscious thought just as subvocal or inner speech—then, in light of the aphasia evidence, it was a reasonable hypothesis that ideas that were unconscious had been cut off from their associated word-representations. Since he assumed the reflex nature of the neural apparatus and the association of ideas, Freud was led to the further hypothesis that, in hysteria, the energy from an unconscious idea that could not be discharged in speech was channeled through associations to other, inappropriate somatic outlets.

Finally, Freud's hypothesis that certain ideas were "in the unconscious," that there was an unconscious system, rested on the topographic aspect of his metapsychology. As noted in chapter 2, brain anatomy and physiology indicated that higher or central mental processes probably should not be regarded as having particular anatomical locations. Although the neurons in a particular region of the brain might currently be serving a particular function, what distinguished them as a system was not their location, but their distinctive functional connections to other systems of neurons. Notice, however, that Freud's account of what distinguished unconscious ideas was cast in terms of connections to other systems of neurons. These ideas were cut off from their word-representations, and so from speech and consciousness. Given this account and an approach that divided the mental apparatus according to functional interconnections, unconscious ideas would have some claim to be regarded as belonging to a special mental division.

This claim was reinforced by another consideration. Although this feature achieved greater prominence later, even in the early works, it was clear that Freud believed that unconscious ideas involved a kind of mental functioning that differed from normal processes. As observed in the last section, he regarded hysterical symptoms as following the more primitive mental processes of reflexes and association, and not the sophisticated principles needed to cope with reality. In part, this was because hysterical symptoms (and dreams) did not appear to follow rational principles, and reflexes and associations were the default assumptions for mental processes. Evolutionary approaches to psychopathology lent additional support to this view. Among others, Jackson and Meynert believed that mental illnesses occurred when newer centers of the brain were disturbed and their functions taken over by older, more primitive forms (Ellenberger 1970:535). Thus, beyond their distinctive connections, or lack of connections, to other systems, unconscious ideas seemed to operate on different principles that suggested that they belonged to an evolutionarily older part of the mental apparatus. So both functional and evolutionary considerations pointed in the direction of an unconscious system within the mind.

Once again, Freud's hypothesis of an unconscious system was no deductive inference, even granting the general and local assumptions that he might reasonably have made. On the contrary, it was an imaginative synthesis of contemporary results and approaches: the psychiatry of hysteria, the psychology of aphasia, the plausible link between language and conscious thought, the functional and evolutionary approach to mental systems, and the constant background assumptions of reflexology and associationism. Still, each of these pieces enjoyed considerable independent support, and it hardly weakened their claims to show that they could be accommodated in a single overarching hypothesis. Freud's explanation for hysterical symptoms was speculative, but certainly no more speculative than its rivals;[6] and, as noted, he immediately began searching for additional confirming evidence.

In 1915, Freud offered a systematic presentation of his views in "The Unconscious." There were few dramatic changes, but some aspects received further elaboration. He began with a review of the evidence. Posthypnotic suggestion, hysterical systems, jokes, bungled actions, dreams, and gaps in normal thinking all testified to the need to assume active but unconscious ideas (S.E. XIV:166–69). Memory itself suggested that we had many ideas of which we were not currently conscious. Still, the critical point for psychoanalysis was that some ideas were inaccessible to consciousness. They were not just currently out of conscious awareness, but were unable to become conscious, in the absence of a change in the functional organization of the mind brought about by therapy or some accidental intervention. So Freud proposed a threefold distinction: currently conscious ideas, ideas that were not conscious, but could be, which he located in the preconscious, and ideas that could not become conscious and so belonged to the unconscious, in the distinctive psychoanalytic sense of "unconscious." Although a third, preconscious, system was added, he regarded it as sharing the same principles of operation as the conscious system (172–73). The fundamental distinction was still between normal conscious processes and ideas that could not be brought to consciousness under standard conditions.

Freud appealed to anatomy to repudiate again the suggestion that the conscious system should be located in the cortex and the unconscious in subcortical parts of the brain ("Preface to Bernheim," 1888, S.E. I:84; "The Unconscious," 1915, XIV:174). To date, anatomy had not been able to match higher functions with particular regions of the brain, so the distinction between the systems was functional and had to remain so for the present. His list of the special characteristics of unconscious mental processes is fairly familiar: They were governed by primary processes (the movement of energy among ideas on the basis of past associations), exemption from mutual contradiction, timelessness, and the replacement of external by psychical reality ("The Unconscious," 1915, S.E. XIV:187). Although the negative characteristics had been filled out somewhat by evidence from symptoms and dreams, the main thrust was still the lack of relation to reality, what Janet had described as the lack of *"fonction du réel"* (Ellenberger 1970:376).

Freud's topographic divisions of the mind underwent important modifications in *The Ego and the Id*. To understand these developments, we must first come to grips with the centerpiece of his account of human mentality, the theory of sex.

Repression and Libido Theory

In *Freud: Biologist of the Mind*, Frank Sulloway raises the most basic question about Freud's theory: Why sex? His answer is that sex had already been made preeminent by evolutionary biology and that Freud drew heavily, but stealthily (to protect his claims to originality), on that pervasive tradition. Sulloway's case for the overriding importance of evolutionary biology in recommending sex to Freud is compelling. Without disagreeing with that fundamental point, I will argue that sex had another significant and related attraction. Because of its ties to such diverse fields as physiology, psychiatry, and sociology, sex opened up the possibility of a unified treatment of mental phenomena.

According to Freud's own frequent retellings of the history of psychoanalysis, the importance of sex was forced on him by the clinical evidence. In "Sexuality in the Aetiology of the Neuroses" (1898), he announced that in every case the most immediate and significant causes of the neuroses were factors involving sexual life (S.E. III:263). An earlier paper, "The Aetiology of Hysteria" (1896), had reported the presence of sexual factors in all eighteen cases that he had been able to analyze (S.E. III:200). He conceded that he was not the first to link sex and neuroses, but understated the support for this view.

As noted earlier, Briquet had tried to test the common view that hysteria was caused by erotic frustration in 1859. Freud himself wrote an encyclopedia article on hysteria in 1888 (presumably offering the currently accepted wisdom), which included the observation that "[i]t must be admitted that conditions related *functionally* to sexual life play a great part in the aetiology of hysteria (as of all neuroses) . . ." (S.E. I:51).[7] His distinguished collaborator, Josef Breuer, pointed to the importance of sex in neuroses without elaborate explanation or defense: "The sexual instinct is undoubtedly the most powerful source of persisting increases of excitation (and consequently of neuroses)" (*Studies on Hysteria*, 1893–95, S.E. II:200); "*the great majority of severe neuroses in women have their origin in the marriage bed*" (246).

The first citation from Breuer indicates a major virtue of sex in explaining the neuroses. In the population seeking medical help, neurotic symptoms tended to be severe and enduring, implicating a potent and continuing causal agent. As we saw in chapter 2, evolutionary biology had suggested that the most pervasive and powerful forces driving animal behavior were probably self-preservative and sexual instincts. A different aspect of the clinical picture suggested the special relevance of sexual instincts: the hypothesis of unconscious ideas.

Why were some ideas unconscious? Charcot and others favored a hereditary disposition toward a splitting of consciousness (Ellenberger 1970:144). Originally, Freud agreed with Charcot. In his encyclopedia article on hysteria, he stated that "[t]he aetiology of the *status hystericus* is to be looked for entirely in heredity . . ." (1888, S.E. I:50). Later, he rejected this position, noting that any serious argument for heredity must be statistical and that had not been given ("Heredity and the Aetiology of the Neuroses" 1896, S.E. III:144).[8] Besides this sound point, Freud had other cogent objections to focusing on heredity. Why should we try to explain adult behavior by appealing to the history of the race rather than to the history of the individual, since "the latter period would be easier to understand and could claim to be considered before that of heredity" (*Three Essays on the Theory of Sexuality*, 1905, S.E. VII:173)? Further, even if its influence were greater, since heredity was fixed, factors lying within the life of the individual had more practical importance ("Heredity and the Aetiology of the Neuroses," 1896, S.E. III:146). For, unlike heredity, life experiences might be prevented or dealt with through therapy. Given the weaknesses of the heredity approach, it seemed reasonable to seek experiential conditions that might cause ideas to be cut off from consciousness (144).

Unconscious ideas had been abroad in intellectual circles at least since Leibniz (1714:644). The usual view was that such ideas were too weak or too faint to attract attention. If some unconscious ideas could cause hysterical symptoms and posthypnotic behavior, however, then they appeared to be quite powerful. With other psychotherapists, Freud assumed that *in the normal case* ideas strong enough to guide action were or could become conscious. So, some special conditions had to explain why ideas were not available to consciousness. Where Charcot and Janet thought of the situation in terms of a hereditary disposition of the mind to split or to fall into unusual states, Freud's conception was more dynamic (Ellenberger 1970:144–45). The normal tendency of ideas to become conscious was blocked by an interfering factor, a force he named "repression." This was Freud's most important dynamic hypothesis: Within the mind there was a force, or family of forces, capable of locking up ideas in the unconscious system.

If heredity should not be presumed to bear the entire explanatory burden and (strong) ideas normally attracted consciousness, then the puzzle of unconscious ideas became, Why were some ideas repressed? Given the traditional links between neurosis and sex and, presumably, with hints from patients, Freud and Breuer perceived the excluded ideas as relating to sexual matters. They observed that sexual experiences and longings were barred from polite discussion and thwarted by social convention. Both offered moving descriptions of the forceful clash—seemingly, violent enough to cause mental illness—between natural sexual desire and social arrangements that left it unsatisfied. Prior to marriage, strict celibacy was required, at least for women. If early indoctrination in the evils of sex did not prevent a woman from enjoying marital relations, then a growing family and the absence of acceptable means of contraception soon led both husband and wife to fear intimacy. Freud expressed a fervent hope that medicine would one day solve the problem.

> It cannot be denied that in any marriage Malthusian preventive measures will become necessary at some time or other; and, from a theoretical point of view, it would be one of the greatest triumphs of humanity, one of the most tangible liberations from the constraints of nature to which mankind is subject, if we could succeed in raising the responsible act of procreating children to the level of a deliberate and intentional activity and in freeing it from its entanglement with the necessary satisfaction of a natural need. ("Sexuality in the Aetiology of the Neuroses," 1898, S.E. III:277)

Breuer observed that the antagonism between societal sanctions and natural sexuality was most acute in the case of particularly moral girls. Some adolescent girls were like the boys in being able to deal with the sexual ideas that crowded in on them at puberty. But girls who had been reared to believe that sex was something dirty and beneath their ethical standards had no choice but to try to fend off these sexual ideas by repressing them, by banishing them from thought as well as from word and deed (*Studies on Hysteria*, 1893–95, S.E. II:245–46).

If the problem of unconscious ideas was to explain what life experiences could lead to repression of what ideas, then sexual ideas and their suppression by society were the obvious candidates. Since not all civilized people were neurotic, or not obviously or clinically so, some further factor was required. In "Heredity and the Aetiology of the Neuroses," Freud distinguished three different types of causes:

> (1) *Preconditions*, which are indispensable for producing the disorder concerned but which are of a general nature and are met with in the aetiology of many other disorders; (2) *Concurrent Causes*, which [are also general] . . ., but are not indispensable . . .; and (3) *Specific Causes*, which are as indispensable as the preconditions, but are of a limited nature and appear only in the aetiology of the disorder for which they are specific. (1896, S.E. III:147)

His account incorporated the widespread belief in the importance of hereditary taint by listing it as a precondition. Much less impressed by the claims for illness, accident, and exhaustion, he relegated such factors to concurrent causes. The novel contribution, as he stressed, was the attempt to provide specific causes for various neuroses.

In *Studies on Hysteria*, Breuer and Freud had offered a causal hypothesis: "*Hysterics suffer mainly from reminiscences*" (1893–95, S.E. II:7), that is, memories excluded from consciousness. Breuer's concluding discussion was more specific in noting that "what are mostly in question are ideas and processes connected with sexual life" (210). A year later, on the basis of eighteen cases, Freud narrowed and universalized this hypothesis: The specific cause of hysteria was "*a precocious experience of sexual relations with actual excitement of the genitals, resulting from sexual abuse committed by another person . . .* [in] *earliest youth* ("Heredity and the Aetiology of the Neuroses," S.E. III:152). He gave an analogous account of obsessional neurosis on the basis of six cases (three that were "pure" or unmixed with other recognized mental disorders). Here the specific cause was precocious sexual experience in which the child was not merely passive, but a lustful participant. He speculated that such behavior was probably the result of an earlier passive experience, a hypothesis that would explain the fact that many cases of obsessional neurosis were not pure, but involved hysteria (156). More briefly, both hysteria and obsessional neurosis were brought about by childhood seductions.

Besides similar etiologies, Freud believed that hysteria and obsessional neurosis had a similar mechanism. Abnormal behavior was produced by the repressed memory of precocious sexual experiences. (Hence, he referred to these as *"psycho*neuroses" ["Abstracts of Scientific Writings," 1896, S.E. III:254].) By contrast, he did not take either neurasthenia or anxiety neurosis to be psychical or ideogenic. "Neurasthenia" was the name given to a somewhat vague clinical syndrome: "fatigue, intracranial pressure, flatulent dyspepsia, constipation, spinal paraesthesias, sexual weakness, etc." ("Heredity and the Aetiology of the Neuroses," 1896, S.E. III:150). He linked it to immoderate masturbation. In massing the evidence for the specific cause of anxiety neurosis (classified by irritability, anxious expectation, anxiety attacks, sweating, tremors, vertigo, phobias, paraesthesias (150)), he was much less casual. After presenting instances and rebutting alleged counterexamples in earlier works, he concluded that this condition was always caused by enforced abstinence or unsatisfying sexual intercourse (151).

Freud summarized his findings about specific causes in his second most important dynamic hypothesis: Pathological conditions produced by each of these major neuroses *"have as their common source the subject's sexual life, whether they lie in a disorder of his contemporary sexual life or in important events in his past life"* ("Heredity and the Aetiology of the Neuroses," 1896, S.E. III:149). However, this account had an important qualification. Although heredity was only a precondition and sexual difficulties specific causes, "[these] can replace each other as regards quantity, [so] that the same pathological effect will be produced by the coincidence of a very serious specific aetiology with a moderate disposition or of a severely loaded nervous heredity with a slight specific influence" (147). Perhaps Freud saw hints of tradeoffs between strength of hereditary factors and degree of sexual frustration in his clinical work. But presumably this idea was given important support by his assumptions that brain processes (normal and abnormal) had a quantitative character and that, since sexuality had a somatic basis, it too could be regarded quantitatively.

How reasonable were the two fundamental and intertwined hypotheses of Freud's dynamic theory, repression and sex? As noted in passing, the case for repression rested on four well-supported points: the existence of unconscious ideas, the widely held view that action-guiding ideas were normally accessible to consciousness, the arguments against heredity as the sole agent, and the fact of societal suppression of sexuality, particularly in the case of women. In terms of numbers, the case for sex was fairly impressive. Precocious sexual experience in eighteen separate cases of hysteria and six of obsessional neurosis was some evidence for a link. Freud was less explicit about the cases of anxiety neurosis, but implied that the number was substantial. Still, (at least) four serious objections can be raised about the clinical evidence implicating sex.

Although Freud was at pains to give precise descriptions of the presenting symptoms of these neuroses, current readers will question whether distinct illnesses have been isolated. If these are not specific diseases, however, then any claim about specific causes is extremely dubious. This criticism can be blunted by appealing to the current *Diagnostic and Statistical Manual of Mental Disorders* of the American Psychiatric Association (1987). A glance at this material reveals that Freud's efforts at classification were quite reasonable even by today's standards of psychiatric nosology.

Careful study of the case material raises a second objection. As others have noted, Freud was directive in psychoanalytic sessions and often suggested sexual causes to his patients, so his results were laden with experimenter bias (Glymour, forthcoming:78). Although this objection casts grave doubts on the *truth* of Freud's views, my concern is with their reasonableness. As Grünbaum documents, Freud was aware of the danger of suggestion (Grünbaum 1984:133; *Introductory Lectures on Psycho-Analysis*, 1917, S.E. XVI:466–47). He believed that he avoided this error, because patients were so loath to discuss sexual experiences that he could not induce them to in the absence of factual bases (e.g., "The Aetiology of Hysteria," 1896, S.E. III:204). It is easy to see Freud's naiveté on this point as very convenient and to believe that he should have had higher standards of empirical evidence. Although both these criticisms are warranted, the state of the field provides some mitigation. Compared to standard alternatives—hypnosis and suggestion, with or without hypnosis—the technique of encouraging or even helping patients to free associate would not have seemed particularly manipulative.

The third objection imputes a different sort of naiveté. Why did Freud believe lurid tales from manifestly abnormal patients? In part, this came from his faith in the cathartic method. If, as he and Breuer believed, symptoms disappeared when patients recalled and worked through traumatic events, then it would seem that the previously unavailable memory must have been the cause of the symptoms, since the effect ceased when the cause did ("Preliminary Communication," 1893, S.E. II:7).[9] He also defended himself against this charge by appealing to two other considerations. Occasionally, another party could confirm the patient's recollection ("The Aetiology of Hysteria," 1896, S.E. II:206). Further, in all cases, the patient's demeanor in describing these events indicated a strong reluctance to do so (204; "Heredity and the Aetiology of the Neuroses," 1896, S.E. III:153).

Beyond Freud's explicit efforts, the best defense against the gullibility charge is the fact that he came to reject his patients' claims! Much has been written about the abandonment of the seduction theory. In the main, I follow Sulloway's plausible and well-documented account (Sulloway 1979:206–7, 215–17, 313–15, 514–15, 516–18). Freud had always recognized three potentially fatal objections to his position. One might think that attacks on children were too rare to account for the frequency of neurosis ("The Aetiology of Hysteria," 1896, S.E. III:207). Worse still, in light of Mill's methods, there seem to be documented cases of *normal* adults who remember being seduced as children (209). Finally, were childhood sexual activity almost universal, "the demonstration of its presence in every case would carry no weight" (210). Freud parried these criticisms by claiming that sexual attacks were more frequent than commonly believed, but by no means universal, and by noting that, even in somatic diseases, pathogens did not invariably bring on illness (207–10). The view that heredity was a precondition provided useful support for the last point.

Sulloway believes that Freud's unacknowledged reading of Albert Moll's careful studies demonstrating that precocious sexual activity, including seduction, need not lead to neurosis was the decisive factor (Sulloway 1979:312). When Freud officially renounced the seduction theory, in 1905, he cited normal case histories compiled by Havelock Ellis and others as the reason for the change (*Three Essays on the Theory of Sexuality*, 1905, S.E. VII:140, 190–91). Although this seems quite straightforward, an aura of mystery has been cast over this episode because, in 1897, he wrote to Fliess that he no longer believed his patients' neurotic stories (Masson 1985:264). Why did he delay conceding this point in print?

I will not join the efforts to psychoanalyze Freud's motives for waiting, because the logic of the situation seems sufficient to resolve this issue. His tone to Fliess was quite confident, but it was only a letter. Many theorists confidently assert claims in private correspondence that they would never consider publishing at that time. As just indicated, Freud was always aware of the potential sources of defeating evidence for the seduction hypothesis. What complicated the situation was the fluid role of heredity. How much slippage between instances of seduction and neurosis should it be assumed to explain? Presumably, as more mismatches were reported, Freud's doubts came to assume the form of a defensible position. Further, his own emerging account of psychosexual development implied the universality of childhood sexuality. Further still, at some point in this time interval, he must have realized that his fundamental dynamic hypothesis about the psychoneuroses—that they were caused by repressed sexual "memories"—was perfectly compatible with this development. On his own theory, the contents of the unconscious were not governed by principles of reality, so the mistake did not threaten his general program. Sexual fantasies could be substituted for sexual memories. Assuming these three factors were critical—the accumulating evidence of normal adults who had been seduced in childhood,[10] the commitment to childhood sexuality, and the formulation of a hypothesis accommodating the apparently inconsistent data—the time lag does not seem extraordinary.

Although abandoning the seduction theory showed Freud's willingness to doubt patients' tales, the episode raises a fourth, potentially devastating, objection. Given the weight he placed on clinical evidence, why did his doubts about patient reliability not lead to more widespread doubts about sexual etiologies and about the method of free association itself?[11] At least in principle, seduction is a public act. In surrendering this doctrine, he gave up the only source of independent evidence for sexual etiologies of the psychoneuroses—and these hypotheses were the bedrock of all his theories.

Without speculating about personality or appealing to the work on dreaming, two quite different considerations explain—and, to a fair extent, justify—Freud's persevering with sex. The simpler is that the fall of the seduction theory impugned very little of the clinical evidence. Only the skimpy corroborating evidence from nonpatients had to be jettisoned. Cures and the reluctance to discuss these matters would still testify to the role of repressed sexually loaded "memories" or, better, fantasies as specific causes. The second factor was by far the more important. In describing his own work, Freud often cast himself as the ultimate Millian Empiricist: His claims for sex did not spring from some philosophical system, but rested entirely on the evidence of the clinic. Despite his frequent genuflections at the altar of Empiricism, there can be no question that Freud placed sex at the center of his doctrines largely for theoretical and systematic reasons. So far, I have presented only his official arguments in favor of the dynamic forces of sex and repression. But it is impossible to assess the plausibility of these claims accurately, without looking more closely at the weighty theoretical factors that recommended sex (and consequently repression) to him as the basic forces governing human mental life.

Why Sex Was Ideal

To begin to understand how sex actually fitted into Freud's thinking, recall two methodological directives and one substantive doctrine that have already been considered. For good reasons rooted in his materialism, he believed that any psychological theory had to be biologically plausible. This implied, in particular, that it had to be neurologically plausible. It also implied a more specific methodological claim: A completed psychological theory should have an economic part that described in general ways the flow of energy through the system. Turning to substantive matters, on the widely shared reflex picture of the nervous system, external forces, from outside the body or within it, were required to drive the apparatus. The suggestion gleaned from evolutionary biology that animal behavior was strongly influenced by self-preservative and sexual instincts seemed to provide an obvious answer: A reflexive neural system needed something to energize it, and these instincts were available to supply the juice. After Darwin's discussion of instincts, many books offered lists of instincts and putative descriptions of their nature (Murphy 1949:116). Among others, William James tried to define instincts and to enumerate essential human instincts (James 1892:258ff.). As Sulloway notes, a number of prominent psychologists and psychiatrists, including Krafft-Ebing, Moll, Thomas Clouston in England, and G. Stanley Hall in America, came independently to the idea that sexual and self-preservative instincts and only they were sanctioned by the biological sciences (Sulloway 1979:254). This was obviously Freud's view as well. Although others might postulate as many instincts as they liked, evolutionary biology clearly discriminated, by providing excellent reasons to regard these two as the most fundamental and the most powerful.

Freud's translators have slightly obscured the intimate relation between his reflex conception of the nervous system and his support for sexual instincts by translating *"Trieb"* as "instinct" even though he carefully distinguished *"Triebe"* and *"Instinkte."*[12] Their rationale was that "drive" had too many distinct, current meanings, but "instinct" was vague and indeterminate (S.E. I:xxv). Although this might be true, "drive" has the advantage of reflecting what Klein aptly described as Freud's "energic" conception of the mental system in general and libido in particular (Klein 1976:15). To preserve this connotation, I use "instinctual drive."

As with the pleasure principle and the Unconscious, Freud did not provide a systematic discussion of instinctual sexual drives until quite late, but the construct was there from the beginning. In the *Project*, he noted that endogenous stimuli originated from major needs, hunger, respiration, and sexuality (1895, S.E. I:297). An 1894 draft of an uncompleted book on the major neuroses mentioned internal versus external sources of excitation, constant versus ephemeral excitation, and the theory of sexual substances (S.E. I:187). His coauthor Josef Breuer moved freely from "endogenous sources of excitation" to "instinctual sexual drives," observing that excitation involved chemical changes and (as noted) that sexual drives were undoubtedly the most powerful source of increases in excitation (*Studies on Hysteria*, 1893–95, S.E. II:199–200).

The elegant fit between the needs of a reflexive nervous system and the apparent endorsement of sexual instincts by evolutionary biology was obviously a critical factor in leading Freud to libido theory, the hypothesis that the neural system was partly driven and largely influenced by instinctual sexual drives. Presumably, he reasoned that if evolutionary biology were right that sex was a behavior-guiding instinctual drive and neurophysiology were right about how the nervous system worked, by having some kind of energy flowing among neurons, then seemingly instinctual sexual drives must have some direct or indirect means of affecting the flow of something among neurons. So there had to be libido, whether it was chemical or electrical in nature and whether there was just one kind or many. Although this argument again was not logically tight and, as we will see in chapter 6, involved some serious oversimplification, the premises made the conclusion plausible.

Despite several attempts to retreat from this fact (*Three Essays on the Theory of Sexuality*, 1905, e.g., S.E. VII:131), Freud explicitly recognized that the principal argument for libido came from biology (and neurophysiology). In 1914, he noted that

> the hypothesis of separate instinctual ego drives and instinctual sexual drives (that is to say, libido theory) rests scarcely at all on a psychological basis, but derives its principal support from biology. ("On Narcissum," S.E. XIV:79; amended translation)

In 1932, he recalled that

> [w]e told ourselves we should probably not be going astray if we began by separating two main instincts or classes of instincts in accordance with the two great needs—hunger and love. However jealously we usually defend the independence of psychology from every other science, here we stood in the shadow of the unshakable biological fact that the living individual organism is at the command of two intentions, self-preservation and the preserva-

tion of the species, which seem to be independent of each other, which, so far as we know at present, have no common origin and whose interests are often in conflict in animal life. (*New Introductory Lectures on Psycho-Analysis*, 1933, S.E. XXII:95)

Psychoanalysis was always constrained by the "unshakable biological fact" that there were two major classes of instinctual drives. When, to the despair of his followers, he proposed the "death instinct," he reversed his earlier position and lumped sex and self-preservation more or less together as one class of instinctual drive (*Beyond the Pleasure Principle*, 1920, S.E. XVIII:52). Since it never attained the status of orthodoxy, I will not consider the Eros/Thanatos duality. As noted, Freud's uneven treatment of libido and self-preservative instincts derived from the link that he and others saw between neuroses and sexual difficulties and also, presumably, from the observation that his patients had all the food that they wanted.

Besides the critical support from evolutionary biology and psychiatry, work in sexology gave Freud reason to believe that sexual urges might move from the domain of common wisdom to that of scientific theory. Apparently, sexual behavior was not a uniform phenomenon, but could be resolved into the effects of more basic component instinctual drives. This richer understanding of sexuality also raised a serious theoretical question. Given the polymorphous character of sexuality, how could instinctual sexual drives be distinguished from others? When Freud tackled this question directly, in *Three Essays on the Theory of Sexuality* and again in "Instincts and Their Vicissitudes," he gave a somewhat equivocal answer. Instinctual sexual drives were identified by their sources (1905, S.E. VII:168; 1914, XIV:122–23). Were these "sources" meant to be the somatic sources of the release of excitation, that is, the erotogenic zones? If so, then the matter was not fully resolved, since bodily areas that Freud claimed to be erotogenic were not standardly associated with sexuality. Hence, it was no proof that instinctual sexual energy was involved to trace the source to the mouth, for example. At this point, he brought in another factor that had appeared previously in his writings, the idea of a special sexual chemistry (*Three Essays on the Theory of Sexuality*, 1905, S.E. VII:168; "Instincts and Their Vicissitudes," XIV:123; cf. "Some Points for a Comparative Study of Organic and Hysterical Motor Paralyses," 1893, I:167). Later in the *Three Essays*, he devoted a section to available chemical hypotheses. Observation of castrated and infertile males made it clear that sex cells (sperm and ova) were not the principal sources of sexual excitation. Other secretions from gonads and perhaps from the thyroid gland appeared to be implicated. In a 1920 revision, he enlarged the thyroid hypothesis and adduced experimental evidence in its support (S.E. VII:215). Nevertheless, he was not prepared to commit himself to this hypothesis. He appended a note to this discussion in which the relation between his metatheoretic directives and particular substantive hypotheses is very clear.

> I may add that I attach no importance to this particular hypothesis and should be ready to abandon it at once in favour of another, provided that its fundamental nature remained unchanged—that is, the emphasis which it lays upon sexual chemistry. (S.E. VII:216)

As we saw in the case of the pleasure principle, he had some sensitivity to the danger of borrowing current hypotheses from other fields. Again he tried to avoid it by adopting a more generic account, so that all he needed was that current views turn out to be roughly right. Unfortunately, as we will see in chapter 6, even this was too much to ask.

Libido theory was a dynamic hypothesis, since it offered a qualitative description of the forces governing mental life: They were primarily sexual. But part of its attraction was undoubtedly that it provided a natural bridge to an economic account of the amount of excitation and the manner of its operation. Freud stayed with sex because he believed that it was the key to constructing a comprehensive theory of mental life, as specified in his metapsychological principles. It lent itself to a possible economic treatment and so fitted with neurophysiology and biology. Further, psychiatry had sanctioned the hypothesis of unconscious ideas. The reflexology of psychology and neurology had made it plausible to believe that the cause of mental illness might be excess energy pouring into the system. Aphasia studies had suggested a possible mechanism for keeping ideas conscious: Psychical energy was diverted from flowing to the word-representation associated with an idea that caused pain when conscious. Because of societal sanctions, sexual ideas induced conflict and pain and were suppressed in speech.[13] Freud regarded psychoanalysis as standing between psychology and biology in the order of sciences, because it forged a link among all these findings. The linchpin of that link was sex.

It was precisely the ability of sex and libido theory to draw connections among all these seemingly disparate results of contemporary science that convinced Freud that he had to be right. His critics would complain that psychoanalysis was a tissue of speculation, woven together from too many different hypotheses drawn from too many different fields. Although each one might be reasonable in itself, it was hopelessly improbable that each link in the chain was sound. Freud's position was exactly the opposite: The ability of libido theory to reveal systematic interconnections among all these facts was its strength. Interdisciplinary theorists should be on Freud's side up to a point. As long as the individual claims were sound and the libido hypothesis itself reasonable, then the fact that it revealed connections among previously unconnected facts must be to its credit.

Beyond these significant attractions, sex had two further compelling claims. Sexology offered a great deal of qualitative material for Freud to draw on in developing his own theories of sex. The extent of those borrowings will be clear in the next section. The last virtue of sex I consider was noted by the sexologists. Krafft-Ebing began his *Psychopathia Sexualis* by extolling the brighter side of the sexual instinct, which, in unfortunate cases, was the cause of such misery and degradation.

> If man were deprived of sexual fulfillment and the nobler enjoyments arising therefrom, all poetry and probably all moral tendency would be eliminated from his life.
>
> Sexual life no doubt is the one mighty factor in the individual and social relations of man which discloses his powers of activity, of acquiring property, of establishing a home, of awakening altruistic sentiments towards a person of the opposite sex, and towards his own issue as well as towards the whole human race.
>
> Sexual feeling is really the root of all ethics, and no doubt of aestheticism and religion. (Krafft-Ebing 1903:1)

Although Krafft-Ebing's claims may seem wildly overstated to us, they were strongly implied by three well-entrenched views that we have already encountered. Most obviously, sex convincingly met the methodological standard that any explanation of our "higher" accomplishments must trace their lineage to conditions shared with "lower" animals. Further, both sociology and anthropology assumed that marriage was a pivotal institution in civilization. According to sociology, however, marriage itself was "rooted in the family [or, dropping the euphemism, in sex]." On theoretical grounds, then, sex had a serious claim to figure in the explanation of a variety of civilization's achievements; in addition, Krafft-Ebing (and others) had observed that homosexuals frequently made outstanding contributions to the state and the arts. Given these assumptions from anthropology, sociology, and sexology, an adequate theory of sex promised to bring together results, not just from neurology, biology, and psychology, but from all the mental sciences.

To return, at last, to the crucial question answered only partially in the last section: How reasonable were the twin dynamic hypotheses of repression and sex? The critical considerations in favor of repression were the hypothesis of unconscious ideas, the flaws with the claims that mental illness was entirely hereditary, and the dramatic evidence provided by Breuer's "talking cure." As noted in the last section, the first assumption was widely, if not universally, accepted in psychiatry, and the second argument was well taken. Even granting the weaknesses in the clinical evidence, Freud's hypothesis of repression was no more speculative than the competitors offered, for example, by Charcot and Janet.

Why sex? His own Empiricist posturing to the contrary, Freud's incorrect, but not unreasonable, nineteenth-century reading of the clinical evidence was but part of the answer. Findings from many different sciences, neurophysiology, psychology, psychiatry, sexology, anthropology, sociology, and—preeminently—evolutionary biology all pointed to sex as the key to understanding the origins of human nature and the forces governing it.

Within his own theory, the two fundamental dynamic hypotheses, sex and repression, were made for each other. The considerations that supported repression implied that there were extremely powerful ideas within the mind that were somehow kept from consciousness. Given the apparent importance of instinctive sexual drives in animal life and societal suppression of sexual topics, nothing fit this dual requirement as well as sex. I do not mean to imply that Freud became convinced about the existence of repression and then realized that sex was a possible, or the only possible, explanation of this phenomenon. Reading the early discussions, it is clear that he hit upon the idea of repression at least partly because he recognized his patients' need to defend themselves against sexual ideas (e.g., *Studies on Hysteria*, 1893–95, S.E. II: 116–17, 146). Nevertheless, the independent arguments supporting repression lent further weight to the importance of sex.

Given this massive theoretical support, when Freud thought that he had found that sex was invariably implicated in the psychoneuroses, he inferred that all neurotic symptoms were caused by sexual difficulties. He has been criticized ever since for excessive generalization. If, however, one accepted his premises that the psychoneuroses were specific diseases that must have specific causes, then this hypothesis could be viewed as a bold, but not totally implausible, attempt to get away from the vagaries of medical psychiatry and put matters on a more rigorous scientific basis. Further, were this hypothesis correct, then the severity of neurotic illness would lend additional support to the more general arguments for the importance of sexual forces in the mental economies of normal individuals. The fall of the seduction theory did not shake Freud's faith in the essential correctness of sexual etiologies, because beyond the clinical evidence, that hypothesis had reservoirs of support "from above," from theoretical considerations provided by relevant and well-established sciences.

Psychoanalysis and Psychosexual Development

Repression and sex did not stand alone as isolated dynamic hypotheses. Psychoanalysis was shaped by Freud's efforts to embed these claims in a wider theory of sexuality and psychological development. This best-known part of psychoanalytic theory relied heavily on the work of predecessors and co-workers in sexology. As Sulloway shows in detail, all of psychoanalysis's central sexual concepts—libido, component instincts, erotogenic zones, autoerotism, narcissism, childhood sexuality, bisexuality, diphasic development—were introduced by others (Sulloway 1979:chap. 8, passim). His point is to demonstrate that the carefully crafted image of Freud as a pioneer in the field of sex is preposterous. However, he also establishes something else. Freud's sexual theories were not the product of flights of fantasy, but rested on the solid achievements of forgotten or scorned, but extremely competent, naturalists and theoreticians.

In 1905, Freud presented the basic psychoanalytic position on sexuality in three essays. Although these essays were revised five times from 1910 to 1925, the essentials never changed. The first essay was, as he noted, a synthesis of standard literature on "perversions" and his own and I. Sadger's clinical materials (*Three Essays on the Theory of Sexuality*, S.E. VII:135, n. 1).[14] In summarizing the writings of Krafft-Ebing, Moll, Moebius, Ellis, and others, he highlighted two conclusions. Sexuality was not a matter of a single, univocal instinct, but was best understood as comprising components, which could come apart, as in the "perversions" (162). For example, homosexuality suggested a disposition to bisexuality (143–144). Second, these various sexual instincts could be opposed by mental forces such as shame, disgust, and morality (162). In normal cases, these countervailing forces prevented the component instincts that were expressed in "perversions" from becoming manifest.

Freud reiterated that clinical experience indicated that psychoneuroses were always tied to sexual ideas. One difficulty in accepting this hypothesis had been that repressed fantasies discovered in analysis did not always coincide with what was considered normal sexual behavior. The discovery of component instincts and countervailing forces appeared to shed considerable light on the clinical picture. For, on the accepted view of "perversions," there were a variety of sexual instincts and forces capable of restraining them in normal individuals. Hence, it was to be expected that some symptoms would be independent of genital sexuality, but linked instead to experiences and fantasies involving other erotogenic zones (*Three Essays on the Theory of Sexuality*, 1905, S.E. VII:165–71). Besides offering a possible solution to this specific problem, the work on "perversions" provided vital independent evidence for Freud's basic dynamic picture: Within the mind there were powerful sexual instincts that could be effectively blocked from leading to action or awareness by opposing forces.

Since component instincts and the forces that opposed them masked each other in normal individuals, Freud saw psychoanalysis as making an important contribution to sexology. It provided a means of studying "perverse" tendencies where the "perversions" were not manifest but had been transformed into somatic symptoms. He summarized his position in an aphorism: Neuroses were the "negatives of perversions" (*Three Essays on the Theory of Sexuality*, 1905, S.E. VII:165). That is, mental illness resulted when excessively strong "perversion"-producing component instincts encountered unusually strong repressing forces. Today, this proposal seems highly speculative. Against the background of his and Breuer's clinical evidence and the excellent work done on sexology, it was not an unreasonable hypothesis.

Freud concluded the first essay by noting that results in sexology implied that it might be important to study the behavior of children. For, if there were component instincts that normally coalesced into adult heterosexuality at puberty, then they should be more readily observable in children. However, that was all the credit he was willing to give other sexologists for the discovery of infantile sexuality. He began the second essay by deploring the lack of attention to the subject. Sulloway's review of the sexology literature demonstrates that this claim to originality was totally false. Not only had the topic been broached, but many of Freud's specific claims had already been published (Sulloway 1979:chap. 8, passim). Worse still, he had clearly read these books and articles (e.g., Sulloway 1979:303). Although Freud was less vocal in pressing a claim for priority in psychosexual development, the situation was basically the same. He mentioned a few isolated figures without acknowledging that his views were only variations on themes introduced and developed by others.

According to Sulloway's account, these were the available facts and theories about infantile sexuality and psychosexual development that Freud failed to acknowledge. Both nativists and associationists had linked "perversion" to sexual precocity. For the former, childhood sexuality was a sign of hereditary taint; for the latter, it was the cause of later "perversions." With the documentation of childhood sexual activity among normal adults, these views were replaced with an account in the evolutionary mold. Given the variety of forms of reproduction among lower animals—including intercourse ending in females devouring males and asexual reproduction—sexual instincts seemed to be incredibly plastic. Further, since some lower organisms must have been our ancestors, humans probably inherited a variety of sexual instincts. According to the biogenic law, early forms would be repeated in immature humans. Hence, the apparent perversity of childhood sexuality, including its oral and anal character, bisexuality, and sadism were to be expected as parts of normal development. So much was a function of heredity; however, life experiences could affect the particular forms that "perversions" took. Anthropological studies confirmed the new biological approach. Among "primitive" peoples, children engaged in what was transparently sexual play.[15] Moreover, "perversions" were found among all peoples and all historical epochs, suggesting that these behaviors were not perverse from the standpoint of nature, but only from that of modern adult Europeans (Sulloway 1979:chap. 8, passim).

Three Essays on the Theory of Sexuality dealt with infantile sexuality and psychosexual development in separate essays. However, Freud's views on these matters were so closely intertwined that I treat them together. In essence, his views were a synthesis of standard sexology, his work on neurotics, and his libido theory. Children brought germs of sexual activity with them in the form of polymorphous component instincts. These were reinforced by live experiences, paradigmatically, nursing at the mother's breast. Component instincts found expression in behavior from the ages of two to five. At that point, through natural forces, such as pity and shame, and societal prohibitions, they were repressed and sublimated, producing a latency period during childhood. (This repression induced an amnesia for infantile sexuality, which was why, he contended, the subject has not been explored.) Sublimation enabled libidinal energy to fuel social and creative efforts. Although repressed, memories of childhood sexual experiences exerted a lasting influence on sexual patterns, particularly on choices of sexual objects. In normal cases, a boy's affectionate relation with his mother and a girl's with her father set the pattern for later heterosexuality.[16] At puberty, component instincts were amalgamated into adult sexuality, that is, into genital, heterosexual activity.

Freud identified several patterns in the complex ontogeny of sexuality, including "diphasic" development, that is, a burst of early childhood sexuality, followed by a latency period, followed by a second onset of sexual activity, and the familiar stages of erotogenic development, the oral or cannibalistic stage, which gave way to the sadistic-anal organization, which in turn yielded to the genital sexuality needed for reproduction. Psychosexual development explained both why human beings were prone to mental illness and why the illnesses took particular forms. All neuroses were rooted in sexual difficulties and these arose because

> [j]ust as on any other occasion on which the organism should by rights make new combinations and adjustments leading to complicated mechanisms, here too there are possibilities of pathological disorders if these new arrangements are not carried out. Every pathological disorder of sexual life is rightly to be regarded as an inhibition in development. (*Three Essays on the Theory of Sexuality*, 1905, S.E. VII:207–8)

That is, every neurosis was a result of fixated sexual development or regression to an earlier (and phylogenetically older) state. Why did these "fixations along the long path of development" occur (235)? Despite his resistance to hereditary explanations, the striking number of syphilitic fathers among his patients led Freud to lay the preponderance of blame there. Given an abnormal sexual constitution, strong "perverse" tendencies might meet with fierce repression, bringing on illness; more happily, they might be sublimated into outstanding creative achievements. Although repression and sublimation were major determining factors, accidental experiences, especially sexual precocity, could reinforce unbalanced sexual instincts and cause illness. They also determined the specific neurotic symptoms (235–43).

Freud's metapsychological directives led him to try to complete his theory of sexual instincts and psychosexual development by sketching the biological basis of these phenomena. Although these matters were unsettled, he offered some parameters. The accumulation of sexual substances—semen—might explain sexual activities of adult males, but was clearly inapplicable to the cases of women, children, and castrated males. If there were component instincts in children, for example, then there had to be some source of sexual energy beyond mature gonads (*Three Essays on the Theory of Sexuality*, 1905, S.E. VII:214). As already indicated, he speculated about the role that the thyroid gland might play in sexuality and about how it might interact with the sex glands proper.

The theory of psychosexual development exemplifies how perfectly psychoanalysis incorporated the ideals and results of nineteenth-century science. Like most nineteenth-century theories, it was historical or genetic. Present conditions were explained by tracing their development from earlier conditions. More specifically, it conformed to the standards of evolutionary naturalism: Higher achievements were shown to result from the baser human endowment of sexual instincts, and these were tied as closely as possible to a biological basis. Even more specifically, it incorporated the widespread assumption of recapitulationism: Distinctively human pathologies (the neuroses) were the result of errors of development from earlier forms—earlier in the life of the individual and in the history of the race. Finally, psychoanalysis took over a large number of specific results from sexology. Freud's claims about infantile sexuality, psychosexual development, repression, sublimation, fixation, and regression seem fantastic only because he expunged the scientific research supporting them from the public record of his work (Sulloway 1979:7 and chap. 8, passim). Apparently, it was more important to him to be regarded as an original thinker than to present the strongest possible case for his views. This was a moral failing, however, not an epistemic one. As he developed these core dynamic principles of psychoanalysis, they enjoyed reasonable support from contemporary scientific evidence and theories. Even Sulloway, who is largely critical, thinks that Freud's work is best understood as an extensive synthesis of sexology, which also transformed the field by relating it to his own work in psychopathology.

> Freud recognized every possible combination of hereditary predisposition with environmental determinism. His flexibility on the degree of "innateness" or "acquiredness" in sexual pathology was a novel and fruitful position. . . . [it] allowed him, above all, to adopt and exploit the best theoretical ideas advanced by the two opposing camps in contemporary sexology. (Sulloway 1979:319)

Neonates, Neurotics, and Neanderthals

One more piece of Freudian theory needs to be supplied before we can return, finally, to his mature topographic account in *The Ego and the Id*, the analysis of "primitive" customs. Although Freud thought about issues in anthropology during the 1890s (e.g., Letter to Fliess, 1897, S.E. I:257:Sulloway 1979:364–65), he did not draw his reflections together until 1913 in *Totem and Taboo*. In an earlier essay, he was explicit about the relevance of "primitive" peoples to psychoanalysis: "Impressive analogies from biology have prepared us to find that the individual's mental development repeats the course of human development in abbreviated form . . ." ("Leonardo da Vinci and a Memory of His Childhood," 1910, S.E. XI:97). As observed in chapter 2, the standard assumption was that contemporary "primitive" societies were just like prehistoric societies. Given the biogenetic law, theories about infantile sexuality and psychological development could thus be tested and confirmed by anthropological evidence. Moreover, if neurosis was always a matter of fixated development or regression, then the blueprint of human psychological development that underlay the progress of the race and the course of individual lives could be approached from three different angles—by studying children, neurotics, and "savages."

In the Preface to *Totem and Taboo*, Freud explained that his purpose was to attract the attention of students of social anthropology, philology, and folklore, on the one hand, and psychoanalysts, on the other, to encourage "a belief that occasional co-operation between them could not fail to be of benefit to research" (1913, S.E. XIII:iii). He also cautioned that he did not regard his accounts as definitive. Instead, they were intended to demonstrate the possibility of psychoanalysis illuminating social anthropology. From the other direction, the apparent ease with which psychoanalytic theories could be applied to anthropological data provided them with potential additional confirmation. In this context, Freud was not concerned to appear original. His purpose was better served by presenting his hypotheses in the context of similar but less satisfactory alternatives.

Freud examined three central problems: taboos (especially incest avoidance), totems, and exogamy. Why did these institutions exist in all "primitive" societies? The strength of his analysis was that it provided one overarching explanation for the cooccurring phenomena. Further, the keystone of his account was a plausible conjecture of Darwin's: Primitive humans lived in small bands with one male dominating a cluster of females. James J. Atkinson noted that this hypothesis implied that younger males would be expelled from the band and have to find sexual partners beyond its bounds, thus producing exogamy. He also observed that the patriarch of such a group must fear the band of males as they mature, since they would attack, depriving him of "both wife and life" (quoted in *Totem and Taboo*, 1913, S.E. XIII:142n.).

Freud's hypotheses about totems appealed to the work of Robertson Smith. Smith noted that totemic meals were always part of the institution. Totems were standardly animals, and Smith reasoned that the totemic meal probably derived from a sacrifice of the totem animal. The ritual surrounding totemic meals suggested that through jointly sacrificing the animal, participants had all become members of a clan (*Totem and Taboo*, 1913, S.E. XIII:132–39). To these available theories, Freud added just three insights from his work on the neuroses. From his work on phobias, in particular, the well-known case of "Little

Hans," he believed that large animals were often symbols for the father. Analyses had also convinced him that sons were ambivalent toward their fathers. Their affection for their mothers created potential conflict with their fathers, yet they also loved their fathers and identified with them, the situation he memorialized as the "Oedipal complex." When these views were combined with the Darwin-Atkinson and Smith claims, the following scenario seemed plausible. Prehistoric humans lived in primal hordes. In this context, boys' incestuous feelings toward their mothers led to their expulsion from the group and, eventually, when they returned as rivals, to the killing and devouring of the aging father. Freud believed that this traumatic event had momentous consequences. Since they also loved their father, they set up a totem animal to symbolize him and forbade its death, thus inaugurating an institution that we have come to call "religion"; further, from their sense of guilt, they renounced their sexual rights to female relatives and tried to overcome their rivalrous feelings toward each other, thereby establishing the beginnings of morality and social feeling. On this account totemism and exogamy were firmly linked, as they had been in early anthropological accounts. Further, both the taboo against incest and that against killing the totem rested on ambivalent feelings. Freud compared the rituals surrounding taboos with those of obsessional neurotics to argue that, in general, taboos reflected deep emotional ambivalence.

To us, Freud's hypothesis is the proverbial "Just So" story without Kipling's wit. Still, at least in 1913, his intentions were modest. He had no illusions about producing a totally satisfactory theory. Moreover, he concluded by raising two serious difficulties for himself. Social psychology had no real answers to the question of how customs were handed down from one generation to another, and this left a huge gap in his account between the primordial killing and later totemic observances. Further, in the case of obsessional neurotics, rituals were not always tied to deeds, but were sometimes linked to mere wishes, so it was not even clear that psychoanalysis supported the reasoning!

These caveats are unlikely to placate current readers. The idea that "primitive" people belonged in a natural kind that included babies and neurotics and the assumption that it was possible to achieve a scientific understanding of the very beginnings of civilization are too remote from contemporary views. They were, however, part of Freud's intellectual milieu. Against this background, it was reasonable to be concerned that psychoanalysis be consonant with the best available research in anthropology and sociology and to use that work to try to extend its claims. With some appreciation of the influence of sexology and anthropology on Freud's dynamic principles, we can return to topography and the culmination of his theorizing in *The Ego and the Id*.

The Development of the Ego

Toward the beginning of *The Ego and the Id*, Freud observed that his previous work had been one-sided, for he had said little about how the mental system that included principles for dealing with reality functioned (1923, S.E. XIX:19). That defect was to be remedied by a systematic presentation of some major emendations of his topographic theory. It may be easiest to understand Freud's theory of the ego system by beginning with the problem that he was trying to solve and with generally accepted constraints on solutions.

Apparently, mature human beings are capable of pragmatic rationality. This would include both delaying actions until an appropriate time and performing actions that tend to achieve some of their goals. At a minimum these capacities require some type of value system and an ability to apprehend reality and evaluate it with respect to possible actions. How are these mental achievements possible? A theorist could not simply posit the requisite abilities, because this move was unacceptable in nineteenth-century science. In that intellectual context, capacities for having goals and for dealing with reality needed to be explained by showing how they had evolved from less problematic structures.

Other than the obvious roles of perception and memory, and matching perceptions to desired states, Freud had little to say about how people achieved satisfactory cognition. His focus was on how human beings became individuals with goals and values, how they developed individual personalities. It is tempting to think that he should not have tackled this problem. Given what was known in the nineteenth century and even what is known today, the question seems very difficult and likely to lead to speculation. Although I am sympathetic to this criticism, two points can be made in Freud's defense. Evolutionary accounts promised to explain the development of very complex physical structures. Since psychical structures must also have evolved from earlier structures and their encounters with the environment, there was reason to hope that evolutionary considerations could shed some light on how human beings came to possess characters or personalities. Further, it was not unreasonable to believe that a science of mental pathology had to rest on an understanding of normal development. Freud thought that psychoanalysis could never be a science unless it determined how normal character traits and rational behavior developed from the animal endowment of human beings and the natural and social environments (*Introductory Lectures on Psycho-Analysis*, 1916–17, S.E. XVI:362–63).

If we lay aside objections to the project itself and compare Freud's efforts with rivals, then his theory of the ego appears surprisingly logical. As always, the central choice for theorists was among inheritance, acquisition, and some combination of the two. Like eye color, values might simply have been inherited, but this hypothesis was unsatisfactory for two reasons. It appealed to an unknown and undocumented cause, and it offered no hope of answering a central question on the nineteenth-century intellectual agenda: How did human beings as a race come to have values? Acquisition could be a matter of individual life experiences or enculturation, but the latter was the standard view. Children acquired values by familial and/or social indoctrination. However, this position had the same two drawbacks as simple nativism. It failed to explain how "original" parents or societies acquired values. Worse still, it offered no insight into the psychological mechanism, but merely posited an unexplained capacity for education. If children had no values at all, including no wish to please their parents or to conform to the norms of society, then how would telling them what was expected help?

Freud tried to explain the development of values in children by appealing to the two dominant instincts of evolutionary biology. Nutritive and sexual instincts came together at the mother's breast, thus producing an extraordinarily strong attachment that was the prototype of every later love relation (*Three Essays on the Theory of Sexuality*, 1905, S.E. VII:222). In the case of "normal" boys, which he used as the model for both sexes, allegedly the following developments occurred. Love for the mother had to be given up, at least partially. First, the infant was weaned; then he recognized that he would never be permitted to gain sexual satisfaction from his mother, since that prerogative was his father's alone. To allay the pain produced by this loss, his mental system took on traits and values possessed by the mother, through a mechanism of identification. It was never made entirely clear how identification operated, but the idea was that the mother's personality was already represented in the boy's mind and that these representations came to be regarded as belonging to his own character.

Since love for the mother was so strong, Freud hypothesized that the child managed to overcome it only by internalizing his father's critical attitude toward it. Again, this was accomplished by taking his mental representations of his father's traits to represent himself. The identification was strengthened by his sexual similarity to his father and by the fact that, since children were allegedly bisexual, he also loved his father. At the same time, however, he disliked his father, because he perceived him as a rival and as preventing the pleasure he craved from his mother. So, the identification was not total and his father's personality was regarded as a somewhat alien part of himself. Nevertheless, a sexually "normal" boy identified more strongly with his father than with his mother.

To account for the original acquisition of values, Freud appealed to phylogeny and referred to his own hypothesis from *Totem and Taboo*. The vicissitudes of the human race—in particular, externally necessitated repressions and sublimations of erotic desires—had created a rich "archaic heritage" in the mind (that is, contents acquired through the experiences of ancestors and passed to subsequent generations through Lamarckian inheritance). Children inherited this material and they also reexperienced it in the reactions of their parents to their libidinal attachments. Thus, what was lowest (in the common opinion) was actually the source of what was highest, our sense of morality, religion, and fraternity (*The Ego and the Id*, 1923, S.E. XIX:36–37). Putting these three pieces together, this was Freud's account: Nutritive and sexual needs led boys to have deep attachments to their mothers, which set up sexual conflict with their fathers; finally to resolve this Oedipal situation, a boy had to incorporate his mother's and father's values into himself, values that derived partly from their life experiences and partly from the archaic heritage of the race; life experiences affected him, but since they were interpreted through his parentally acquired value system, all later developments of his personality bore the stamp of his parents.

If this was how the ego developed, then, Freud realized, his earlier topographic account had to be inadequate. He had taken the conscious part of the mind to have a number of functions: It apprehended reality and was concerned with self-preservation; it was critical, rational, and controlled access to motility; it was also that part of the apparatus that was identified as the person himself, its values were his values. Freud began to doubt his division when analyses revealed what he took to be an unconscious sense of guilt. Unconscious guilt could be attributed to neither the unconscious nor the conscious system, so he made a fundamental alteration in his topography. Although the property of being conscious or unconscious still had the deepest significance for psychoanalysis, his mental divisions could not follow this property. What distinguished the "Unconscious" system was not that its contents were uniquely unconscious, but that they were primitive, including both the basic biological endowment of human beings and their archaic heritage (*The Ego and the Id*, 1923, S.E. XIX:36–38). So the "Unconscious" became the "id." By contrast, the ego, which took over the functions previously assigned to the Conscious (and Preconscious) system, was that part of the mind that was not inherited, but shaped by encounters with reality. However, some of its functions were also unconscious. Most importantly, its critical faculty and values were largely unconscious, because they had developed by assimilating parental traits in order to deal with the repression of Oedipal desires and also by primitive preverbal identifications with parents. Because this mental cluster within the ego was extremely significant for personality and unusual in being unconscious yet created by life experiences, Freud distinguished it as a special system, the "superego." In postulating a superego, he believed that he could resolve both the therapeutic puzzle about unconscious guilt and the general issue of how an amoral infant developed a value system.

Postponing objections for a moment, the theory of the ego and the id had several virtues. As he had done in sexology, Freud rejected simple nativism and simple acquisition to offer an account that gave due credit to each claimant, while avoiding their common failings. He sketched an account of how children acquired values from experience, by appealing to the instincts of sex and self-preservation and to the fact that they had mental representations of their environments, including parental traits. Moreover, details about how experiences led to specific traits could sometimes be filled in from analyses of neurotics. He explained how the race acquired values by invoking the inheritance of acquired characteristics. Over time, as succeeding generations underwent the same experiences, such as being expelled from the primal horde by the dominant male, traits like fearing and respecting powerful males became ingrained in young male humans. Unlike a blank appeal to heredity, this approach opened the prospect of further enlightenment from social anthropology. Further, as in sexual pathology, Freud allowed inheritance and experience to fill in for each other. So, to the obvious but unvoiced objection that not all children were nursed, he explained that phylogenetic inheritance was so strong in this area that "it makes no difference whether a child has really sucked at the breast or has been brought up on the bottle . . . the child's development takes the same path" (*An Outline of Psycho-Analysis*, 1938, S.E. XXIII:188).

Despite these advantages, Freud's theory was vulnerable to three obvious criticisms. A standard objection has been that although he allowed that extremely painful or pleasurable experiences could alter values at any time in life, he placed too much emphasis on early childhood. However, the special importance of childhood was supported by several independent considerations. Since he did not see how the events of an individual life could be sufficient to account for character, heredity had to play some role. Assuming the biogenetic law, that influence would be strongest in childhood. Second, a value that was inherited or acquired early would be very influential, because experiences would be interpreted through it, so it would affect subsequently acquired values. Finally, if a value were unconscious, then, in the absence of therapy, it would be immune from rational revision. Only the last motivation depended on Freud's own theories. As noted, however, there was fairly widespread support for unconscious ideas, and it was reasonable enough to believe that an idea that could not even be thought could not be rationally evaluated. Freud's stress on childhood was a bold and novel departure only in the sense that it followed a number of widely accepted assumptions in biology, social anthropology, and psychiatry to their logical conclusion.

A second obvious criticism is that Freud relied heavily on work in social anthropology when he should have recognized the excessively speculative character of this field. Further, he appears to have converted his 1913 hypothesis about the killing of the father by sons expelled from the primal horde into a fact in 1923! Freud did engage in rampant anthropological speculation. In a section of a paper he characterized as a "phylogenetic fantasy," he endorsed Sandor Ferenczi's links between anxiety, conversion hysteria, obsessional neuroses—and the Ice Age (Freud 1915:13–16)! However, he never published that paper; it is one of the lost metapsychological papers. Nor did he employ details from his account of the primal horde in outlining the theory of the superego. He still referred to his "hypothesis" in *Totem and Taboo* that the denouement of the primal horde stage was brought about by Oedipal forces (*The Ego and the Id*, 1923, S.E. XIX:37, 38). All he assumed was that the human archaic heritage resided in an unconscious, "primitive" portion of the mind, the id, and that it contained values produced by many repressions and sublimations of base human desires (36, 38). Granting Lamarckian inheritance of psychological traits, the former assumption followed from his characterization of the ego system as that part of the mind that expresses the influence of the external (physical and social) world. Nothing that was innate could be part of the ego. In assuming that religion, morality, and social sense—what was "best" in human beings—evolved from what was basest, he did not embrace any particular anthropological hypothesis, but merely a fairly widespread working assumption of the field, evolutionary naturalism. What he argued was that his hypothesis fulfilled the basic requirements laid down for an explanation of our "higher" natures, but he did not think that it had been established. The distinctive aspects of Freud's position were that human value systems were partially unconscious and developed in each individual through the resolution of the Oedipal complex. These theories derived, not from anthropology, but allegedly from his clinical work.

This is the third obvious area of criticism. The theory of the superego rested on the clinical "discovery" of the Oedipal complex, and that foundation was insufficient to support it. Were its assumptions correct, the criticism would be valid, for reasons already noted in discussing the general problem of the clinical evidence. But the assumption is wrong. Nothing was more central or more original in psychoanalysis than the postulation of the Oedipal complex and its "heir," the superego, and Freud tried to portray his reasoning as a straightforward inductive inference from the clinical evidence. However, as he often pointed out, his clinical discovery was directly related to two biological considerations widely taken to be facts: the long period of a child's dependency on its parents (which he had implicated in the development of morality as far back as the *Project* [1895, S.E. I:318]) and diphasic sexuality ("A Short Account of Psycho-Analysis," 1924, S.E. XIX:208; cf. *The Ego and the Id*, 1923, XIX:35, n. 1). Suppose we grant a flowering of infantile sexuality at somewhere between two and five. Since parents were often the only available objects of love,[17] it would not be surprising if a child's first attachment were to them. Part of the diphasic theory was that early sexual manifestations underwent suppression and/or sublimation. Given jealousy and also availability, it was reasonable to assume that the agents of suppression were the parents, in particular, that each tried to damp down the child's libidinal attachment to the other.

To these biological and commonsense assumptions, add a distinctive, but not unreasonable, Freudian claim. The unconscious ideas that a number of psychiatrists took to be the bases of neuroses were in that state because they had been repressed. Although convinced of the fact of repression, Freud had considerable difficulty in understanding how it was possible. Since sexual activity was pleasurable, why should individuals avoid sexual ideas and behavior? The Oedipal complex and the superego provided an elegant solution to this problem. Because of their first choice of a sexual object, children's sexual ideas had been driven from consciousness by parental suppression. Children compensated for this loss by assimilating parental values and character traits. As a result, when sexual ideas returned with a vengeance at puberty, adolescents (and later adults) had elements within their personalities that would repress sexuality without further external pressure.

When viewed in the context of diphasic sexuality, the origin of values, and the problem of repression, the hypothesis of the Oedipal complex and the superego was, once again, no wild guess, but an imaginative synthesis of recent discoveries and puzzles. Although not brought together formally until 1923, most of the essential pieces of this account, the Oedipal complex, the efforts to understand repression and the origin of morality, the centrality of sex, and diphasic development, had been part of Freud's working arsenal since the late 1890s and early 1900s (see e.g., Letter to Fliess, 1897, S.E. I:253). Over time, phylogeny and Lamarckian inheritance emerged as another important source of support. Given infantile sexuality and the triangles that ensued, Oedipal attachments and suppressions would have been experienced over and over again in the history of the race, creating a massive deposit of inherited incestuous desires and repressions ("From the History of an Infantile Neurosis," 1918, S.E. XVII:119). The universal presence of incest taboos was some indication of the strength of this inheritance ("The Resistances to Psycho-Analysis," 1925, S.E. XIX:220). Finally, Freud also appealed to literature—to Sophocles, Shakespeare, and Diderot. Although this strikes current readers as quintessentially unscientific, it was not so clear in the nineteenth and early twentieth centuries. If enduring plays often rested on ancient myths and myths were testimony about the practices and beliefs of ancient peoples (Wundt 1916), then literature had the potential to offer confirmation for hypotheses about phylogenetic inheritance.

Despite Freud's preferred mode of presenting his ideas, the theory of the Oedipal complex and the superego did not simply emerge from his analytic work. Analyses only testified to the importance of early sexuality to neuroses and filled in details about varieties of the Oedipal complex. The background into which those details were fitted was provided by strict determinism, evolutionary naturalism, the growing recognition of unconscious ideas in psychiatry, phylogeny and Lamarckian inheritance, diphasic development, the overwhelming importance of sex, and a smattering of literature. When these theoretical factors were added to clinical evidence from neurotics, then the idea that infantile sexuality was the father of adult sexuality, values, and mental health was not an unreasonable proposal.

Finally, in assessing the reasonableness of the Oedipal hypothesis, it is important to consider the role that Freud assigned to it in the science he was trying to found. The label "Oedipal complex" applied to a vaguely defined set of syndromes that were united on only three points. It was unconscious, it always involved erotic love for parents or parent-substitutes, and its resolution (or lack of same) had momentous consequences for future psychological development, including sexual preferences, values, and neuroses. On all other points, Freud was flexible and frequently amended previous accounts.[18] Alternatively, he viewed the "Oedipal complex" as a research project. Although convinced that something meeting these three descriptions was part of the development of all humans, he recognized the complexities of love relations and so did not claim to know the details or possible variations (e.g., *The Ego and the Id*, 1923, S.E. XIX:33).

Summary

In this chapter I have attempted three interrelated tasks. Besides the theory of dreams (the subject of chapter 5), I take the core doctrines of psychoanalysis to be the Oedipal complex, the pleasure and reality principles, the unconscious system, libido and repression, and psychosexual development. In each case, I have indicated how the doctrine depended on work in other disciplines. I have also tried to explain why each was a more or less reasonable working hypothesis in the context of nineteenth-century scientific advances, views about the goals of scientific explanation, and standards of evidence. Finally, I have tried to show how each of these doctrines either fulfilled a requirement of Freud's metapsychology (e.g., the pleasure principle) or was attractive to him precisely because of its ability to unite results from different disciplines (e.g., libido theory). Freud's large corpus included a number of speculative works. He offered case histories based on scanty literary remains, hypotheses about the history of religion and civilization, and a defense of a new instinct, the infamous "death" instinct. I make no claims for the probity of any of this. However, such essays usually began by pointing out the hypothetical nature of the research. All I have tried to defend were the hypotheses seriously advanced as the framework of psychoanalysis.

To avoid confusion, I should clarify the limited nature of that defense. I have not suggested that any of these doctrines is true. Nor have I argued that it was reasonable for Freud to persevere with his hypotheses anywhere near as long as he did. A fortiori, I have not implied that anyone ought to believe them today. I have not even tried to present Freud's theories as the best available at the time he originally formulated them. Contemporaries had many valid reservations about his work. Moll questioned the truth of seduction stories; Krafft-Ebing doubted whether a "cathartic" recounting of a trauma could produce a cure; Breuer and many others did not see why sex had to be the *sole* pathogen in neurosis, even granting its extreme importance (Sulloway 1979:315, 81, 85). For reasons we have seen, sex was a very attractive candidate, but it was not the only possible explanation of higher mental life.

Given the influence of psychoanalysis, it is tempting to hold Freud to a higher standard. It was not enough to make scientifically reasonable hypotheses that, in many cases, enjoyed a substantial amount of support by nineteenth-century standards. This temptation rests on a confusion. A famous scientist offering a theory with the potential to change the lives of thousands must adhere to extremely high scientific standards. Throughout most of the development of psychoanalysis, however, this was not a burden Freud had to assume. Fame and influence came later, when the central doctrines of psychoanalysis were already firmly in place. The evidential base of psychoanalysis could have been firmer, but these principles were not the improbable and irresponsible speculations they seem to current students of human cognition. They were merely plausible working hypotheses—but they were at least that.

Finally, I will try to bring together the disciplinary interrelations that have been noted throughout the chapter. These can be represented by the type of schematic diagram used in chapter 2 to illustrate different conceptions of the relations among the disciplines. Freud took psychoanalysis to lie between biology and psychology and the mental sciences. In particular, he took it to be constrained and inspired by brain anatomy and physiology, psychophysics, and the theory of evolution from below, and to psychology and child psychology from above. The relation to psychiatry was somewhat strange: Psychoanalysis was constrained by its solid results but was supposed to replace it. In addition, psychoanalysis stood in reciprocal relations of inspiration and support with a variety of disciplines: sexology, anthropology, and, less centrally, history of civilization, *Völkerpsychologie*, and mythology. The results of psychoanalysis also needed the be extended by brain anatomy and physiology, biology, sexology, and anthropology. Putting all these relations together produces a rather complex picture, figure 4.1.

Given the complexity of this diagram, I have not indicated the weaker relations of support and inspiration where the stronger relations of constraint and extension are present. Nor have I separately represented the influence of Freud's three metapsychological principles. The effort to find functional/evolutionary divisions in the mind is captured in the relations to evolutionary biology, psychology, anthropology, *Völkerpsychologie*, mythology, and history of civilization. My claim is not that the search for mental topography led Freud to these disciplines, but that the influence was reciprocal. Because of the influence of these disciplines, a functional division seemed natural and, given his explicit adoption of this metapsychological principle, he sought further enlightenment from these fields of study. The same relation holds between Freud's economic metapsychology and the biological sciences. Recent discoveries in neurophysiology reinforced

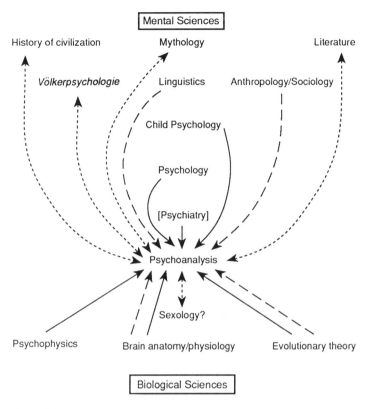

Figure 4.1
Freud's view of the relation of psychoanalysis to other disciplines. The bottom-to-top layout indicates ontological priority. Solid arrows indicate relations of constraint and guidance and run from the constraining to the constrained disciplines. Dotted arrows indicate the weaker epistemological relations of support and inspiration, running from the supporting to the supported disciplines. Dashed arrows represent relations of explanatory extension and run from the extending to the extended disciplines. The ontological positions of sexology and psychiatry are disputable. Insofar as sexology was to be grounded in sexual biology, it was ontologically more basic than psychoanalysis, although one might argue that at the time Freud was writing, its results were only a matter of psychological observation. In the case of psychiatry, some regarded it as directly tied to brain anatomy and physiology, but others did not; and, again, at the time, its results were based on psychological observation.

his conviction that psychoanalysis needed to be grounded in the biology of the brain, and this decision led him to seek further information about energy flowing among neurons. The pattern was repeated for dynamic forces. Sexology, psychology, and social anthropology offered hypotheses about dynamic principles governing ideas and mental systems, thus validating the approach and providing a source of substantive principles.

Earlier I noted the potential of psychoanalysis for uniting work in psychology and biology. The diagram illustrates how many other areas of inquiry could be brought under the umbrella of psychoanalysis and so perhaps support and extend its claims. If Freud saw psychoanalysis as occupying something like this position in relation to the achievements and programs of late nineteenth-century science, then we can appreciate why he believed that he was on the threshold of a major advance in understanding human mentality. Results and approaches in different disciplines seemed to fit together and reinforce each other, producing, in William Whewell's term, a "consilience" of evidence and disciplines. Given so great a consilience and so many directions to extend and corroborate psychoanalytic research, it might have been hard to foresee how his program could fail utterly.

Chapter 5
Interpreting *The Interpretation of Dreams*

The preface to the third English edition (1931) of *The Interpretation of Dreams* makes clear the place of this book in the eye of its author: "[This book] contains . . . the most valuable of all the discoveries it has been my good fortune to make. Insight such as this falls to one's lot but once in a lifetime" (S.E. IV:xxxii). Disciples and detractors alike share Freud's estimate of the centrality of the dream book to psychoanalysis. Aficionados reach for sufficiently laudatory epithets, with Peter Gay comparing it to the *Origin of Species* as a "revolutionary classic shaping modern culture," Marshall Edelson claiming that it is "one of those major works of insight that changes forever the reader's view of himself, others, and the world," and Ernest Jones seeing it as the "entirely novel and unexpected" result of Freud's "momentous," "unique," and "heroic" self-analysis; Richard Wollheim settles for "masterpiece"; even Frank Sulloway describes it as "unparalleled" and offering "remarkable insight" (Gay 1988:3; Edelson 1975:30; Jones 1961:209, 228; Wollheim 1971:41; Sulloway 1979:334). To those who fail to see Freud's charm, however, this book symbolizes (if they'll pardon the expression) everything that is wrong with psychoanalysis. Clark Glymour maintains that it was in the dream book that Freud turned from "scientist towards mountebank" (Glymour 1983:69). Frederick Crews concurs: "Freud was already a pseudo-scientist from the hour that he published *The Interpretation of Dreams*" (Crews 1988:250). Contrasting his contemporary, brain-based theory with Freud's, J. Allan Hobson claims that the latter has no evidential base, offers a convoluted argument, is incompatible with modern data, and is clinically stultifying with complex and arbitrary interpretations (Hobson 1988b:289).[1] Hobson's coworker Helene Sophrin Porte speaks for many when she labels the dream theory simply an "impostor" (Porte 1988:333).

Masterpiece or impostor? Such widely divergent opinions can probably never be fully reconciled. Nevertheless, in this chapter I provide an account of how dream interpretation related to the rest of psychoanalysis, which explains why it has been the lightning rod for critical appraisal. To Freud's supporters, my interpretive strategy will seem suspect. I have presented a fairly full account of his theory of mind without making any use of the dream material. In their view, my approach amounts to offering an interpretation of *Hamlet* without considering the Prince of Denmark. I pursued this order of exposition, because I wish to argue that dream interpretation was entirely theory driven. Having achieved some grasp of Freud's interdisciplinary theoretical commitments, we can, I will argue, understand all the prima facie implausible features of his dream interpretation. This result is anathema to supporters, because it is essential to their position that dreams were an objective or theoretically neutral source of evidence for psychoanalytic theory.

On the other hand, Freud's critics will be appalled by the conclusions that I draw from the dependence of dream interpretation on the rest of psychoanalysis. Unlike Crews, I do not infer from the fact that Freud's theory is formed by borrowings from nineteenth-century science that he was a pseudoscientist and a liar, with an unfortunate tendency to "intellectual *ejaculatio praecox*" (Crews 1988:236, 246). Not surprisingly (I hope), I argue that its thorough grounding in the approaches and results of nineteenth-century science gave dream interpretation a fleeting chance of achieving scientific status. I also argue for a more unsettling claim. Although agreeing with critics that Freud's strong theoretical commitments led him to take neutral data as confirmation, I demur from the conclusion of pseudoscience. The proper role of theories is to make otherwise bland data salient and comprehensible, even though this process can sometimes result in useless data being seen as probative.

As in previous chapters, I draw on the work of others in tracing the influence of particular nineteenth-century sciences on dream interpretation. This allows me both to take advantage of good work that has already been done and to avoid the charge that *I* see the theory of dreams as an instance of interdisciplinary theory construction only because that is my general position on psychoanalysis. My argumentative strategy, outlined in chapter 1, is to try to confirm my general interpretation by demonstrating its ability to explain Freud's work on dreams. Where I differ from other students of this episode is in seeing dream interpretation as having many sources beyond Freud's neurophysiology and Jackson's evolutionary functionalism. Psychology, psychiatry, sexology, anthropology, and linguistics also made key contributions, while the background assumptions of strict determinism, evolutionary naturalism, and interdisciplinary theory construction provided an aura of plausibility for the whole project. Crews concurs on the last point, but casts it in a very negative light: "[What] actually shaped Freud's thought . . . [was] for example, the prevalence of premature attempts to unify evolutionary theory, neurophysiology, and psychology along biogenetic lines . . ." (Crews 1988:238). It is now clear that Freud's attempt to construct a complete interdisciplinary theory of mind was premature. To sustain a charge of pseudoscience or even bad science, however, it is necessary to show that a reasonable investigator should have recognized the futility of the cause *then*.

Physiological Mechanisms and Assumptions

Dreams occur. Only the most skeptical or cautious would question the existence of the phenomenon of dreaming and assume only dream reports. Hence, the most basic question is, Why do we dream at all? Hobson argues that Freud's now outmoded neurophysiology provided him with a ready answer to this question. Freud assumed that the neural system was constructed like a reflex, but that energy from external and endogenous stimuli was not all discharged in daytime motor activity. This surplus energy was thus available to fuel nocturnal mental life (Hobson 1988b:285–86; cf. *The Interpretation of Dreams*, 1900, S.E. V:567). Further, the system was constituted by matter that had an inherent tendency to throw off energy (see above, p. 70), so energy would flow around the system seeking an outlet. Hence, the mind was not completely quiescent in sleep. Hobson also notes that the Freudian brain would be in a difficult position. Stimuli would bombard it, causing a rise in overall energy level that produced pain. Since it could not defend against invasion by stimuli or always rid itself of unwanted energy, it needed mechanisms of defense against pain (Hobson 1988b:285–86).

Porte explains how a fundamental tenet of Freud's dream theory derived from a rather different neurophysiological assumption. Freud accepted Jackson's hypothesis about the construction of the brain in evolutionary layers. In madness or other abnormal states, mental functions would be taken over by phylogenetically older layers. Given the phenomenological picture of dreams, as illogical and fragmentary, they were obvious candidates for the effects of older "primary processes" (Porte 1988:335–38). That is, dreaming appeared to involve a regression to more primitive modes of thought. As Sulloway and Porte observe, the Jackson regression model was originally adopted in the *Project;* the surplus energy repression model did not make its appearance until *The Interpretation of Dreams* (Sulloway 1979:327–28; Porte 1988:337–38; cf. *Project for a Scientific Psychology*, 1895, S.E. I:338–39).

Porte sees these two ideas from neurophysiology as not only determining Freud's theory, but also saddling it with intractable inconsistency. What was the theory? Were dreams the result of distortion by
censorship or merely the reflection of the characteristic lack of reality
of primary processes? Alternatively, were displacement and condensation primary processes or the tools of the censor (Porte 1988:337–
38)? Although I will not try to remove all the tensions in Freud's
account, I think Porte's dilemma is more apparent than real. An idea
was made unconscious by being cut off from its normal associations,
including its word-representation. That is, it entered the Unconscious
by undergoing a functional change. Having suffered this change, it
was unavailable for rational, conscious thought, but could still function by accidental associative connections. These primary processes
could produce, among other things, the putting together of different
but associated ideas (condensation). If the new condensed idea was
sufficiently unlike the old one to arouse the former's normal associations, then it could become conscious. Hence, one could characterize
condensation as both a primary process and an agent of censorship.
It was the latter in the sense that an idea could get past the censor if
it had been sufficiently combined and condensed (see *The Interpretation
of Dreams*, 1900, S.E. V:595–97). Wundt noted that preexisting structures could take on new functions (Wundt 1902:325–26). In the terminology of modern evolutionary theory, the primary processes were
co-opted into the service of censorship and thereby helped to protect
the system from pain.

Further, repression and regression were different but complementary processes. The former referred to the effort to keep an idea out
of consciousness and the latter to the primitive pattern of functional
relationships that an idea so exiled could participate in (*Introductory
Lectures on Psycho-Analysis*, 1916–17, S.E. XVI:314–42).[2] Alternatively,
in Freud's theory, the two neurophsyiologically inspired models, surplus energy plus repression and regression, were yoked together in
such a way as to complement each other. Repression was offered as
one explanation of why some minds at some times undergo regression;
regression was supposed to explain why repressed ideas behaved in
such illogical ways.

As Freud noted, his account of dreaming involved repression and
three kinds of regression, temporal, topographic, and formal (*The
Interpretation of Dreams*, 1900, S.E. V:548). He said little about formal
regression, but his topographic claim is interesting. Visual and other
dream images were critical phenomena for any theory of dreams to
explain. According to standard reflexology, perceptual images led to
motor activity directly or through the mediation of some type of

thought processes. All agreed, however, that (for the most part) motor activity was blocked in sleep. Freud combined those three ideas in a single bold hypothesis: Because motor activity was blocked, the energy that would propel it was shunted back through the reflex, reversing its normal path, and ending up in a perceptual dream image. Porte observes that Freud was in no position to offer any evidence for this hypothesis, but concedes its prima facie plausibility (Porte 1988:325–26). Although Freud never abandoned the idea of topographic regression to perceptual imagery in dreams (cf. *New Introductory Lectures on Psycho-Analysis,* 1933, S.E. XXII:19), it remained a suggestive hypothesis, rather than a central tenet of his theory.

In all three cases, surplus energy plus repression, temporal regression, and topographic regression, the same pattern was repeated: Freud's understanding of certain neurological theories and hypotheses led him to see them as offering possible explanations for recognized features of dreams. Dreams occur, but typically are forgotten. These two puzzling facts could be explained by surplus energy plus repression. Surplus energy and the reduction of the censor's power in sleep could account for why they happen at all; the reemergence of the fully awake censor would explain why they usually disappear from wakeful recollections. The wild illogicality of dreams would be expected, were they a reflection of more primitive mental processes, which Freud had reason to believe existed alongside later structures. Finally, on the hypothesis that reflex pathways could be run in reverse, there would be a link between two widely recognized facts about dreaming, the lack of mobility and the presence of imagery.

Raymond Fancher and Frank Sulloway maintain that Freud's neurophysiological assumptions also determined the central hypothesis of his theory, that all dreams were wish fulfillments. Indeed, both argue that this allegedly empirical claim follows *deductively* from his brain physiology, although the details of their putative deductions differ somewhat. Fancher believes that Freud reasoned as follows: If energy could enter the nervous system only from external and endogenous stimuli, and the senses were nearly shut down in sleep, then only endogenous stimulation could instigate a dream. When energy entered the nervous system from instinctual needs, it followed paths of previous satisfaction. That is, it (partially) revived earlier perceptions, producing a hallucinatory or wishful state (Fancher 1973:83, 99–101). Sulloway emphasizes Freud's claim in the *Project* that secondary processes were diminished during sleep (Sulloway 1979:327; cf. 1895, S.E. I:335–39). Wishful, hallucinatory images flourished, because reality testing took a nightly holiday. If we put these pieces together, we can construct the following argument:

1. Dreaming requires some stimulus to the nervous system.
2. Only endogenous stimuli can enter the sleeping nervous system.
3. Endogenous stimuli revive perceptions associated with previous satisfaction of the endogenous needs, thereby producing wishful images.
4. Wishful images can be blocked only by the operation of secondary processes.
5. In sleep, secondary processes are shut off.

C1. Therefore, the underlying biological cause of dreaming is endogenous stimulation arising from biological needs, and the phenomena of dreaming, visual and auditory images and the like, represent those needs as being fulfilled. (1–5)
C2. Therefore, dreaming is wish fulfillment (reformulation of C1). Q.E.D.

Fancher and Sulloway are correct on the two essential points. Freud's neurophysiological investigations and hypotheses led him to embrace 1 through 5, and C2 is a deductive consequence of those assumptions. These results cast grave doubts on the orthodox suggestion that Freud's work on dreams led to the discovery of his most distinctive theories (e.g., Jones 1961:228). On the other hand, they do not render his work on dreams pseudoscience or even nonempirical. Premises 1 through 5 are not logical axioms, but scientific hypotheses. Hence, they cannot guarantee the truth of C2. C2 needs to be established on empirical grounds. If this could be done, then the truth of C2 would provide additional confirmation for hypotheses 1 through 5, in the standard hypothetico-deductive fashion.

The neurophysiological foundations of Freud's theory do not make the dream book pseudoscience, but they do explain the curious and often annoying way in which he argued. In a twelve-page chapter, "Dreams as Wish-Fulfillments," he offered only slender anecdotal evidence that some dreams could be seen as the fulfillments of wishes. Yet, at the beginning of the next chapter, he proclaimed his hypothesis that *all* dreams were wish fulfillments and proceeded to rebut apparently contradictory evidence. On its face, this makes no sense. Why cling to a barely supported hypothesis that seemed to have many counterexamples? Against the background of his neurophysiological assumptions, however, at least part of Freud's strategy was perfectly sound. Given the strong theoretical grounds for believing that dreams had to be instigated by biological needs that produced images of satisfaction, it was reasonable to try to reconcile this hypothesis with the mixed observational data. Such a reconciliation would have had two highly desirable consequences: a theoretical understanding of dreams and additional confirmation of plausible neurophysiological hypotheses. So Freud persevered.

Unfortunately, he gave his readers no reason to follow, beyond the charm of his style. Perhaps this was because he would have rather been seen as highly original than present a convincing argument. Perhaps he hid the neurophysiological foundations of his theory, because he was a cryptobiologist bent on offering a physiological theory impersonating a psychological theory. Or, perhaps, even though the hypothesis of wish fulfillment follows from Freudian neurophysiology, he did not accept it for that reason, either because he no longer accepted the neurophysiology or because he held it on independent grounds.

Only the last conjecture will rescue the orthodox view that the theory of dreams was not a consequence of Freud's theoretical commitments, but their inspiration. However, this hypothesis is clearly wrong. Freud did not give up his basic neurophysiological views; he reiterated them in the famous seventh chapter of the dream book, which was retained in nearly unaltered form through all eight editions (see especially, *The Interpretation of Dreams*, 1900, S.E. V:564–69). To suggest that he adopted wish fulfillment on other grounds, even though it was a deductive consequence of a set of hypotheses he clearly accepted, is to opt for miraculous coincidence.

I offer a different conjecture. Although there were other sources of support, such as popular opinion and Wilhelm Griesinger's anticipation (*The Interpretation of Dreams*, 1900, S.E. IV:143), Freud came to believe that wish fulfillment was the best hypothesis largely on neurophysiological grounds. He did not hide these considerations, but, for various reasons, placed them at the very end of the dream book, in a highly abstract discussion of theoretical issues. Some of these reasons have already been considered. Despite his belief that psychoanalysis should be inspired and constrained by biology, Freud was wary of tying it too closely to specific neurophysiological hypotheses. So the seventh chapter does not discuss neurons and Q, but provides a more general account of the mental apparatus, its sources of stimulation, reflex nature, stages of development, cathexes, and two distinct systems, the primary, which was operative in dreaming, and the secondary, which dealt with reality. Further, at this stage of his career, Freud was no longer in a position to make any contributions to the neurophysiological basis of dreaming, and many of his remarks suggest that he believed that nobody else was turning the general framework of neurophysiological assumptions into specific substantive hypotheses about mental functioning either (e.g., "The Unconscious," 1915, S.E. XIV:174–75). So the focus of his discussion was on those areas where he believed that he could make contributions, in particular, the analogy between dreaming and neurosis and the interpretive techniques that he used in trying to make sense of patients' dreams. When he tried to extend and confirm particular hypotheses, he looked, not to neurophysiology, but to psychiatry, sexology, anthropology, and linguistics.

I offer this conjecture, because it explains a great deal of the otherwise puzzling argumentative structure of the book. Among other things, it explains why he persevered with wish fulfillment, why the seventh chapter is important, but curiously disengaged from earlier discussions, and why he was anxious to seek confirmation for specific claims in other sciences. On this picture, the theory of dreams was something of a mess. Its central hypothesis rested on a foundation of general neurophysiological principles; its central constructs of regression and repression were also partially inspired by neurophysiology. Yet Freud believed that this field might not advance enough in the foreseeable future to suggest or support more specific claims. Hence, details about dream formation and techniques of dream interpretation had to be supplied from other sources.

Given Freud's interdisciplinary approach, however, this messy appearance would not be disheartening. Using details from various mental or social sciences to fill in a neurophysiologically grounded theory skeleton would be perfectly reasonable, if there were good reason to believe that these sciences would all be part of a complete and integrated theory of the mind. If each of the pieces was right, then eventually they would all fit together. As we have already seen, Freud's reflexology and Jackson's hypothesis about the brain being composed of phylogenetically different layers were respectable scientific positions during the 1890s, as the dream theory was taking shape. I turn now to some of the other contributing areas of inquiry.

Psychology, Psychiatry, and Sexology

Convinced that dreams must be wish fulfillments or at least that this hypothesis must be given a chance to prove itself, Freud adopted a strategy for dealing with seeming counterexamples. He proposed to distinguish between the manifest content of dreams, provided by dream reports, and their latent content. More than any other single turn in Freud's twenty-three volume argument for psychoanalysis, it is this move that leads critics to cry "foul" or even "fraud." The importance of the move is clear. Without it, there is no compelling need for dream *interpretation*.

Was this fateful turn a turn to pseudoscience? At a superficial level, the evidence against Freud is compelling. He adopted this distinction and so embarked down the murky path of dream interpretation precisely to save the wish fulfillment hypothesis. The move can hardly be labeled deception, however, since he told the reader exactly what he was doing. First he observed that anxiety dreams render the general hypothesis of wish fulfillment not just false, but absurd. Then he explained that these seemingly conclusive objections could be met by making the proposed distinction (*The Interpretation of Dreams*, 1900, S.E. IV:135). Unless he believed his readers to be fools, he must have assumed that this argumentative strategy was not patently unscientific. And it was not—if it could be established that the distinction between manifest and latent content was not ad hoc, but could be seen to be plausible independently of the hypothesis at issue. Alternatively, what he needed to show was that despite its long heritage as quackery, dream interpretation could be put on a scientific basis and so supply independent evidence for the distinction.

Part of Freud's faith in the possibility of dream interpretation came from background assumptions. As a strict determinist, he believed that every crazy aspect of every dream must admit of some explanation. So even if "*Traüme sind Schaüme*" ("Dreams are froth" [*The Interpretation of Dreams*, 1900, S.E. IV:133]), the froth must be explicable, though not necessarily interpretable. He appealed to Mary Whiton Calkins's statistical survey of her own and another's dreams over a six-week period to dismiss external sense perception as a major contributor to dreams (IV:221). He also considered internal somatic causes. The weakness with these theories was that they could not connect particular dreams with particular somatic causes. A dream of falling had, for example, no obvious connection with any bodily state during sleep. One way to get around this difficulty was to suggest that dreams were the mind's interpretations of bodily stimuli. So, for example, the motion of the arm falling away from the body in sleep might be interpreted as falling from a height (IV:37–38). Rival psychical hypotheses faced a similar problem. It was not obvious how to connect waking interests, for example, with the particular contents of dreams. Thus, on all the available hypotheses, the gulf between putative explanations and the reported contents of dreams had to be bridged by some sort of connecting linkage.

A second assumption (shared by such contemporary theorists as Hobson and Francis Crick and Graeme Mitchison) was that dreams must have some function (*The Interpretation of Dreams*, 1900, S.E.

V:573ff; Hobson 1988b:5; Crick and Mitchison 1983:111). Since that purpose (or those purposes) could not be gleaned from the wild and varied contents of dreams, it seemed necessary to look deeper into the functioning of the mental apparatus for connecting links between dreams and the needs of the organism. Although neither of these assumptions implied that dreams were interpretable, they strongly suggested that dreams could not be explained so long as they were taken at face value.

Besides these background assumptions, I think Freud embraced dream interpretation for two reasons. First, the difficulty of connecting dream contents with somatic sources led him to think that the connecting links had to be mental. As he took pains to point out, this claim was consistent with the view that they were also physical, since

> [e]ven when investigation shows that the primary exciting cause of a phenomenon is psychical, deeper research will one day trace the path further and discover an organic basis for the mental event. (*The Interpretation of Dreams*, 1900, S.E. IV:42)

Although eventually all mental phenomena, including the dream and its instigator, would be shown to have a physiological base, existing knowledge was inadequate to make direct links between dreams and somatic conditions. This left a would-be dream investigator with a choice: He could look for mental intermediaries that could themselves be tied more directly to a biological foundation (either to a biological purpose or to a general principle of neurological functioning) or he could wait for brain physiology to develop. Perhaps the latter course would have been wiser, although progress is still very slow ninety years later. That does not make the former unscientific, however, if independent support could be found for proposed mental links.

With the decision to pursue mental intermediaries, Freud committed himself to an interpretive theory. He would try to explain a reported dream by appealing to other mental states that had brought it about. It is important to realize from the outset, however, that this interpretive project differed dramatically from many current paradigms of interpretation. Just how different it was can be seen by noting that Freud's fundamental method of dream interpretation was free association (*The Interpretation of Dreams*, 1900, S.E. V:359–60). Although I will discuss this technique in more detail shortly, the essential point is that free association disclosed largely *accidental* associations. So interpreting a dream was not primarily a matter of rational reconstruction, of seeing how, given the agent's beliefs and desires, having a dream with this content was a reasonable thing to do. Although dreams had content, and so were intentional in Brentano's sense

(Brentano 1874), they were not intentional in the sense that they were something the dreamer intended to do.[3] Alternatively, interpreting a dream was a matter not so much of rationalizing its contents, but of explaining them.

The second push to dream interpretation came from the analogy Freud saw between dreaming and psychopathology. Hobson lists five psychological features of typical dream reports:

1. formed sensory perceptions (akin to hallucinations);
2. cognitive abnormalities (akin to the inconstancies and uncertainty in cognition that characterize delirium and dementia);
3. uncritical acceptance of all such unlikely phenomena as real (akin to delusions);
4. emotional intensifications (akin to those seen in panic anxiety); and
5. amnesia (akin, again, to that seen in organic syndromes). (Hobson, 1988b:287)

As he observes, these features invite comparison with mental illness. This was an invitation that Freud could not resist.

Trends in nineteenth-century science made it plausible to put children, "savages," and the mentally ill in the same category. Each could be seen as manifesting primitive forms of human mentation that were normally invisible, because overlain by rational thought. Given its presenting "symptoms," dreaming seemed to be a further example of the workings of the primeval mind. If that were true, then the interpretation of dreams—tracing dreams back to the mental states that gave rise to them—would enable theorists to see how this primeval mind functioned and, in odd states, still did function. Dreams could be, as Freud hoped, the *"royal road to a knowledge of the unconscious activities of the mind"* (*The Interpretation of Dreams*, 1900, S.E. V:608). From the other direction, if the same primitive functioning were manifested in childhood, madness, and remote societies, then general hypotheses about dream formation that stood behind particular interpretations could be confirmed by child psychology, psychiatry, and anthropology. The very reason that convinced Freud of the potential value of dream interpretation also gave him hope that, at last, the game could be played with the net up.

In Freud's time, as now, association was the default assumption for explaining connections among mental states. When aspects of the environment were experienced together, the ideas caused by them tended to become associated, especially if the experience was accompanied by pleasure or pain. As noted in chapter 4, in the *Project* (1895) Freud appealed to the recent discovery of separate neurons to offer a speculative neurophysiological model of association: Ideas became associated, because when they were experienced together, both were filled with Q and simultaneous filling tended to facilitate the flow of Q between them; when Q ran from one neuron to another, it broke down the contact barrier between them, leading to easier future passages. So psychology proposed and neurophysiology did not resist association as a basic principle of mental functioning. For irrational thought processes, such as those exhibited in psychopathology and dreaming, it was reasonable to suppose that it was the main principle, since there were no apparent connections of logic or sense. Freud's belief that the primary tool of dream interpretation must be association had considerable theoretical plausibility.

His more specific association hypothesis also enjoyed prima facie plausibility, and even more today, perhaps, than when he offered it. Experience would set up a vast number of associations. Why did latent dream thoughts follow one of these paths of association rather than another? Although he did not express it this way, Freud's answer was quantitative. A dream content element had to be associated with many different underlying dream thoughts. The connections between dream thoughts and surface elements were not one-one, but many-many. Each thought was represented by several elements, and each element represented several thoughts. An element made it into a dream if it had a sufficient number of associations to exceed some threshold or, perhaps, if it had more associations than rivals (*The Interpretation of Dreams*, 1900, S.E. IV:283–84). Although there is no hard evidence that the human mental apparatus operates in this fashion, Freud's proposal is similar to some recent connectionist models, in particular, to nets that exhibit threshold effects and to "winner take all" designs (Feldman and Ballard 1982).

Theoretical considerations made it plausible to believe that manifest dream contents should be traced to latent dream thoughts along paths of association. Such high-level principles could, however, offer no guidance in specific instances. To interpret a dream, it was necessary to find the actual associates of its surface elements that were peculiar to the life history of the individual. Although Freud presented the method of free association as if it were discovered through his and Breuer's clinical work, it followed clearly, if not deductively, from associationism and the hypotheses of repressed wishes.

Suppose there were good reason to believe that the instigator of a dream was always a repressed wish and that the contents of a dream were related to its underlying thoughts by paths of association. One way to get out the strongest associates to the dream's surface elements would be to ask the dreamer to say whatever came to mind when thinking about these elements. To prevent the associates from being blocked, one might also ask the dreamer to adopt an uncritical attitude (cf. *The Interpretation of Dreams*, 1900, S.E. IV:101). Later, Freud elevated this technique to the "fundamental rule of psychoanalysis," that "whatever comes into one's head must be reported" (e.g., "The Dynamics of Transference," 1912, S.E. XII:107).

Much of the apparent arbitrariness of dream interpretation comes from its foundation in associationism. In principle, anything can be associated with anything; in practice, we often lack sufficient knowledge of the history of the individual to predict particular associations. So associative explanation usually takes the unattractive form of postdiction (which plagued Skinnerian behaviorism as much as psychoanalysis). Given some reason to believe that two mental states (or behaviors) are connected, it is simply assumed that they were regularly or affectively experienced together. On the other hand, Freud claimed that associationism was what saved dream interpretation from being "arbitrary" and incapable of yielding a "certain result" (*An Outline of Psycho-Analysis*, 1938, S.E. XXIII:169). To assess whether associationism was a strength or weakness of dream interpretation, it is helpful to separate the metaphysical and the epistemological issues: Was it reasonable to believe that dream contents were in fact connected to other mental states by paths of association? Was it reasonable to believe that we could come to know these connections through the method of free association?

So far I have argued that Freud's metaphysical position was a reasonable hypothesis. Since dream contents had to come from somewhere and purely somatic sources seemed implausible, it was reasonable enough to assume mental intermediaries, and the obvious mechanism for (irrational) connections among mental states was association. Freud offered three explicit defences of the method of free association in the guise of replies to a predictable criticism. He put the objection forcefully: Given the ease with which putative associates could be found, it only took a bit of ingenuity to trace back a path from several dream elements to the same underlying dream thought (*The Interpretation of Dreams*, 1900, S.E. V:527). The most important argument, as Grünbaum stresses, turned on putative cures (Grünbaum 1984:230–31). Associations to symptoms or to dream contents put forward by free association had been confirmed when conscious acceptance of the associate produced relief from symptoms (V:528). Freud also appealed to two types of internal validation. Connections were sometimes found to one element that were then confirmed by their surprising connections with others; further, the proposed latent dream contents were always "purposive"; they had some obvious significance for the dreamer (V:527–30; also IV:148).

I considered the issue of confirmation by cures in note 9 to chapter 4. Although Grünbaum is right that, in the absence of control groups, even real cures could confirm neither diagnoses nor treatments, Freud's mistake in thinking that they did does not distinguish him from many reputable medical researchers. On the question of internal validation, however, Glymour's and Grünbaum's negative appraisals seem fully justified (Glymour 1983:67; Grünbaum 1984:174). Free association alone permitted only ad hoc selection among potential associates, and significance was too common to permit any serious pruning.

Freud needed and actively sought ways to confirm and constrain the deliverances of free association. In his *Introductory Lectures on Psycho-Analysis*, he claimed that experimental research on association had "played a notable part in the history of psychoanalysis" (1916–17, S.E. XV:109). He described the experimental paradigm for association experiments introduced by Wundt.

> [A] *stimulus word* is called out to the subject and he has the task of replying to it as quickly as possible with any *reaction* that occurs to him. It is then possible to study the interval that passes between the stimulus and the reaction, and the nature of the answer given as a reaction, possible errors when the experiment is repeated later, and so on. (109)

The Zurich school, led by Freud's former disciple and current antagonist Carl Jung, had performed a number of these experiments, some of whose results appeared in *Studies in Word Association* (1906). Without trying to speculate about how influential such experiments were on Freud's thinking (see *The Interpretation of Dreams*, 1900, S.E. V:532), two points seem clear. First, free association could be viewed as a variant of Wundt's experimental design. The only essential difference was that subjects had to try to adopt an uncritical attitude. Second, it is not obvious how association experiments could confirm hypotheses about *particular* associates.

Suppose that free association suggested that a certain patient associated ideas A and B. If that subject were now tested in Wundt's experimental paradigm, she might well reply "B" when given the stimulus "A." However, this result might show nothing more than that this association was now active in her, after therapy. If she did not say "B," that would not prove that there was not a strong link between A and B, since she might be repressing B! Thus, although Freud was apparently eager for help from experimental psychology,

in this instance, it could provide no confirmation for putative interpretations. Given the difficulty with individual testing and the dearth
of knowledge about individual histories, the only real hope for constraining free association was to find general principles of dream
interpretation.

We seem to have come full circle. The interpretation of dreams was
supposed to be a source of information about the functioning of the
primeval/unconscious mind. In order to prune associates down
enough to offer interpretations, however, Freud had to appeal to
principles of how the system functioned that had been proposed by
other disciplines, such as psychiatry and sexology. Dream interpretation seemed unable to make any independent contribution to the
project.

Without denying the potential seriousness of this problem, I think
that Freud had two plausible rejoinders. Although principles derived
from other disciplines had to be invoked to eliminate associates, free
association was, in theory, a genuine source of candidate associations.
Further, general principles did not provide unique analyses of dreams.
Even if there were reason to believe that the underlying wish was of
a sexual nature, for example, that would not isolate any particular
wish. So, ideally, free association could be informative. Further, more
specific principles of functioning might be discovered through the
analysis of particular dreams. These would include principles such as
condensation and the representability of particular ideas in dream
images.

A key move in the search for general principles to constrain free
association was Freud's analogy between dreaming and psychopathology (e.g., *The Interpretation of Dreams*, 1900, S.E. IV:92). Human beings
have many more dreams than they remember, and this fact must be
explained by any adequate theory. Besides the surface similarities
noted by Hobson, Freud saw a link between the forgetting of dreams
and the forgetting of unconscious material in psychopathology and
everyday life. Psychiatry had posited the existence of unconscious
elements in the mind to explain symptoms of psychopathology. According to his own version of this doctrine, these elements were kept
out of consciousness by the forces of repression. Given the striking
similarities between madness and dreaming, why not make the same
assumption about the forgetting of dreams? During waking life, dream
material was repressed; individuals were conscious of it during sleep
only because repressing forces were somehow diminished.

Although this was only a speculative analogy, Freud pursued it
vigorously. If the same system found expression in dreams as in
psychopathology, then the latent content of dreams would be the

fulfillment of repressed sexual wishes. Hence, a dream interpreter should pay particular heed to those deliverances of free association that bore on sexual matters. Since links to sexuality could always be found, Freud saw dream interpretation as confirming his sexual theory of the neuroses, while the latter was illuminating the nature of dreams. In this instance, the threat of circularity is particularly clear. The theory of the neuroses was used to guide dream interpretation, which was then supposed to provide confirmation for psychoanalytic diagnoses. I return to this problem below.

Rather than rely on descriptions of this method, Freud provided many samples to explain as much as illustrate dream interpretation. I chose this one more or less at random from the index of dreams.

> *I came up to my house with a lady on my arm. A closed carriage was standing in front of it and a man came up to me, showed me his credentials as a police officer and requested me to follow him. I asked him to allow me a little time to put my affairs in order.* (The Interpretation of Dreams, S.E. IV:155)

Freud questioned the dreamer about the grounds for his arrest and elicited the reply "infanticide." After further probing it turned out that his informant (a jurist friend, not a patient) had spent the previous night with a married woman and had practiced coitus interruptus. Freud interpreted the dream as follows:

> [Y]our dream was a fulfillment of a wish. It gave you a reassurance that you had not procreated a child, or, what amounts to the same thing, that you had killed a child. The intermediate links are easily indicated. . . . No doubt, too, you know Lenau's gruesome poem in which child murder and child prevention are equated. . . . [At this point the dreamer confided that he happened, apparently by chance, to think of Lenau that morning.] An after-echo of your dream. And now I can show you another incidental wish-fulfill-ment contained in your dream. You came up to your house with the lady on your arm. Thus you were bringing her home, instead of spending the night in her house as you did in reality. (The Interpretation of Dreams, 1900, S.E. IV:156)

Given the moral chasm between birth control and infanticide, the interpretation seems farfetched. When viewed through Freud's the-oretical commitments, however, it could not be more straightforward. Elements in the dream must be tied back to some wish relating to sex. As in all cases, Freud also used specific knowledge about the recent and, if available, ancient history of the dreamer to limit the space of possibilities. That is, his practice incorporated the common observation that dreams usually include elements from the day's waking life ("day's residues") and the psychological theory that people often dream about things that are worrying or frustrating them. With these clues, especially the fact of coitus interruptus, he felt that there must be a connection between avoiding procreation and infanticide (even though infanticide offered no rational solution to the dreamer's concerns, since pregnancy would reveal the affair). After speculating about several ways in which this association might have come about, Freud's hypothesis was given surprising confirmation by the dreamer's admission that he had been thinking about Lenau only that morning. The case was a perfect confirming instance of his theory: a manifest content, "infanticide," that made no sense on its own, a likely candidate for the latent content, the wish to avoid procreation, and a plausible explanation of how an associative link was formed between them, Lenau's striking poem.[4]

Other dreams were not so easy. A man who nursed his father and was grieved by his death reported the following dream to Freud:

> *His father was alive once more and was talking to him in his usual way, but* (the remarkable thing was that) *he had really died only he did not know it.* (*The Interpretation of Dreams*, 1900, S.E. V:430)

This was Freud's analysis:

> While he was nursing his father he repeatedly . . . had what was actually the merciful thought that death might put an end to his sufferings. During his mourning . . . even this sympathetic wish became a subject of self-raproach. . . . A stirring up of the dreamer's earliest infantile impulses against his father made it possible for this self-reproach to find expression as a dream; but the fact that the instigator of the dream and the daytime thoughts were such worlds apart was precisely what necessitated the dream's absurdity. (430–31)

This analysis was quite typical, and I will use it to make three different points. As with many of Freud's analyses, it depended on a highly sophisticated description of the dreamer's sexuality: The dreamer's Oedipal wish to marry his mother had led to an enduring death wish against his father. In a way, this dependency is hardly surprising, since Freud had made a serious study of sexology and its discoveries of childhood sexuality and component instincts. Reading such interpretations, however, it is clear that he could not have discovered childhood sexuality through analyzing dreams. Unless he had already assimilated and extended the work of sexology on this topic, the dream would be completely impenetrable. As with the basic wish fulfillment hypothesis, the distinctive claim that dreams expressed the fulfillment of infantile sexual wishes was theory driven.

This dream also illustrates the ease with which rival interpretations could be formulated. Seemingly, the dream admitted of a much simpler analysis that would still be compatible with the wish fulfillment hypothesis. Why not see it as expressing the dreamer's wish that his father were still alive, coupled with some sort of recognition that this could not be true? Freud would have rejected this alternative on the grounds that it contradicted two other aspects of his theory: The wish to have his father alive again was conscious, not repressed, and not obviously sexual. Eschewing simpler lines of interpretation, he appealed to the therapeutic "discovery" that symptoms often expressed the underlying unconscious idea in reverse and to his contribution to sexology, the Oedipal complex, to propose a different analysis. The dream expressed the sexually based Oedipal wish that his father would die, but rather than have this come out as the thought that his live father was dead, it was reversed in the manifest content that his dead father was alive.[5]

The third point relates to each of the first two. Especially in interpretations of patient dreams, Freud availed himself of his own and other theories of sexuality to tie apparently neutral contents to some aspect of sex. Sexology had revealed that sex was a much more pervasive feature of human life and had many more diverse expressions than might initially be suspected. Unfortunately, this expansive view of sex tended to nullify the constraints on association proposed by the analogy between dreaming and mental illness. Limiting candidate associates to those connected to the sexual sphere was no help when almost anything could be so connected. Hence, the possibility of constructing rival interpretations remained wide open. And, again, we seem to have a circle. Freud clearly saw the interpretation of dreams as confirming and expanding the work of sexology, even though theories of sexuality were involved in producing those interpretations.

A number of theories provided the foundations for Freud's distinctive approach to dream interpretation. His own neurophysiology and Jackson's evolutionary functionalism stood behind wish fulfillment and, to some degree, repression and regression. The method of free association was supported by both psychological theory and its experimental practice. His researches into the neuroses implicated unconscious sexual wishes as the instigators of dreams, and sexology stressed the importance of childhood sexuality. In all these critical respects, the dream theory was theory driven. This, however, is the good news. For these theoretical underpinnings were reasonably respectable. Associationism is still regarded with respect today, although it is perhaps not clear why. Sexology had made genuine discoveries about the many guises of sexual expression, and the theory of component instincts had some plausibility. Even Freud's theories of the neuroses were regarded as serious science, although subject to number of criticisms.

Let me now return to the charge of circular reasoning. Even if these theories were respectable enough in themselves, it is easy to see Freud's use of them as illegitimate. Dream interpretations were supposed to confirm and extend theories of sex and of the neuroses, even though the latter were used in framing interpretations.[6] However, this issue is less simple than it appears. Whether he was arguing in a circle or using three different ways of studying the unconscious to constrain and confirm each other's results depends on the answers to four questions: How well confirmed were theories of the neuroses independently of dream interpretation? How well confirmed were principles of sexology? How reasonable was it to believe that free association produced genuine associates? How well did these three approaches work together to explain actual dream data?

Given positive answers to these questions, the case appears to be one of mutual support. In light of then current knowledge of the neuroses and of sex, a subset of the associates actually elicited by the manifest contents would be expected, and hence would be the true latent content. On the other hand, if psychoanalysis, sexology, and the method of free association were themselves doubtful, then the treatment of dream interpretation would be blatantly circular. Opinion about Freud's work is polarized in part because of his interdisciplinary approach. For those who give some credence to each discipline's contribution, the fact that he integrated them in a unified theory reinforces faith in the parts and inspires it in the whole. But skeptical doubts also multiply in the face of this kind of theory construction until the whole enterprise appears hopelessly speculative.

Freud believed that associations between ideas could be established on the couch or by experiment. He also believed that his theory of the neuroses and various principles of sexology were well established. The real problem was not that he relied on these theories, but that they did not give him enough details to make contact with the data. To sustain a defense of mutual support, the last of the above questions also had to be answered positively. Apparently, he saw these theories as working together to yield explanations that fit dream data quite well. This, however, was a mistake. Rather than enabling an analyst to sift through the products of free association to get down to the likely underlying dream thoughts, sexology undermined the point of using psychopathology to understand dreams. For psychopathology led to sexual wishes, but as Freud understood sexology, sex was both polymorphous and ubiquitous—hence the familiar and correct observation that too many equally plausible (or implausible) interpretations were possible.

Anthropology, Philology, and Literature

Despite his confident tone, Freud was not insensitive to the lack of adequate constraints on free association and sought help from other areas of study. As already noted, several currents in nineteenth-century thought suggested that children, madmen, and contemporary "savages" manifested the workings of a primeval mind from which higher thought processes evolved. Recapitulationism implied that contemporary children actually passed through a stage of primeval mentation; Jackson and others took the contemporary brain to possess vestiges of earlier structures (which would provide a physical basis for children's repetitions). Freud alluded to this position several times (*The Interpretation of Dreams*, 1990, S.E. IV:127, 247, and V:548) and cited the authority of Havelock Ellis, James Sully, and Friedrich Nietzsche in its defense (IV:60, V:548). He presented Ellis's account of how it bore on the study of dreams, which was exactly his own view.

> Ellis . . . speaks of [dreams] as "an archaic world of vast emotions and imperfect thoughts," the study of which might reveal to us primitive states in the evolution of mental life. (IV:60; cf. *Introductory Lectures on Psycho-Analysis*, 1916–17, S.E. XV:199)

If dreams were relics of primitive mental life, then anthropology or prehistoric archaeology might enable us to understand some of the connections produced during free association. This was certainly Freud's plan, to add to the resources of dream interpretation by drawing on the discoveries of anthropology. In the *Introductory Lectures on Psycho-Analysis*, he dedicated one chapter to the archaic and infantile features of dreams. However, he had virtually nothing to say on the former topic (1916–17, S.E. XV:199ff.) Given the lack of usable work on prehistoric peoples, the only anthropological evidence he could invoke was his own theory from *Totem and Taboo*!

Like others in the nineteenth century, Freud believed that myths and literature based on myths were important sources of evidence about the archaic mind. Still, his original use of *Oedipus Rex* in the dream book was quite tentative.[7] In the very first edition (twelve years prior to *Totem and Taboo*), he cited it as confirmation of his psychological theory that all children experienced feelings of love for the opposite-sex parent and hatred for the same-sex parent (1900, S.E. IV:261). Although it stretches over four pages and can seem circular, the argument was very simple. The hypothesis of universal Oedipal impulses in children was confirmed by Sophocles' play, because it was possible to explain its enduring appeal (despite unfashionable doctrines about fate, choruses, and so forth) on the assumption that such impulses were universal, and this was also confirmed by dreams (IV:262). However, *Oedipus Rex* was not just a bystander as dream interpretation and child psychology mutually supported each other. Given the Oedipal hypothesis from his own child psychology, the continuing interest in the play was predictable, and so offered a bit of confirmation.

Freud also hinted at possible stronger confirmation. Earlier, he had suggested that myths and legends gave inklings about the primeval ages of human society, when fathers oppressed sons and sons emasculated fathers (*The Interpretation of Dreams*, 1900, S.E. IV:256). He would have assumed that childhood recapitulated the mental life of primitive peoples. Given these points, he could have offered a richer explanation of the surprising appeal of the play. The Oedipus legend probably represented some prototypical activity of a much earlier time, an actual falling in love with the mother and hatred of the father. Since childhood recapitulated the mental experiences of prehistoric times, children also went through these emotions. The memories of childhood were retained in the unconscious and so spilled out in neurotic symptoms and dreams.

There was, however, a crucial missing link in this account. Where was the evidence that prehistoric men actually had incestuous feelings for their mothers and consequent hatred of their fathers? None was available in 1900 beyond the play and various myths, so he had to settle for the relatively weak argument described above and hints of stronger connections. In a note added to the 1919 edition, the hints were finally redeemed. His own work in *Totem and Taboo* showed that if we assumed an actual Oedipal situation among primitive peoples, then we could explain incest taboos, exogamy, and the father figures characteristic of religion. In *Totem and Taboo*, Freud's account of life in the primal horde was described as a hypothesis, which faced some obvious objections (1913, S.E. XIII:157ff.). By 1919, he was much less tentative.

> Later studies [*Totem and Taboo*] have shown that the 'Oedipus complex' . . . throws a light on undreamt-of importance on the history of the human race and the evolution of religion and morality. (*The Interpretation of Dreams*, S.E. IV:263, n. 2)

If a hypothesis threw this kind of light on central questions of anthropology and sociology, then those fields could provide significant confirmation for it. This was clearly how Freud saw the matter. Further, a number of prominent anthropologists took his psychological reflections seriously, despite early skepticism about the speculative character of his anthropology (Wallace 1983:chaps. 4 and 5, passim). The addition of anthropology to the dream interpreter's arsenal widens the gulf between evaluations of the enterprise even further. For many current readers view psychoanalytically inspired anthropology as having not a single reliable datum or theory to offer dream interpretation or psychoanalysis more generally.

By contrast, philology was able to provide Freud with a number of useful and independently derived theories. It also supplied significant moral support. Many scholars believed that linguistic evolution proceeded according to strict, discoverable laws. If dreaming was a function of a primitive unconscious system, then its language would be that of early hominid ancestors. The hope was that linguistic studies might enable theorists to trace language and thinking back to their earliest forms. Müller described comparative philology as the key to the early history of humans, since it could furnish scholars

> with information by which the earliest development of the human mind, the origin of religion, the growth of civilization and the elements of social life amongst the old Arian tribes, may be traced. (cited by Leopold 1987:506)

At the beginning of his work on dreams, Freud was quite resistant to the technique of symbol interpretation (*The Interpretation of Dreams*, 1900, S.E. IV:99–100). Later, he adopted the view that it had to supplement free association (V:359–60). Still, he warned that most attempts to interpret symbols were arbitrary, because they lacked any technique based on a scientific understanding of the phenomena (IV:226). He hoped to avoid this problem by using a number of sources to supply or confirm symbolic relations, ranging from philology, myths, fairy tales, and legends, to jokes, children, ordinary linguistic usage, and studies on Korsakoff patients (V:346–47, 384; *Jokes and Their Relation to the Unconscious*, 1905, S.E. VIII:20; *Introductory Lectures on Psycho-Analysis*, 1916–17, XV:158; *New Introductory Lectures on Psycho-Analysis*, 1933, XXII:23, 24).

Among Freud's symbolic interpretations, his appeal to opposites is particularly annoying for nonbelievers: "Full" could mean empty, "potent" could mean impotent. This allowed great latitude in constructing interpretations—to say the least. However, he found surprisingly strong confirmation for it. In 1884, the philologist Karl Abel had argued that the Egyptian language used antithetical meanings of words. Freud quoted Abel's discussion at length in "The Antithetical Meanings of Primal Words" (1910). I reproduce only the first part.

"Now in the Egyptian language, this sole relic of a primitive world, there are a fair number of words with two meanings, one of which is the exact opposite of the other. Let us suppose, if such an obvious piece of nonsense can be imagined, that in German the word 'strong' meant both 'strong' and 'weak' . . ." (cited in S.E. XI:156)

He also provided Abel's ingenious explanation for the phenomenon. Concepts depend on comparison, on, for example, the contrast between strength and weakness.

"Since the concept of strength could not be formed except as a contrary to weakness, the word denoting 'strong' contained a simultaneous recollection of 'weak', as the thing by means of which it first came into existence. In reality this word denoted neither 'strong' nor 'weak', but the relation and difference between the two, which created both of them equally. . . . Man was not in fact able to acquire his oldest and simplest concepts except as contraries to their contraries, and only learnt by degrees to separate the two sides of an antithesis and think of one without conscious comparison with the other." (cited in S.E. XI:157–58)

Abel's discussion was perfectly suited to Freud's needs. He stressed the antiquity of the Egyptian language and the fact that this pattern was common only in very old languages. He presented not only data, but a very plausible theory to explain them. And the work was completely independent of psychoanalysis—although not of the nineteenth-century attitudes that shaped it. If Abel was right (and if dreams were an expression of archaic forms of thought and language), then the language of dreams should be ambiguous between antithetical meanings, however much this added to the difficulty of interpreting them.

Freud also cited the work of Hans Sperba, who argued that sexual needs were the foundation of language and hence that all primal words had sexual meaning (*The Interpretation of Dreams*, 1900, S.E. V:352, n. 1; *Introductory Lectures on Psycho-Analysis*, 1916–17, XV:167). Again, he noted that this work was independent of psychoanalysis and so especially welcome as confirmation.[8] Not all of Freud's appeals to linguistics were explicit. For example, he often claimed that dreams were unable to express logical relations (*The Interpretation of Dreams*, 1900, S.E. IV:312, V:660). In 1933, he finally drew the analogy between dreaming and primitive languages lacking grammatical structure: Both were unable to express such subtle relations. Although he gave no source, a discussion in Wundt's *Völkerpsychologie* indicates that primitive languages were widely believed to be lacking in grammatical categories and syntax (Wundt 1916:67ff.).

In trying to understand what a word represented in a dream, Freud claimed that it was far more important to consider its sound than its spelling (*The Interpretation of Dreams*, 1900, S.E. V:406). This appears to be an arbitrary stipulation. In fact, the important regularities discovered by historical linguistics concerned sound changes (Robins 1968:182ff.). He also suggested that we could decode dream symbolism by looking at the syntactic inventions of children and by considering analogical extensions of words and phrases (e.g., IV:303, V:386). Analogy and the well-known tendency of children to overregularize were acknowledged to be important forces in linguistic evolution (Antilla 1972:106; Robins 1968:188). The implicit argument was that symbol interpretation should be guided by the same general principles that had been found to govern historical transitions among linguistic forms. This made sense, on the assumption that the agency responsible for the production of dreams exemplified the same laws as earlier mental systems that created and molded language.

Philological considerations also provided useful support for several of Freud's hypotheses about "dream-work." He believed that three mechanisms bore the primary responsibility for constructing dreams: condensation, considerations of representability, and displacement of affect (*The Interpretation of Dreams*, 1900, S.E. V:445; see also 488ff. on "secondary revision"). In his work on jokes and slips of the tongue, he presented numerous examples that turned on the superimposition of one word on another. An example in English will give the flavor. Thomas De Quincey allegedly remarked that old people tend to fall into their "anecdotage," an obvious combination of "anecdote" and "dotage" (*Jokes and Their Relation to the Unconscious*, 1905, S.E., VIII:21–22). Jokes and slips provided an existence proof of verbal composites, but they did not imply that dream contents should also be understood in terms of a process of condensation. Freud believed that this inference was warranted, because the materials were strikingly similar: "We cannot doubt that in both cases [dreams and jokes] we are faced by the same psychical process, which we may recognize from its identical results" (29).

Why do dreams involve hallucinations of particular scenes and items? To gain some insight into pictorial representation in dreams, Freud again turned to philology. Three considerations seemed to promise help. The course of linguistic evolution "makes things easy for dreams," as he put it (*The Interpretation of Dreams*, 1900, S.E. V:407). Many words (and phrases) that once had concrete and pictorial meanings later acquired abstract meanings. This would make it easy to express wishes in hallucinated scenes. So, for example, in German "*Schrank*," literally "cupboard," can also be used to indicate a limit or restriction. Using this clue, Freud interpreted a man's dream of his brother in a box or cupboard as expressing a wish that he should restrict himself (V:407). Idiomatic expressions are also apt to have pictorial literal meanings. The Freudian corpus offers many examples, including "*Der Hafer sticht mich*," whose idiomatic meaning, "Prosperity is spoiling me" could be expressed in a dream about a horse rolling in a field of oats, each of which was tied to a pig's bristle, for the literal meaning is "The oats are pricking me" (V:407 and n.).

Second, concrete words that lent themselves to pictorial expression were especially useful in the dream-work, because they were also richer in associations than abstract terms (*The Interpretation of Dreams*, 1900, S.E. V:340). Freud did not explain why he thought so, but presumably it was due to their greater antiquity. Finally, he presented a linguistic hypothesis of his own as a potential solution to the general and vexing problem of the symbolic relation: "Things that are symbolically connected to-day were probably united in prehistoric times by conceptual and linguistic identity. The symbolic relation seems to be a relic and a mark of former identity" (V:352). In support, he cited the work of Sperba discussed earlier and studies of G. H. von Schubert and Sandor Ferenczi, which both suggested that common symbols extend across different (current) languages (V:352 and n. 1, and n. 2).

Given the general historical approach and specific recapitulationist theses of his time, Freud's speculative hypothesis would have seemed much more plausible then than it does now. Further, as he pointed out, his appeal to language to explain how dream thoughts were turned into pictures and, hence, how pictures could be translated back into abstract thought had a great advantage over standard symbolic dream interpretation. Each interpretation could be verified by appeal to established linguistic usage (*The Interpretation of Dreams*, 1900, S.E. IV:342).

Philology did not determine Freud's hypotheses about the dream-work as surely as neurophysiology determined wish fulfillment. Nevertheless, the potential of language to relate the abstract to the concrete and to build new forms out of old ones allowed him to see order in the chaotic materials of dreams. Without the example of language and its apparent strict orderliness, it is unlikely that he would have thought of condensation (linguistic and nonlinguistic) or representability as lawful processes in a science of dreams.

In the case of the third mechanism of primary dream-work, displacement of affect, Freud was explicit about its foundation in another field: The attachment of an inappropriate affect (emotional value) to a particular idea in a dream would remain an enigma unless the results of psychoanalysis were considered. Analysis (bolstered by the neurophysiological model of energy moving from one cluster of neurons to another) revealed that ideas and their normal emotional accompaniments could come apart, so the mystery of inappropriate affect disappeared (*The Interpretation of Dreams*, 1900, S.E. V:460, 461).

So far, I have highlighted the etymological contributions of comparative philology. As the previous citation from Müller makes clear, it had a much broader compass. Philology studied literary monuments in order to classify them into proper linguistic and historical categories (Pedersen 1962:79); comparative philology applied the comparative method to these results in an attempt to discover universal features of the growth of human mentality and civilization.

In one form or another, the project of using literary and cultural artifacts to unearth earlier forms of mental and social life appeared in the work of many scholars whom Freud admired. Henry Thomas Buckle explained that "[l]iterature, when it is in a healthy and unforced state, is simply the form in which the knowledge of a country is registered" (Buckle 1857–61:151). So, if it would be useful to gain some insight into the knowledge and thought patterns of previous epochs, look at their literary monuments. Edward B. Tylor echoed this view: To understand early civilization, scholars need to look at survivals, directly expressive language, myths, and ceremonies (Tylor 1891:v). Wundt took the topic to a more theoretical plane. It was impossible to understand the development of higher mental processes without considering the origin of such factors as language, civilization, and religion. These, however, were the products not of individual minds, but of cultures, so it was important to gain insight into early civilizations. This could be done through intensive study of each of their cultural products, language, art, myth, and religion. Since "the various mental expressions, particularly in their earlier stages, are so intertwined that they are scarcely separable," however, it is better to try a synthetic approach that considers these phenomena in their interconnection (Wundt 1916:3–7; citation from 6). Wundt presented the purpose of the enterprise in the form of an open question, to determine "whether or not mental development is at all subject to law" (xiii). There is little doubt, however, that his own bet was on the affirmative side.

Given this intellectual milieu, it is hardly shocking that Freud thought of literature, and especially of myths and legends, as possible sources of confirmation for psychological hypotheses. Literary monuments would reveal not just the thoughts of their authors, but the mental categories of the whole culture. If the hypothesis to be proved was that, among primitive peoples, fathers were feared and hated, then numerous or widely known stories involving patricide would seem to be positive evidence.

Freud's incorporation of literature into psychoanalysis is sometimes portrayed as a move away from science, as a midlife recognition that mental phenomena could not be understood in scientific terms, but must be dealt with on a literary model, either as providing the same sort of insight that literature gives into reality or that critics have into literature. This is exactly backward. He did not abandon science in favor of literature—he tried to co-opt literature into the service of science, as did several of his distinguished contemporaries. Literature represented, not an alternative mode of understanding, but an alternative source of evidence about the universal laws of mental development.

If Freud did not change from scientist to literary critic, then his increasing use of symbol interpretation should not be understood in terms of this hypothesized change. As the editors of the *Standard Edition* note, the most significant additions over the eight versions of the dream book were the expanded discussions of symbolism. These indicated a growing confidence in the possibility of tracing symbols and perhaps also a growing recognition that free association had to be supplemented. What I have argued is that this confidence had some basis in fact. The general view that the development of language followed regular patterns, the actual discovery of the common genealogy of Indo-European languages, the existence of comparative philology as a discipline, and the particular contributions of people like Abel and Sperba made it possible to hope that early forms of language and their distinctive means of representation could be unearthed. If the language of dreams was closely related to this archaic language, then these discoveries would simultaneously provide the long-sought keys to dream symbolism.

As with psychiatry, anthropology, and sexology, however, Freud's theoretical hopes and expectations exceeded what comparative philology delivered. The 1914 edition of *The Interpretation of Dreams*, acknowledged the importance of symbolism by adding a new section (chapter 6, section E) in which material from the 1909 and 1911 editions was reorganized in a more systematic presentation. It began by recounting the many sources of symbols: folklore, myths, legends, linguistic idioms, proverbial wisdom, and current jokes (S.E. V:351). But the examples that followed were not carefully tied to any particular source and certainly not to actual philological discoveries. In most cases,

Freud simply relied on their intuitive obviousness to the reader, King and Queen for father and mother, trees and umbrellas for the male sexual organ, and so forth. If symbol interpretation were made this easy—the meaning of the symbols could just be read off by the average person—then what accounted for the two millennia of disagreement documented in this historical chapter? Worse still, when he provided documentary support, he often appealed to Wilhelm Steckel, whose method he described as "intuitive" and unscientific, or to K. A. Scherner, whose lack of a serious method he lamented in an earlier chapter (V:350, IV:226).

Over the editions Freud invoked other authorities, but these were usually disciples, Otto Rank, Hans Sachs, or Alfred Robistek, for example, publishing in one of the house organs of psychoanalysis. In one passage he attempted to marshal experimental evidence for psychoanalytic interpretations.[9] K. Schrötter put subjects under deep hypnosis and then suggested that they dream about various kinds of sexual intercourse. When they did dream, the symbols that appeared were those predicted by psychoanalysis. Freud reported similar experiments by G. Roffenstein (*The Interpretation of Dreams*, S.E. V:384). He also discussed work done by Betlheim and Hartmann, who told sexual anecdotes to Korsakoff patients (patients suffering from alcohol-induced dementia). When the patients repeated the anecdotes, they tended to use symbolism, in particular stairs for intercourse, that had been predicted by psychoanalytic dream interpretation (V:384). Freud took these experiments to be confirmation, and they did offer preliminary support. To provide genuine independent confirmation for the many dream symbols proposed by psychoanalysis, however, the experiments would have had to be both more extensive and more systematic.

It is not hard to see why opinion is sharply divided over the value of Freud's dream symbolism. He conceded that many details were missing or uncertain. In a central and much-discussed case of dental content symbolizing masturbation, for example, he remarked on his continuing inability to provide a convincing account (*The Interpretation of Dreams*, 1900, S.E. V:387). Despite such difficulties, Freud had great faith in the big picture. It would not matter much if some rough and ready decodings did not stand up. There was reason to believe that dream symbols were relics of a primeval language and that this language could be approached through many different avenues, including psychoanalytic studies of neurotics. So, eventually, the details would be cleared up. Supporters presumably share this faith. By contrast, doubters can only be appalled at the lack of detailed, independent evidence supporting any of the proposed symbolic relations.

When it came to specifics, common intuition and psychoanalysis were the principal evidence for symbolic relations in dream interpretation—and vice versa.

Dreams and Theories

We now have a fairly complete picture of how dream theory fitted into the rest of psychoanalysis. As can be seen in figure 5.1, this theory exemplified Freud's construction of psychoanalysis from interdisciplinary borrowings.

I will use this diagram to make three different points. The most obvious is simply a summary of arguments that have been given throughout this chapter: In all essential respects, Freud's dream theory was theory driven. I have also argued the second point in passing. This type of theory construction tends to inspire very different evaluations, because confidence in, or doubts about, particular pieces ramify when the parts are brought together in a single theory.

In the diagram, dream theory is represented as the intersection of many branches of psychoanalysis. This representation is accurate, because the theory incorporated many diverse but key doctrines of psychoanalysis. Still, it might seem that this highly problematic part of Freud's work could be excised. Suppose that dreams were senseless. It might still be true that all people and especially neurotics were governed by unconscious sexual wishes, that there were clear stages of psychosexual development including the Oedipal phase, that the nervous system tried to rid itself of excess energy, and so forth.

The diagram indicates why this approach is untenable. Arrows of support, constraint, and confirmation go in both directions. At least in the cases of sexology, evolutionary anthropology, comparative philology, and psychiatry, dream interpretation needed to give as well as to take. To see why, consider what psychoanalysis itself had to contribute to the project of figuring out how human mentality developed and currently functioned. Freud was extremely widely read and had an agile imagination, so he was able to synthesize a large body of work from other disciplines. Once he left Brücke's laboratory, however, he had only two direct means of acquiring information about the mind, the analysis of neurotic patients and the interpretation of dreams. Freudians are right in defending the probity of clinical evidence and in prizing dream interpretation. For without its two unique sources of evidence, psychoanalysis would have no way of advancing the understanding of mental life. On this point alone, supporters and critics are in complete agreement—although they draw diametrically opposed conclusions from it.

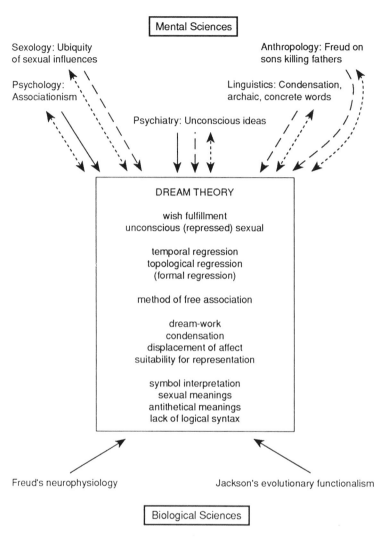

Figure 5.1
Freud's dream theory and its connections with other disciplines. Solid arrows indicate relations of constraint and guidance and run from the constraining to the constrained disciplines. Dotted arrows indicate the weaker epistemological relations of support and inspiration, running from the supporting to the supported disciplines. Dashed arrows represent relations of explanatory extension and run from the extending to the extended disciplines.

Following current practice, I have used the terminology of "pseudoscience" to present the debate over Freud's dream theory. Recent work in philosophy of science suggests that this classification may not be very helpful. As Larry Laudan has argued, all proposed criteria of demarcation between science and nonscience have been successfully attacked (Laudan 1983). So there is no reliable standard by which to judge. Laudan does not rue the lack of precise boundaries around science, because he believes that it is still possible to ask important normative questions about theories and projects such as, Is a theory well confirmed? Are its assumptions warranted?

Dropping the rhetoric of "pseudoscience," detractors can still maintain that the dream theory was paradigmatically bad science, supporters that it was a lasting achievement. One advantage of exploring how Freud pieced this theory together from work in various disciplines is that it exposes the weaknesses of both these extremes. I start with the positive side.

If Freud was inspired to offer this theory and continued to adhere to it on the basis of the interdisciplinary considerations I have documented, then it cannot be regarded as a lasting achievement. There is no reason to believe that it is true. As will become clear in chapter 6 and 7, the disciplines Freud relied on did not develop in the ways he expected, so that over time the theoretical supports for dream theory disappeared. Of course, it *might* still be true, even though it is not true for the reasons Freud thought. This is merely a theoretical possibility, however, and not a serious defense.

Defenders should take a different tack and argue that the theoretical superstructure of dream theory can just be abandoned, because discoveries from couch and bed can stand on their own. By now, the problem with this strategy should be obvious. As I have argued, the good parts of dream theory were its theoretical foundations. Specific dream interpretations were badly underdetermined and poorly supported, either by appeal to common sense or by appeal to psychoanalytic hypotheses, which were themselves partially defended by invoking the work on dreams. Perhaps the sole exception to this dismal accounting is the discovery of condensation. Particularly for condensed words, it is very hard to think of plausible alternatives, and Freud may well have described a common feature of dreams that later researchers need to study (Crick and Mitchison 1986:238–39).

At this point, the dream theory seems to be egregiously bad science. Not only was it theory driven, but the theories drove Freud to take neutral data as confirmation, year after year, dream after dream. As noted at the beginning, however, this failing is more common than epistemologists would like to believe. Primatology furnishes an example that is somewhat similar to the dream case. For many years, field workers documented various patterns of dominance and aggressive behavior in males of different primate species. As in dream theory, evolutionary biology seemed to provide a compelling rationale. For males, many matings are a good way to reproductive success; a male who is aggressive and so able to dominate females and rival males will achieve differentially more matings. Looking for such patterns, primatologists were able to find behaviors that seemed to instantiate them. More recent studies show that these behaviors are better understood in terms of different categories, that aggression and dominance are neither as prevalent nor as critical as previously believed, and that earlier work simply overlooked many examples of cooperative behavior (Strum 1987).[10] Stephen Jay Gould describes an example from a very different field. Convinced that nature did not take leaps, Charles Doolittle Walcott classified the arthropods of the Burgess shale in established conventional groups in 1912. When they were definitively reclassified in the 1970s, only two of his twenty-two genera turned out to be legitimate members of their groups (Gould 1989:109).[11]

Given Laudan's general point about the absence of demarcation criteria, this result is not surprising. Even theory-driven spurious confirmation is an imperfect indicator of bad science. What matters is how good the theories were and how reasonable it was to interpret the observations as confirmation. Throughout the chapter, I have argued that many of the theories on which dream theory rested, the evolutionary layer theory of the brain's construction, Freud's own neurophysiology and psychiatry, associationism, sexology, and comparative philology, were sound enough to serve as supports. On the other hand, I have joined Freud's critics in pointing out the excessive slack between the dream data and the construals applied to them. This, perhaps, is where the case for bad science should be made. Before coming to a final verdict, however, it is illuminating to take a page from Hobson's book and compare Freud's theory with his own, which is probably the most developed theory of dreaming currently available.

I provide only the barest overview of the physiological work that led to Hobson's theory, and interested readers should consult his own review of the literature (Hobson 1988a:parts II and III). In 1953, Aserinsky and Kleitman discovered a correlation between dreaming and rapid eye movements during sleep, the now famous REM sleep. In 1959, Jouvet localized the region of the brain that initiated REM sleep in the brain stem (Hobson 1988a:19). Three years later, he established a correlation between REM sleep and the presence of a distinctive EEG pattern, ponto-geniculo-occipital (PGO) waves. Even more dramatically, he showed that REM sleep could be enhanced in cats by introducing drugs that mimic the action of acetylcholine (Hobson 1988a:153–54). In 1985, Gillin reported a series of experiments in which human REM sleep and consequent dream reports were successfully manipulated through intravenous infusion of cholinergic drugs (Hobson 1988a:201). Besides these specific results, Hobson's theory differs from Freud's in being based on a very different conception of neurons. As he emphasizes, Freud took neural tissue to be reflexive, to require stimulation from the outside. In fact, neurons have their own energy stores within them, and the whole neural system should be seen as capable of self-activation (Hobson 1988b:283).

I will compare Hobson's activation-synthesis hypothesis with Freud's dream theory in respect to three questions: What is the cause of dreaming? Why, in general, do dreams have the unusual features that distinguish them from waking life? What accounts for the particular anomalies present in specimen dreams? Freud claimed that unconscious sexual wishes cause dreams. Hobson argues that dreams are the result of the brain's autoactivation, specifically, that they are caused by cholinergic brain-stem mechanisms (Hobson 1988:202).

Freud and Hobson agree about the phenomenon to be explained. Dreaming involves sensory hallucinations and delusion (because the fantastic is unquestioned); dream narratives include impossible happenings, compound or indeterminate characters, and incoherent sequences of events. Freud explained these bizarre features by hypothesizing that the surface contents of dreams were disguised representations of unconscious sexual wishes and that they exhibited a primitive, prelogical phase of human mentation. Whatever its faults, the manifest/latent content distinction had the advantage of addressing both halves of the problem, why dreams were so weird, yet not completely random. To account for the semicoherence of dreams, Hobson turns to synthesis. Chemical signals from the brain stem activate the visual and motoric cortices, causing hallucinations of sights and movements. Since the brain is designed to integrate information, it struggles to place an interpretation of these random inputs (Hobson 1988a:15). Synthesis thus explains both the coherence and the strangeness of dreams, because it "denotes the best possible fit of intrinsically inchoate data produced by the auto-activated brain-mind" (Hobson 1988a:204). Hobson adds that in dreaming, the mind-brain has been switched into a different mode of operation (Hobson 1988a:205, 1988b:307).

Since sexuality was thought to be ubiquitous, Freud's theory had a serious shortcoming. It was too easy to link dream contents—whatever they were—to some aspect of sexual life and so to a latent sexual wish.

Hobson's hypothesis has exactly the same drawback. Given one mechanism for chaos and one for order, activation-synthesis can explain any amount of either one. Nor is it enlightening to claim that dreaming is different from waking, because in REM sleep the brain is in a different state of activation (even though this may be true) (Hobson 1988a:258). Both theorists need to provide more precise descriptions of the production of dream contents. Freud tried with the "dreamwork." Condensation, displacement of affect, and considerations of representability were supposed to provide more specific answers to the question of how latent contents turned into incoherent manifest contents. Hobson offers a dual approach. At the narrative level, he sides with Jung in believing that the meanings of dreams are transparent. They are to be explained in terms of the dreamer's experiences, concerns, and associations. The narrative aspect is then supplemented by explanations of the peculiar or formal characteristics of dreams. To develop this side of his theory, Hobson has drawn up various systems of classification for the unusual features of dreams and is trying to get some sense of their frequency.

He has also formulated hypotheses to explain the specific kinds of bizarreness encountered in dreams. In sleep, people do not get external inputs that inform them of such basic conditions of the outer-world as orientational unity, contextual congruity, and linearity of cause-effect relations between events. Further, the internally generated stimuli lack these three parameters. Although they are still organized into scenarios by the sleeping brain, the scenarios are inherently unstable, perhaps because of the lack of attention and memory capacity during sleep (Hobson 1988a:268). To illustrate how his theory works, Hobson applies these five factors (lack of orientational unity, contextual conditions, cause-effect sequence, memory, and attention), plus the tools of narrative analysis, to a specimen dream from the journal of the "Engine Man," a man who recorded his dreams on 100 successive nights between July and October of 1939.

Hobson is able to account for many elements of the dream. Unfortunately, it is not hard to see why this will be the result, whatever the dream. As Freud did with condensation and displacement of affect, Hobson turns apt descriptions of the materials of dreams—lack of orientational unity, contextual conditions, and normal cause-effect sequences—into explanatory factors. The dream-work of condensation explains why dream elements are condensed, the lack of orientational unity explains why they lack a unified orientation, and so forth. Where these factors fail to account for a feature, Hobson appeals, as Freud did, to a mélange of commonsense remedies: diminished or absent capacities, recent or past experiences, particular concerns—

and the psychologist's best friend in need, association (Hobson 1988a:272–81; see also the analysis of his own "Mozart" dream, 220–22).

I do not draw this painful comparison to criticize Hobson or to imply that no progress has been made in the last ninety years. Contemporary researchers now have some crucial understanding of physiological mechanisms involved in dreaming. What the comparison shows, I think, is how treacherous dream contents are as a scientific subject matter. They have just enough regularity and common sense has just enough palliatives to make them seem law-governed. Recognizing this danger, many dream theorists do not try to explain contents at all, but simply try to account for the state of dreaming. So, for example, Francis Crick and Graeme Mitchison offer the following hypothesis. They assume that the brain can be understood as a connectionist net. Thus, when people experience certain patterns, particular connection strengths are established among the nodes of their neural nets. Dreaming introduces random stimulation, thereby causing a weakening of these connections or "reverse learning." Reverse learning is useful, because nets can become so overloaded with connections that new patterns are not learned efficiently, but merely superimposed on existing patterns (Crick and Mitchison 1986). As Crick and Mitchison acknowledge, the obvious objection to their approach is that it leaves untouched the thematic and narrative unity of dreams, such as it is (Crick and Mitchison 1986:232). They also admit the speculative and theory-driven character of their proposal. Along with other connectionists, they have been led to see dreaming as a type of "washing" mechanism by considering the problem of overloading in connectionist networks. In partial defense, they observe that other recent proposals about the function of dreaming are equally theory driven and speculative (Crick and Mitchison 1986:245–46).

Freud's dream theory was speculative, theory driven, and very loosely connected to the dream data. What I have just argued is that, in these respects, it is typical of theories of dream contents and function. Given the recognized difficulty of dream phenomena, it was unwise to make them so central to psychoanalysis. Further, the treacherous nature of the subject matter does not excuse this cavalier dismissal of alternative interpretations in presenting large numbers of dreams as confirmation for his theory. Further still, unlike contemporary theorists, he did not seem to regard his hypothesis as a hypothesis. He began *The Interpretation of Dreams* by announcing that he would give a proof of a psychological technique for interpreting dreams (1900, S.E. IV:1). In putting great stock in dream theory and in being too cavalier and too confident, Freud fell considerably short of the standards of good science.

However, these failings do not explain the urge to label him a "pseudoscientist." Hobson reveals the real source of complaint in the following outburst:

> The Interpretation of Dreams was antiscientific because Freud so forcefully dismissed all previous writers that he actually aborted an emerging experimental tradition. Psychiatry and psychology have been in Freud's thrall for almost a century. . . . [T]he tenacity of the psychoanalytic view remains impressively obstructive to integrative theorizing. (Hobson 1988a:51)

What is so galling about Freud's dream theory—why many are tempted to call it unscientific, pseudoscientific, or antiscientific—is that it succeeded far out of proportion to the strength of the evidence in its favor.

Critics have tried to paint Freud's unwarranted success as itself a scientific failing: It derived from his magnetic personality, the tight control he exercised over the institutions of psychoanalysis, or his strategy of going over the heads (or, perhaps, under the feet) of the established scientific community to appeal to an uncritical lay audience. Although popular, the first two hypotheses are not very plausible. Freud did not have personal contact with the vast majority of people who came to accept psychoanalysis, and he could only control those who already wished to become members of the psychoanalytic community.[12] Insofar as the third hypothesis is meant as a criticism, it is also wide of the mark. Writing for the educated public is not a failing in scientists. As John Dewey pointed out long ago, scholars should try to make their learning available to the larger society.

Freud did not live in an age of mass communication, and he gave relatively few public lectures. The obvious source of his influence was his remarkable literary talent. He was a gifted writer, and he had a very good story to tell, even if the direct evidence for some key parts (i.e., the theory of dreams) was quite weak. In the Introductory Lectures, Freud explained the secret of his success.

> [Psycho-analysis can] attract general interest in a way in which neither psychology nor psychiatry has succeeded in doing. In the work of psycho-analysis links are formed with numbers of other mental sciences, the investigation of which promises results of the greatest value: links with mythology and philology, with folklore, with social psychology and the theory of religion. (1916–17, S.E. XV:167)

This self-diagnosis was exactly right. What attracted the educated public to psychoanalysis was its grand sweep, its seeming ability to bring so many aspects of mental life that people cared about—personality, social relations, religion, values, and, of course, sexuality—within the purview of a single unified theory.

Psychoanalysis became excessively influential, because it promised to put order into the generally chaotic picture of mental life. Phenomena as diverse as art, ritual, dreaming, and social mores could all be seen as part of a pattern. That pattern was elegant, simple enough in its basic lines to be grasped quickly, yet complex enough in its detail to permit application to an endless variety of seemingly disparate facts: the expression of sexual instincts as modified by individual heredity and experience, on the one hand, and interpersonal and social influences, on the other. Moreover, this new systematic understanding of mental life did away with scientifically dubious distinctions between mind and body, humans and other animals. Mentality was seen as an outgrowth of sexuality, and sex was firmly rooted in biology. An internal secretion produced by some bodily organ or organs, libido, drove the mental apparatus by the amount and direction of its flow.

By drawing on many areas of study, Freud was able to construct a systematic theory of mental life that seemed to explain a vast array of data in terms of a few simple principles, principles that rested on an apparently solid foundation in biology and neurology. Aided by an able pen, this combination probably guarantees popular success for a candidate science of the mind. As we will see in part II, its interdisciplinary and systematic character also made psychoanalysis "impressively tenacious," as Hobson puts it. Lack of progress or outright failure in one or two areas could be ignored, because there were always other disciplines to turn to and an elegant explanatory scheme that promised too much to too many to be lightly surrendered.

PART II
The Consilience That Failed

Chapter 6
Biology: Disappointment and Disaster

At least in the United States, psychoanalysis is no longer a thriving scientific research program in either psychology or psychiatry. Freudian analysts still practice, theorize, and contribute to journals, but they are a dying breed. In his Presidential Address to the American Psychoanalytic Association in 1969, Samuel Ritvo complained that "[t]he psychoanalytic societies are organizations of middle-aged and old men" (cited in Fine 1979:123). He was right. For example, of the 274 members of the New York Psychoanalytic Society that year, 2 were under forty. The average age of the 63 members who belonged to faculties was sixty-one (Fine 1979:124). Looking beyond psychoanalytic organizations, few psychology departments offer courses wholly or partly on Freud; current texts mention him, if at all, only to provide historical background for more recent theories of personality. When today's psychoanalysts leave practice or academic posts, it is hard to see where their replacements would come from.

In these last two chapters, I try to show how Freud's interdisciplinary approach contributed to the fall of psychoanalysis. This is not the complete explanation. Forty years of questioning the effectiveness of psychoanalytic treatment has undoubtedly discouraged aspiring therapists from joining the program. However, psychoanalysis is not just a school that flourished and faded. It is widely regarded as the paradigm of bad science, a theory so obviously false that its proponents must be deluded or devious or perhaps both.

I argued in chapter 5 that the most plausible explanation for the "oversuccess" of psychoanalysis was its systematic character. It held out the promise of a simple, comprehensive theory of mental life firmly rooted in the biological and physical sciences. The same factors, I will argue, account for its spectacular failure. For those who were in a position to know, the interdisciplinary props supporting the system were simply not there, either because they failed to materialize or because they were actually refuted. To these scientists, Freud's grand system rested on nothing at all.

The interdisciplinary structure of psychoanalysis did not just make it vulnerable to the charge of empty puffery. I will show how Freud's expectations for certain disciplines and his reactions when those expectations were disappointed made psychoanalysis both more likely to fail and less likely to be respected as a serious science. In examining these interdisciplinary errors, I will also take up the second task of the book, which is to use Freud's example to reveal potential dangers of current interdisciplinary work in cognitive science. This chapter will detail how poorly his biological bets fared in the first three decades of the twentieth century. Chapter 7 will trace what was, from the psychoanalytic point of view, the disappointing course of the social sciences during this same period.

Neurological Complications

Psychoanalysis was anchored in physiology by a few simple assumptions. Due perhaps to its inherent irritability, neural matter functioned as a reflex. When energy came in, the nervous system reacted by trying to discharge it, either immediately or after some necessary delay. Discharge of energy produced pleasure, retention of excess energy, pain. Besides external stimulation through sensory receptors, the neural system received energy from endogenous sources. In particular, somatic sources of instinctual sexual drives released something, presumably a special chemical substance, into the system, which produced an outpouring of energy into the neural mechanism. Sources of sexual energy would shut off only if the sexual needs of the organism were fulfilled. When sexual needs went unsatisfied, the neural system would be put under strain due to excess energy pouring into it.

As noted in chapter 4, three of these assumptions were quite reasonable at the time they were originally adopted. Many believed that neural matter was reflexive and that it received endogenous stimulation; Darwin supported common sense in assuming the existence of sexual instincts. However, the contribution from Fechner was speculative, and Freud's way of integrating these ideas was only a hypothesis. Even if neural matter were reflexive, excess energy were felt as pain, and sexual needs resulted in chemical signals being sent to the brain, it hardly followed that these signals overloaded the system, producing pain. This hypothesis was compatible with reasonable physiological assumptions and it forged an interesting link among them and with apparent clinical findings relating neuroses to sex, but it needed independent corroboration.

What I will argue is that as physiology developed, this essential corroboration failed to materialize. Hence, it became less and less reasonable to believe that psychoanalysis was properly grounded in biology. Before turning to these developments and their ramifications, let me anticipate an objection. A standard interpretation maintains that Freud gave up neurophysiology in the 1890s. Further, his own neurophysiology, the *Project for a Scientific Psychology*, was unavailable until 1953. So it might be claimed that the support of Freud and Freudians for psychoanalysis did not rest on any possible relation to biology. In chapters 3 and 4, I offered textual evidence to show that Freud never retreated from the view that psychoanalysis was grounded in the physiology of the nervous system. Although I have resisted using later psychoanalysts as sources, because Freud's original theories were developed in many different directions, discussions by Otto Fenichel and Franz Alexander suggest that for orthodox Freudians, the ties to biology remained an essential part of the attraction of psychoanalysis. The following citations are from Fenichel's authoritative text, published in 1945:

> Mental functions should be approached from the same angle as the functions of the nervous system in general. They are manifestations of the same basic function of the living organism— irritability. The basic pattern which is useful for understanding of mental phenomena is the reflex arc. Stimuli from the outside world or from the body initiate a state of tension that seeks for motor or secretory discharge, bringing about relaxation.

> Freud suggested that two kinds of excitation should be distinguished: one that is evoked by external, perceptual, discontinuous stimuli and another that arises from continuous instinctual stimuli within the organism. . . . This concept [of instinct] is very illuminating since it is consonant with the reflex pattern as the basis for all mental functions, and it is clearly this concept of instinct that has enabled psychoanalysis to rest on a biological basis.

> The *source* of an instinct is that chemicophysical status which causes a sensory stimulus to bring about excitement. . . . (Fenichel 1945:11, 54, 55)

Although Alexander also presents the relation to biology as a chief virtue of psychoanalysis, his account of the relation is more diffuse.

> The scientific consequence of this new perspective [of psychoanalysis] is that psychology is related to biology.

Life consists in a continuous cycle of supply and output of energy. Energy is consumed and must be regularly replaced and this requires a fresh supply from the environment. In the higher animals, the primary functions of the cerebrospinal and autonomic nervous system is to maintain this dynamic equilibrium, which is upset both by external stimuli and by the process of living itself. . . . A basic tendency of the organism is to keep these psychological tensions at a constant level. Freud borrowed this principle from Fechner and called it the "principle of stability." Its physiological counterpart was first recognized by Claude Bernard and formulated by Cannon in his principle of "homeostasis," the tendency of organisms to preserve internal conditions like temperature and the concentration of body fluids at a constant level.

The advantage to the organism of the principle of economy is obvious. It permits the saving of energy which adaptation to the environment requires. (Alexander 1948:18, 35, 36)

Alexander offered four different possible biological groundings for the pleasure principle: All biological systems consume and expend energy; a primary function of the nervous system is to maintain a dynamic equilibrium; more generally, organisms tend to operate by homeostatic principles; organisms need to save energy to deal with the environment! But, whatever the means, Alexander was confident that the relation of psychoanalysis to biology enhanced the former's scientific status.

Do somatic sources of instinctual sexual drives tax the nervous system by flooding it with energy that can sometimes find reflexive discharge only in inappropriate ways? Although psychoanalysis was a complex theory with many detailed and intertwined claims, this hypothesis was a keystone. If it could not be maintained, then the rest of the structure would collapse. But neither Freud nor his followers ever found any direct evidence for this hypothesis, and advances in endocrinology and neurophysiology made both halves seem considerably less plausible. I start with neural reflexes.

As others have noted, subsequent discoveries revealed that the pleasure principle rested on a mistaken picture of neural action (Holt 1965:108–9; Hobson 1988b:284–86). Freud assumed that the neural system was quiescent, or nearly so, and that when invaded by stimuli, it reacted by discharging the energy introduced by the stimulus. By 1930, however, "it began to be evident that the nerve cell is not physiologically inert, does not have to be excited from the outside in order to discharge" (Hebb 1982:35). It is important to realize how badly this change in the conception of neural action undermined Freud's position. If the nervous system is not driven by energy supplied from sources outside itself, then there would be no particular reason to believe that it tried to discharge this foreign energy or that it was burdened by excessive amounts of external energy. However, both dream theory and the theory of the neuroses assumed the presence of energy needing discharge. This energy was supposed to be the instigator of dreams and the explanation for the tics, paralyses, and other bodily symptoms of neuroses. If the nervous system did not strive to discharge energy, then psychoanalysis had no explanation for these phenomena—and they were supposed to be its core *explananda*.

In 1930, Freud was seventy-four years old. Rebuilding psychoanalysis from the ground up, as this development required, would have been a superhuman task, and it would be harsh to fault him for not undertaking it. His disciples cannot get off so lightly. Although Fenichel was happy to cite the physiological foundations of psychoanalysis, not one of his 1646 sources is a work in basic neurophysiology. Almost all the references are to other psychoanalysts. In 1945, he took his physiology second-hand from Freud. Similarly, although Alexander was impressed by the biological basis of psychoanalysis, he did not take the trouble to consider how, exactly, biology provided support for Freud's theory.

Given the disastrous consequences of the fall of the pleasure principle, it is tempting to think that Freud blundered in relying on physiology. He should not have made a physiological hypothesis so central to his program, but should have transformed himself into the pure psychologist envisioned by some of his followers. As noted, he retreated somewhat from 1890s neurophysiology by using more generic formulations of the pleasure principle in his later writings. This, however, was only a tactical retreat. He did not abandon his physiological foundations and assert that the "psychical apparatus" sought to discharge energy on purely psychological grounds. Particularly in *Beyond the Pleasure Principle* (1920), but even in the very brief discussion in *An Outline of Psycho-Analysis* (1938), Freud's account of the pleasure principle presupposed that his readers accepted the reflex character of the nervous system (see S.E. XVIII:26–27, XXIII:146). For unless they believed that stimuli produced neural energy needing to be discharged, they would have had no reason to find his principle true or even plausible. Had Freud become a pure psychologist, then new conceptions in neurophysiology could not have hurt him. Under these circumstances, however, he would have had either to abandon the pleasure principle or to offer it without any physiological support, and psychoanalysis would have been a very different and much less attractive theory.

It would also not have been an example of interdisciplinary theory construction. For good reasons, Freud wanted his psychological hypotheses to be guided and constrained by what was known about the nervous system, and the reflexive character of neural matter, spinal and cortical reflexes were well established. Where then was the mistake, other than relying on a theory that turned out to be wrong? Although not amounting to blunders, Freud made two related and instructive errors in his use of neurophysiology. By 1930, it was too late, but he should have been aware of potential problems as early as 1906.

That year saw the publication of Charles S. Sherrington's classic, *The Integrative Action of the Nervous System*. Sherrington offered a wonderfully complete and complex picture of what was known about reflexes; seven of the ten lectures have the word "reflex" in their title. The reflex concept was hardly going out of fashion in neurophysiology. Nevertheless, Sherrington's central brief was that it was not enough to understand nerve cells, their modes of conduction, and simple reflexes. As the title implied, the key to future research lay in figuring out how neural reactions, including reflexes, were integrated to produce the smooth performance exemplified in physical activity (Sherrington 1906:2–5).

As many have observed, Sherrington's lectures did not quite live up to their title. There was a great deal of information about particular reflexes and precious little about integration. Still, given the dependence of his theory on physiology, Freud should have familiarized himself with these lectures, and they should have given him pause. The pleasure principle took the individual neuron as a model for the whole; since each neuron seemed to pass off energy imparted to it, so did the system as a whole. This was not a crazy extrapolation. Hobson argues in a similar vein that since individual neurons are self-active, so is the entire system (Hobson 1988b:284). In 1906, however, Charles Sherrington, an undisputed expert, maintained that it was no simple matter to extrapolate from individual neural reactions to the actions of the whole system. On the contrary, this was the great challenge facing neurophysiology.

Sherrington sounded a further warning. Toward the beginning of his first lecture, he explained that "[t]he energy which is imparted to the organism by the stimulus is often far less in quantity than the energy which the organism itself sets free . . . [in reaction to the stimulus]" (Sherrington 1906:5). This should have worried Freudians. Even though their theory could allow some cases of stimuli leading to the release of more energy than they themselves imparted, this could not be true in general, for external and endogenous stimuli were the only sources of energy for the nervous system.

Perhaps Freud was simply ignorant of these developments. Given Sherrington's impact and Freud's wide interests and facility with English, I suspect (but cannot prove) that he had some familiarity with the questions raised about integration. However, they did not lead him to rethink his own position. Although problems remained to be solved in neurophysiology, Freud may have dismissed them as details of interest only to specialists. As long as the neuron doctrine was intact and reflexes were still regarded as the basic unit of neural action, his borrowings from physiology may have seemed quite safe.

This was a mistake. Whether Freud dismissed emerging difficulties as technical or simply did not bother to keep up, he erred in having more faith in the smooth progress of neurophysiology than the experts. Even though the basic concepts of neuron and reflex endured, they needed to be supplemented by higher-level concepts in order to explain the possibility of complex, coordinated action. These complications had the potential to change the simple picture of neural action that Freud had captured in the pleasure principle. This was exactly what the experts, Sherrington in particular, were telling him, but he was not listening.

Although it led to a costly mistake, Freud's attitude toward neurophysiology should not be seen as a blunder. From a distance, it is easy to regard problems in a neighboring discipline as relating only to details and so to have more faith in the resources of its basic concepts than the experts. This is, I believe, an endemic problem for interdisciplinary theory construction. It is also a perfect example of an interdisciplinary error that seems glaring in Freud, but that can pass unnoticed in contemporary discussions in cognitive science. Consider, for example, a recent exchange between philosopher Stephen Stich and computer scientist Paul Smolensky. In a wide-ranging paper, Smolensky tries to chart the implications of recent work in connectionism (or "parallel distributed processing (PDP)," as this style of computation is also known) for issues in cognitive science.[1] He begins by listing several caveats about possible limitations of connectionism. I cite portions of three of these.

> It is far from clear whether connectionist models have adequate computational power to perform high-level cognitive tasks: *There are serious obstacles that must be overcome.* . . . It is far from clear that connectionist models, *in something like their present forms*, can offer a sound basis for modeling neural computation. . . . Even

under the most successful scenario for connectionist cognitive science, many of the [other] currently practiced research strategies in cognitive science would remain viable and productive. (Smolensky 1988:2; my emphasis)

In his comments on Smolensky's paper, Stich proposes to trace the implications for cognitive science "if the project he describes can be carried off" (Stich 1988:53). Stich's argument is that the success of connectionism would go a long way toward establishing two philosophical theses that he has long supported, the elimination of "folk psychology" and the demise of the symbolic paradigm in psychology.

My objection is not that Stich ignores Smolensky's warnings about limitations that may make connectionist success less likely. His ruminations are meant to be hypothetical: If connectionism is successful, then what follows? As Freud's example makes clear, the danger lies in the nature of the warning. Once Sherrington had pointed out that neurophysiology had to expand its horizons beyond individual neurons and reflexes, the fact that Freud's psychological theories were consonant with the simple neuron-reflex picture no longer implied that they were well grounded in physiology—for experts in neurophysiology maintained *both* that the neuron doctrine was true at some level *and* that physiology needed to develop additional theories about the integration of neural activity in order to achieve a tolerably complete understanding of mental processes. By contrast, Freudian neurophysiology simply extrapolated the action of individual neurons to the entire system. Similarly, Smolensky offers reasons to believe that the current resources of connectionism are inadequate. It faces serious obstacles that may require important additions, either in the form of new computational breakthroughs or borrowings from other, more traditional approaches. Under these circumstances, showing that a particular philosophical theory comports well with the basic—but admittedly inadequate—explanatory constructs of connectionism does not provide evidence in its favor. For Smolensky's point is that complex mental processes probably cannot be modeled by the kinds of connectionist networks now available.

Stich is not alone in having more faith in the resources of connectionism than the experts. David Rumelhart and James McClelland make the following observation in discussing the implications of PDP for general issues in cognitive science:

We agree that many of the most natural applications of PDP models are in the domains of perception and memory. . . . However, we are convinced that these models are equally applicable to higher level cognitive processes and offer new insights into these phenomena as well. *We must be clear, though, about the fact that we cannot and do not expect PDP models to handle complex, extended, sequential reasoning processes as a single settling of a parallel network.* We think that PDP models describe the microstructure of the thought process. . . . (Rumelhart and McClelland 1986:144; my emphasis)

In a recent book exploring the implications of connectionism for issues in the philosophy of science, Paul Churchland proposes a PDP theory of explanation. The gist of his account is that explanatory understanding is very like perceptual recognition. Perception can be understood in PDP terms as the activation of a prototype vector. A PDP network that has been trained on a vast array of perceptual stimuli will have a large range of prototype vectors (that is, patterns of activation of hidden units) in its repertoire. Recognition occurs when a stimulus input leads a network to settle into one of the activation patterns in its repertoire. This is Churchland's proposal for understanding and explanation:

> I wish to suggest that those prototype vectors [that represent complex prototypical situations in the actual world], when activated, constitute the creature's recognition and concurrent *understanding* of its objective situation. . . .
>
> Explanatory understanding consists in the activation of a specific prototype vector in a well-trained network. (Churchland 1989:208, 210)

Since scientific explanation is a paradigm of the higher-level cognitive processes Rumelhart and McClelland were discussing, Churchland's proposal flatly contradicts expert opinion. The fathers of PDP are extremely doubtful that their account of the microprocesses of cognition in terms of settling into activation patterns of hidden units can be directly applied to this sort of phenomenon. In disregarding these doubts, Churchland undermines his own case—for he intends to argue that his proposal is plausible, precisely because it is well grounded in recent discoveries and advances in PDP modeling.

Stich and Churchland are able philosophers, knowledgeable about connectionism. Their examples suggest that it is highly likely that theorists will have more faith in the basic concepts of a neighboring discipline than the experts. Of course, an interdisciplinary theorist might get lucky. The experts could be wrong. What Freud's example demonstrates, however, is that when local experts express serious doubts about the adequacy of their own constructs, it is a mistake to make those constructs the measure of theories in related areas. In ignoring such doubts, Freud made it more probable that his theory would fail.

Freud's use of neurophysiology also exemplifies a fallacy made famous by D. O. Hebb. I repeat Hebb's point in this context, because it cannot be repeated often enough: When used by theorists outside of neurology, "CNS" should be understood to stand, not for "central nervous system," but for "conceptual nervous system," a simplified and often out-of-date working model of how the neural mechanism is supposed to function (Hebb 1982:32–41). It is probably impossible to avoid adopting simplified models in trying to demonstrate the relevance of work in one field to problems in another. As Freud's case illustrates, however, unless theorists take account of the fact that what they are using is only a working model, this strategy can lead to disaster.

Freud assumed that the central nervous system functioned as a modified reflex, expelling energy when possible and storing it only to permit the more efficient discharge of incoming energy. This was his CNS. Interestingly, he tried very hard to avoid Hebb's fallacy. He labeled his CNS a "postulate," a "hypothesis," and a "working hypothesis" ("Instincts and Their Vicissitudes," 1915, S.E. XIV:120; *The Interpretation of Dreams*, 1900, V:565; "The Neuro-Psychoses of Defense," 1894, III:60). These labels indicated its provisional status. However, nothing in his manner of constructing psychoanalysis reflected this status. He did not monitor the progress of neurophysiology, nor could the model be overthrown by any of his psychological theories, since they were developed strictly in accordance with it. His defense against Hebb's fallacy was merely semantic; his practice assumed that his CNS was the real central nervous system.

Worse still, Freud actively discouraged his disciples from investigating recent developments in biology.

> I had to restrain the analysts from investigations of this kind for educational reasons. Innervations, enlargements of blood vessels, and nervous paths would have been too dangerous a temptation for them. They had to learn to limit themselves to psychological ways of thought. (Letter to Victor Weizsaecker, 16 October 1932, quoted in Sulloway 1979:439)

Sulloway believes that Freud tried to turn his disciples away from biology and make them into pure (Freudian) psychologists in order to prevent disagreements about his core assumptions (Sulloway, letter, 1991). Another possibility is that he believed that his own strategy was the correct one for psychoanalysis: Abstract from current biological details and controversies and only assume that the basic picture was correct. In any case, once he had built nineteenth-century neurophysiology into the foundations of his theory, he eschewed further physiological investigations that might have permitted midcourse corrections. Even when he encountered complex phenomena that could not be readily modeled in neuron-reflex terms, he did not go back to neurophysiology, but simply embellished his own CNS! To take just two of numerous possible examples, he hypothesized that when an idea became conscious, it acquired an extra amount of energy (a "hypercathexis") and that, in mourning, energy was withdrawn from various ideas in a long-drawn-out and gradual fashion (*The Interpretation of Dreams*, 1900, S.E. V:594; "Mourning and Melancholia," 1917, XIV:256). As he cast them, these issues were neurophysiological and could be definitively settled only by that discipline. In extending his CNS from the armchair, Freud invited the criticism that his theory was hopelessly speculative. More generally, as neurophysiology progressed, his overreliance on his CNS made psychoanalysis appear to rest on more and more outmoded, simplistic, and speculative ideas of neural functioning.

The Sex Instinct: Physiology Fails to Deliver

Turning to the other half of Freud's hypothesis that instinctual sexual drives led to excess undischarged energy in the neural apparatus, the picture is just as grim. The bifurcation of instinctual drives into the sexual and nonsexual (either self-preservative or death) was a fundamental tenet of psychoanalysis. As was clear in chapter 4, Freud saw this distinction as coming out of biology, which taught that "sexuality is not to be put on a par with other functions of the individual" ("Instincts and Their Vicissitudes," 1915, S.E. XIV:125). Further, since the polymorphous character of sexuality made it difficult to find a criterion for distinguishing libido from nonsexual excitation, he frequently raised the possibility of a special sexual chemistry. For the critical libido–excess neural energy hypothesis to be established, physiology would have had to make two major discoveries: one or many markers (chemical or other) of instinctual sexual drives and the fact that whatever was released into the nervous system by these drives was of sufficient relative quantity that, if it continued to pour in unabated over time, it could strain the system.

As Fenichel observed in 1945, "physiology here disappoints us; the instinctual sources are a purely physiological problem, and in this field our knowledge is not yet sufficient" (Fenichel 1945:55). Except that this badly understated the difficulty. Freud first raised the issue of a special sexual chemistry in an unpublished 1894 draft (S.E. I:167). From 1903 onward, the actions of sex hormones began to be recognized (Singer 1959:543). The 1910 edition of the *Encyclopaedia Britannica* reported that experiments and observations led to the conclusion that beyond the production of sex-cells, gonads discharged secretions (hormones) into the blood that led to the development of secondary sex characteristics (vol. 24:746–47). In arguing for the prescient character of Freud's physiology, Karl Pribram and Merton Gill note that recent experiments have established the existence of central receptors that are sensitive to the female hormone estrogen (Pribram and Gill 1976:45). So special chemical secretions relating to an organism's sexuality do emanate from gonads (and other glands) and can impact on the nervous system. To this day, however, none of this work has established that sexual secretions have anything like the profound effect on the functioning of the nervous system that Freud claimed.

As endocrinology advanced, it became clear that hormonal secretions do not act in the way he hypothesized. Most obviously, they do not supply energy to other parts of the body, including the nervous system. Rather, hormones regulate various functions, by triggering or releasing activities in other parts of the body. If the impact of sex hormones on receptors in the brain led to the release of large amounts of neural energy, then Freud's position would still be compatible with results in endocrinology. Again, however, there has never been any evidence that this is true.

The libido–excess neural energy hypothesis was Freud's broadest claim about instinctual sexual drives. He also made more specific claims about component drives. In particular, the theory of psychosexual development rested in part on the assumption that sexual behavior did not have a single biological source, but instead involved a number of distinct yet related types of excitation. Freud never intended his ontogenetic theory to be merely descriptive; he meant to explain why sexuality followed its tortuous path of development by reference to its varied biological components (*Three Essays on the Theory of Sexuality*, 1905, S.E. VII:241). Earlier, I understated what psychoanalysis demanded of physiology: Physiology needed to provide markers for several distinct but related instinctual sexual drives.

Nothing in physiology gave Freud any reason to expect such a development. He got the idea of components of sexuality not from biology but from studies in sexology. I noted the impressive accomplishments of this field in chapters 2 and 4. Varieties of sexual behavior were carefully distinguished and catalogued, and, eventually, a fair amount of theoretical consensus was achieved about their complex biological and experiential origins. Many years later, Kinsey and his followers provided a clearer statistical picture of sexuality, but the descriptive work of turn-of-the-century sexology has never been seriously challenged. The problem for psychoanalysis stemmed from the theoretical claims of sexology. Like the Gestalt theory of perception of the thirties and forties, sexology's data were robust and rich, but there was no experimental or observational means of getting at its theoretical claims. They remained speculative, and when the recapitulationist thinking that supported them was itself discredited, they departed the domain of serious science.

As with his neurophysiology, for those in a position to know, Freud's views about special sexual secretions and their effects on the nervous system became less and less plausible over time. How did psychoanalysis end up in this awkward position? One obvious culprit was the instinct concept itself, a concept that has since been banned from psychology (Burghardt 1973:323). Darwin's discussion of instincts had prompted a number of theorists besides Freud to adopt the position that although instincts seemed free for the asking, at least sexual and self-preservative instincts were sanctioned by the biological sciences. Further, these instincts were perfectly suited to play a role in explanations of higher functions, because they clearly met the requirements of evolutionary naturalism. Still, the weaknesses of the instinct construct were acknowledged even by its supporters. In an article for the 1910 *Encyclopaedia Britannica* on "Instinct," C. Lloyd Morgan laid out the attractions and difficulties of this concept. On the negative side, the term had both a scientific and a lay meaning, and the scientific definition was a matter of some dispute. Indeed, Lloyd Morgan felt obliged to repudiate explicitly the definition provided by G. J. Romanes in the ninth edition of the *Encyclopaedia*. Nevertheless, the potential of "instincts" or "instinctive behavior" was enormous.

> [N]o small part of the interest and value of investigations in this field of inquiry lies in the relationships which may thereby be established between biological and psychological interpretations. (*Encyclopaedia Britannica*, 1910, vol. 14:648)

This was precisely the interest of the concept of instinctual drive for Freud. It was a "frontier" concept between biology and psychology (*Three Essays on the Theory of Sexuality*, 1905, S.E. VII:168; "Instincts and Their Vicissitudes," 1915, XIV:121–22) and, as such, provided for a possible rapprochement between them. Freud was sensitive to the vagueness of the term and pleaded the right of a new science to begin with indefinite concepts (XIV:114). During the twenties, the instinct concept came under increasing attack for its vagueness, and it was subsequently abandoned by psychology (Murphy 1949:405). Vagueness, however, was not the real problem with the psychoanalytic concept of instinctual drive. To see this, consider the two problems that a theory of instincts must resolve. First, it must provide descriptions of instinctual behaviors that reveal them to have that character. Second, it must find innate neurophysiological causes that impel that behavior under certain releasing conditions (Wilm 1925:144–45). Vagueness can be a reproach only for the descriptive half. Presumably, neurophysiological causes cannot be vague; either they are found or they are not found. Given Freud's views about the vicissitudes that instinctual drives underwent, he made no serious attempt to describe instinctual behaviors. He rejected the notion of *Instinkt* in favor of *Trieb* (instinctual drive), just because he did not believe that complex patterns of behavior could be attributed to inherited factors alone. Since psychoanalysis offered no account of "instincts," in the sense of instinctual behaviors, it could not err by doing so in an excessively vague manner.

For psychoanalysis, the crucial part of instinct theory was the second half, not the behaviors that were impelled, but the forces that did the impelling—hence *Triebe* (instinctual drives) that were to be identified by their somatic sources. Freud's error lay not in vagueness but in unwarranted specificity. As he made clear in a section added to the *Three Essays on the Theory of Sexuality* in 1915, "The Libido Theory," libido was a "quantifiably measurable force" that was distinguished "in respect of its special origin" from other kinds of neural energy and so presumably "by a special chemistry" (S.E. VII:217). Sexuality had been made extremely important by evolutionary biology; there were obviously a variety of sexual behaviors; and, as the economic aspect of Freud's metapsychology soundly maintained, any mental activity must have a physiological basis. Still, it was a fallacy to infer from "Every sexual behavior must have some physiological basis" to "There is some source of sexual excitation that impels every sexual behavior."[2] Besides vagueness, a serious drawback of the instinct construct is that it encourages this fallacy. Labeling behaviors as manifestations of an "instinct" invites the hypothesis that there is some reasonably circumscribed physiological basis that they all share. Only this fallacy supported the claim that libido was a specific kind of neural energy, which could be differentiated from all others.

By 1931, Freud realized that he had to retreat from the expectation of a physiologically grounded libido.

> [W]e cannot dismiss the notion that sexual excitation is derived from the operation of certain chemical substances. . . . [Still it is naive to expect biochemistry to provide a simple picture].

Even in sexual chemistry things must be rather more complicated. For psychology, however, it is a matter of indifference
whether there is a single sexually exciting substance in the body
or two or countless numbers of them. Psycho-analysis teaches us
to live with a single libido. . . . ("Female Sexuality," S.E. XXI:240)

This passage is curious. He did not renounce the possibility of a sexual
chemistry ("we cannot dismiss the notion . . ."). And the bottom line
was left ambiguous. Psychoanalysis was compatible with the discovery of one, two, or countless sexually exciting substances. Was it also
compatible with the discovery that these allegedly "sexually exciting"
substances were completely heterogeneous among themselves and
indistinguishable as a group from nonsexual energy?

To see the underlying difficulty, reflect again on the polymorphous
character of sexuality in psychoanalysis. What stood behind the claim
that these superficially diverse behaviors were all manifestations of
sexuality, a claim that was central to Freud's entire program? In some
cases, superficial similarities with recognizable examples of sexual
behavior could be noted, but this move was not always available. The
hypothesis of component sexual drives also provided some theoretical
backing for claims that certain behaviors that were mixed with sexuality in "lower" organisms might be part of human sexuality. Still,
this support was speculative and required supplementing to explain
why these behaviors should be considered sexual in adult humans.

In his most systematic discussion of instinctual drives, Freud admitted the poverty of such approaches.

I am altogether doubtful whether any decisive points for the
differentiation and classification of instinctual drives can be ar-
rived at on the basis of the psychological material. ("Instincts and
Their Vicissitudes," 1915, S.E. XIV:124)

Hence, the glue to hold libido theory together was to come from
biology, from "the chemical characteristics of the sexual processes,
which we suspect, [but] are still awaiting discovery" (*Introductory
Lectures on Psycho-Analysis*, 1916–17, S.E. XVI:320; see also "Instincts
and Their Vicissitudes," 1915, XIV:125). The unity of what psychoanalysis called "sexual phenomena" and so the ultimate correctness
of its claims for sex would be confirmed by biology. Even while la-
menting this fact, Freud clearly admitted it.

Though psycho-analysis endeavors as a rule to develop its theories as independently as possible from those of other sciences, it
is nevertheless obliged to seek a basis for the theory of instinctual
drives in biology. ("The Libido Theory," 1923, S.E. XVIII:258)

In his next discussion of libido theory after questioning its grounding in biochemistry, Freud switched biological horses. Alongside the hypothesis of a special sexual chemistry, he had always stressed the importance of sexuality to evolutionary biology. In a passage cited at greater length in chapter 4, he placed the entire weight of the distinction on the "unshakeable biological fact that the living individual organism is at the command of two intentions, self-preservation and the preservation of the species, which seem to be independent of each other" (*New Introduction Lectures on Psycho-Analysis*, 1933, S.E. XXII:95). Oddly, his last account, in *An Outline of Psycho-Analysis*, appears to revert to the earlier formulations: "There can be no question but that the libido has somatic sources . . ." (1938, S.E. XXIII:151).

As it did to others and for similar reasons, the instinct concept appealed to Freud, because it promised to meet the requirements of both his dynamic and economic metapsychology. "Instinctual sexual drive" was a qualitative description of the forces governing the nervous system that opened up the possibility of a quantitative account of the amount of excitation and its mode of operation. In need of a principled criterion of the sexual and gulled by the instinct concept, Freud made a serious miscalculation. He made his theory dependent on a specific result in another discipline, a result that experts gave him no reason to believe would be forthcoming. This made it both more likely that his theory would be wrong and less likely that it would be respected by knowledgeable scientists.

It is important to be clear about the nature of Freud's mistake. He did not err by making a prediction about what physiology would discover on the basis of his own clinical research and work in sexology. The strongest type of interdisciplinary confirmation is to predict (successfully) an unexpected result in one field on the basis of discoveries in a related field. His mistake lay in building his theory on the presumption that the circumstantial evidence was so strong that physiology had to find libido. He did not predict a physiological discovery; he presumed it and constructed his theory around it. Further, he maintained this presumption (except for the one lapse noted) even as discoveries about internal secretions and their mode of functioning made it less and less reasonable to do so. Finally, as in the case of neurophysiology, he erred in taking a simple (and hypothetical) model of internal stimulation much too seriously. Even at the rhetorical level, he never presented libido theory as a postulate or a working hypothesis that might have to be discarded.

It is equally important to distinguish Freud's error in theory construction from an apparently similar move, exemplified by Darwin. The biological theory of natural selection implied the geological claim that the earth was very old. Unfortunately, the best calculations of the earth's age, those made by Lord Kelvin, put that assumption in considerable doubt. Yet Darwin persevered and in the end turned out to be right, confounding the experts' expectations. Although Darwin was lucky, even if he had not been, he would not have been guilty of the same fallacy as Freud, simply because he was not engaged in interdisciplinary theory construction. He was trying to construct a theory not of the origin of the earth or of life, but merely of the origin of species. So he did not try to enlist theories of the creation of the earth or of life in support of his doctrines. His theory led him to a claim about the age of the earth; he did not base his theory on a presumption about its age. By contrast, the great advantage of psychoanalysis was supposed to be its ability to unify the results of the mental and biological sciences. In the case of libido theory, however, Freud did not borrow results from physiology, but presumed them.

Unlike having too much faith in the smooth progress of neighboring disciplines, presuming a specific and unanticipated result in another discipline is, I believe, fairly anomalous in interdisciplinary theory construction. Still, Jerry Fodor's *Language of Thought* (1975) appears to offer a contemporary example. In the first part of the book, Fodor offers a plausibility argument for the claim that there must be an innate language of thought as powerful as any natural language; later parts are to delineate its properties. This is a specific (and very strong) claim that is outside the bounds of Fodor's home disciplines of philosophy and psycholinguistics. At least at present, the appropriate discipline for such a hypothesis is developmental psychology. So Fodor is resting his theory of the language of thought on the expectation that developmental psychologists will discover that children come with or develop independently of experience all the basic concepts they will ever have.

Like Freud's case for libido, Fodor's argument for an innate language of thought is circumstantial. That is, none of the evidence comes from developmental psychology itself; instead, it derives from a variety of other fields. Many have regarded thinking as a kind of computing. Work in the theory of computation (at the time of his writing, 1975) implied that computing required a representational medium, a symbolic language in which the computations were carried out. Psychological theories of concept acquisition often model it in terms of inductive confirmation. According to standard philosophy of language, mastery of a concept requires knowledge of its extension (the objects to which it correctly applies) (Fodor 1975:59). Putting all these together, language learners can acquire a concept through inductive confirmation, which is a kind of computational process, only if they antecedently possess a representational system powerful enough to express a truth rule for the concept, that is, a rule that determines its extension. Failing this, they could not express the truth rule that they are trying to confirm and so could not learn the concept.

Fodor's argument is analogous to Freud's in another unfortunate aspect. Just as biologists have been wary of the instinct construct, so developmental psychologists have often shied away from the concept of innateness. In both cases, the concept has seemed to local experts to be too unclear and too simplistic to be helpful in scientific discussions. There are also important disanalogies, although one can hardly count in Fodor's favor. If nineteenth-century biologists were agnostic about instinctual sexual drives, contemporary developmental psychologists take language acquisition to be a mixture of native capacities and exposure to natural languages. That is, they explicitly reject Fodor's claim. Perhaps the more important disanalogy is that Fodor does not seem to take his hypothesis anywhere near as seriously as Freud took libido theory. Given Freud's example, that is fortunate. Resting your theory on presumed results in another discipline is probably a good way to guarantee failure.

Relying on the Promise of Connection

After sixty years of complaints that the great defect of psychoanalysis was that it was unfalsifiable, this criticism may seem shocking. Far from making his theory invulnerable to refutation, I maintain that in proposing libido theory, Freud took an inappropriate risk and paid dearly for it. Since the inadequacies of the pleasure principle have also been exposed, Popper's well-known charge that psychoanalysis was unfalsifiable in principle cannot be right, at least for its theoretical parts. Freud and his circle did not follow Popper's directive for science by trying to refute the theory themselves but few scientists do. What is more worrying is that they made so few efforts to confirm either half of the libido–excess neural energy hypothesis. Analytic practice produced many apparent clinical confirmations of a close connection between sexual difficulties and neurosis. However, the libido–excess energy hypothesis and the many economic and dynamic claims it spawned were much more specific: There was a more or less unitary, qualitatively described instinctive sexual force that easily lent itself to future quantitative treatment and could overburden the nervous system. Given the importance of this thesis—it stood behind the claims that there was not merely a correlation, but a causal connection between sexual problems and the neuroses, dreams, slips, jokes, and artistic creation—why didn't the psychoanalytic establishment try to confirm it?

For example, why weren't some of the resources of psychoanalysis directed to work in neurophysiology and endocrinology? Even if Freud's disciples did not wish to don white coats themselves, why didn't they closely monitor developments in these fields? Undoubtedly there are many answers, some having to do with personal interests and abilities, others perhaps with the founder's wish to protect his biological assumptions from revision. One answer impled by some of Freud's discussions is that analysts believed that physiology and especially neurophysiology were simply not advanced enough for it to be reasonable to hope for confirmation from these sources. Hence, the only kind of confirmation possible at the time was clinical. In one sense, this position was correct. So little was known about neural energy and hormonal secretions that it would have been wildly optimistic to expect physiology to be able to explain a putative relation between the two. On the other hand, the fact that developments that might confirm libido theory were highly unlikely in the near future did not imply that those developments that were occurring could be dismissed as irrelevant.

Yet Freud ignored them. Besides having more faith in neighboring disciplines than the experts and allowing his interdisciplinary aims to blind him to the dangers of the instinct concept, he was overconfident about the eventual vindication of the libido–excess neural energy hypothesis. Fenichel's recounting of the hypothesis points to a key source of overconfidence: "This concept [of instinct] is very illuminating since it is consonant with the reflex pattern as the basis for all mental functions" (Fenichel 1945:54). As noted in chapter 4, these two theories, instinctual sexual drives and the reflexive character of the nervous system, fit together extremely well. A reflexive nervous system needed sources of energy; sexual selection was a critical force in evolution; all psychological forces had to have a physiological basis. Libido theory united these facts in a simple and elegant story. Gonads and other internal organs released a substance into the nervous system that provided it with needed energy and constituted the physiological mechanisms by which sexuality influenced behavior and so ultimately evolution. Particularly when psychiatry testified to the importance of sexuality in mental illness and sociology and anthropology tried to trace social institutions and other higher human achievements to biological factors such as sexuality, libido theory emerged as a doctrine capable of uniting an impressive array of important results from different sciences in a single coherent account. The general contours of this account were so clear and the sources of potential support so diverse and plentiful that Freud was confident that the details would eventually be worked out.

His mistake lay in taking the promise of unification and interdisciplinary support for the actuality. For the two pieces of the theory we have been considering, his implicit reasoning was something like the following: Since the reflex theory, if true, made the libido hypothesis quite plausible and since, if true, the libido theory made the hypothesis of a reflexive nervous system quite plausible, then both hypotheses were extremely plausible. The fundamental assumption of an interdisciplinary methodology is that consonance with theories in related disciplines is positive evidence for a particular hypothesis. However, this does not imply that, by itself, fit between two theories is evidence for either one.

Freud erred in not fully appreciating that consonance with a theory in a related discipline is support for a given theory only to the extent that the different theories are themselves independently well supported. As questions began to be raised about the sufficiency of a reflex model, they could not be dismissed by noting how well a reflex model fit with libido theory and the importance of sex to evolution—when libido theory itself was finding little support in endocrinology. Likewise, doubts about libido theory could not be assuaged by pointing to its compatibility with the reflex doctrine, when the latter was also being called into question. As these two critical pieces of psychoanalysis lost their individual plausibility, it no longer mattered how well they fitted together. Yet Freud continued to be impressed by their "consilience" and so invited the common charge that psychoanalysis was an elegant fabrication utterly lacking in empirical support.

This mistake in interdisciplinary reasoning may have been abetted by another. Freud believed that, given their elegant fit, the probability of libido theory, given the reflex character of the nervous system, was higher than the independent probability of this theory. Conversely, he also believed that the probability of reflex theory, given the libido theory, was higher than the independent probability of the former theory. It is easy to see how such thinking might iterate out of control. Suppose that given their mutual fit, Freud incremented the probabilities of both theories. As a result, the two theories would look even stronger. Had he failed to recall the source of this enhanced strength, he might have become even more convinced about the libido theory, in light of its compatibility with the strongly supported reflex theory and conversely. Although I can hardly prove it, I believe that something like this process went on in Freud until he had raised the probability of both theories to near certainty—largely on the grounds that they fitted so well together.

Given the current style of interdisciplinary work, with its emphasis on close collaboration, it is highly unlikely that theorists would ignore developments in related fields, even if their relevance to cherished hypotheses were not immediately obvious. So Freud's cavalier practice is unlikely to be repeated. I am less confident about his fallacious reasoning. Recently, McClelland and Rumelhart have tried to bolster their case for modeling the mind/brain as a PDP network by arguing that such networks can extract the prototypes that have figured in many psychological discussions of concepts and categories.[3] Within psychology, prototype theory is roughly the doctrine that people are able to use concepts by virtue of possessing a prototype, an inner or psychological representation that "(1) reflects some measure of the central tendency of the instances' properties or patterns; (2) consequently is more similar to some concept members than others; and (3) is itself realizable as an instance" (Smith and Medin 1981:169). McClelland and Rumelhart conclude their discussion of PDP simulations of category learning with the observation that "a distributed model of memory provides a natural way of accounting for the fact that memory appears to extract the central tendencies. . . ." (McClelland and Rumelhart 1986:214). That is, they use consonance with the psychological data favoring prototype theories as additional evidence for PDP models.

Terry Horgan and John Tienson reason in the opposite direction. Having cited the virtues of connectionism (or their generalization of connectionism, rules without representation), they argue that the truth of this theory makes it more likely that there are no necessary and sufficient conditions for concept use and that many concepts should be understood as being grounded in prototypes (Horgan and Tienson 1989:169–70). Thus, as prototype theories in psychology make it plausible to try to model the mind/brain in PDP terms, the successes of PDP modeling make it more reasonable to think that cognitive tasks like concept use are supported by prototypes.

Although it is not spelled out explicitly, the interdisciplinary reasoning behind the mutual support provided by prototype theory and PDP models is relatively easy to fill in. Since PDP models are "neural-like," they offer a better model of the brain than, for example, traditional computer models. An impressive amount of psychological evidence suggests that concepts are represented in human beings, not as lists of necessary and sufficient conditions, but as prototypes. Sound methodological considerations imply that all psychological processes must ultimately be grounded in neural hardware. Hence, if neurons process information roughly in the manner of PDP networks (or "neural nets," as they are sometimes called), then since such processes are good prototype extractors, concept use and perhaps other cognitive tasks would function via prototypes. There is nothing wrong with McClelland and Rumelhart's or Horgan and Tienson's interdisciplinary reasoning. The temptation that must be resisted is allowing the mutual support that these theories can provide to reverberate back and forth until both look nearly certain and counterevidence to either is discounted.

Despite its popularity, prototype theory has been subject to trenchant criticisms (e.g., Murphy and Medin 1985; Keil 1989; Gelman and Markman 1987). Most center on its overreliance on perceptual similarity and underestimation of the importance of theoretical considerations in categorization. Turning to the other half of the picture, even advocates of PDP models note that they abstract from many known features of neuronal interaction and so perhaps from features that are crucial to neural processing (Churchland 1989:181–88; Sejnowski 1986:388). Lacking a crystal ball, it is impossible to predict how either of these issues will be resolved and how long the resolutions will take. In the meantime, how much weight should be given to the fact that PDP models and prototype theories fit together in a natural way? This depends on how the independent support for the two hypotheses waxes and wanes. If, for example, the evidential base of prototype theory were to weaken, then its consonance with PDP models could provide only very limited support. A hypothesis that is under attack can be aided by its compatibility with a hypothesis in a related discipline only if it can still provide a significant amount of independent support for itself. Conversely, if both theories were to gain independent evidential strength, then the rationale for incrementing each in virtue of their harmony would be significantly stronger. What Freud's example warns against are the following patterns: Allowing the consonance between prototype theory and connectionism to blind theorists to a lack of evidence for or significant challenges to either or both. If either of these theories fails to establish itself, then the fit between them should not count for very much; if both come under attack, then however much it accords with contemporary methodological predilections, their consonance should count for nothing at all.

Untimely Exits for Lamarckianism and Recapitulationism

Beyond the neuron-reflex idea from physiology and the construct of instinctual sexual drives extracted from evolutionary theory, psychoanalysis incorporated the biological assumptions of recapitulation and the inheritance of acquired characters at many places in its theoretical structure. The theory of psychosexual development was grounded in sexology's "discovery" of component instinctual sexual drives only by the assumption of recapitulation. The variety of sexual behaviors in animals, "primitives," and children could provide insight into adult "perversions" and psychopathologies only if recapitulationism were true. Discoveries about archaic languages could contribute to interpreting the "language" of dreams only by the grace of the recapitulationist hypothesis. Without this hypothesis, anthropological claims about sexual arrangements in "primitive" societies and his own hypothesis of the primal horde could have no bearing on the universality of the Oedipal complex. In brief, if the support provided by Lamarckianism and recapitulationism were withdrawn from psychoanalysis, central parts of its theoretical structure would collapse. Freud understood this dependency quite clearly. Writing about difficulties with the inheritance of acquired characters in the mid-thirties, he frankly confessed that "[he] cannot do without this factor in biological evolution" (*Moses and Monotheism*, 1939, S.E. XXIII:100).

Although distinct hypotheses, Lamarckianism and recapitulationism were closely allied and shared a common fate. Stephen Jay Gould traces the antiquity of the notion of recapitulation and its flowering in the nineteenth century. In broadest outline, recapitulationism was the thesis that there were important parallels between the development of individuals (ontogeny) and the historical development of "higher" forms of life (phylogeny). Before Darwin, recapitulationism was subjected to insightful criticisms by Karl Ernst von Baer. Taking the paradigm case of the discovery of gill slits in human fetuses, von Baer's point was simple and elegant: Why do the presence of gill slits imply that human fetuses replicate the features of adult fishes rather than that related animal forms have common initial stages, which then differentiate with further development? Von Baer's question was never given a satisfactory answer in the nineteenth century, although recapitulationists like Haeckel were able to parry his individual points about features failing to appear at the right time in embryological development by presenting a more complex account (Gould 1977:52–57, 167ff.).

Von Baer's doctrines were set out against the background of creationism, but Darwin was quick to see the implications of embryology for the evolution of species: "Embryology is to me by far the strongest single class of facts in favor of change of forms" (cited in Gould 1977:70). Specifically, Darwin interpreted von Baer's point about common initial stages to provide the key to descent: "Community in embryonic structure reveals community of descent" (cited in Gould 1977:71). To reconstruct actual lineages—to determine not only which species were related, but which came first—Darwin appealed to von

Baer's idea of differentiation from embryonic forms. He again added an evolutionary interpretation. The least developed adult forms, those closest to embryonic stages, were least developed, because they were the ancestral forms (Gould 1977:72).

Darwin's own view of recapitulationism is a matter of some controversy (Gould 1977:72–73; above, chapter 2). Recapitulationism was warmly embraced by many prominent Darwinians, however, including August Weismann. As Weismann noted, recapitulation would explain why some characters seen in juvenile forms had no selective advantage (Gould 1977:102–9). More importantly, recapitulation became the standard means of establishing lineages: Common descent was established by common juvenile forms; ancestral forms were established by the similarity of adults to fetal and juvenile stages; later forms by the differentiation of adult forms from juvenile stages. Given this means of classification, it follows that the adult stages of ancestral forms will resemble the juvenile stages of evolved forms.

If the practice and theory of Darwinism were compatible with recapitulation, Lamarckianism positively supported it. Suppose that more advanced forms have inherited the characters acquired during the lifetime of earlier forms. Three key points follow. First, if the character is to be considered inherited, then it had better appear before the organism matures. Otherwise, why assume that it was inherited rather than acquired? Second, if new and useful traits were acquired during life, then we would expect these developments to postdate the standard development into an adult organism. They would be "terminal additions" to development (in Gould's terminology) and unless the organism's descendants were to undergo ever longer developmental processes, some mechanism would have to allow for a speeding up or condensing of development. As Gould argues, however, the crucial theses to be established by recapitulationism were terminal addition and condensation. Hence, Lamarckian inheritance provided a sketch of how recapitulation might be true, although it offered no specific mechanisms.

Both recapitulationism and Lamarckianism peaked in the 1890s, as Freud was laying the foundations of psychoanalysis (Bowler 1983:59, Gould 1977:100–102). Soon both were to be in trouble. August Weismann destroyed the ecumenicism of late nineteenth-century evolutionists by claiming that the germ plasm responsible for transmitting hereditary information was isolated and so could not be affected by life events. If Weismann's theory were correct, then Lamarckian inheritance was simply impossible (Bowler 1983:41–42). Many criticized Weismann, including Theodor Eimer in Germany. By 1910, however, Lamarck's position was clearly on the wane, largely because it was very hard to test experimentally (Bowler 1983:60). An experimental defense of the inheritance of acquired characters was mounted, but it ended in the disastrous affair of Paul Kammerer and the midwife toad (Bowler 1983:93–99). By the end, Lamarckianism was shown to have three fatal weaknesses. It could not compete with the experimentally based Mendelian school; it never found a mechanism for transmitting acquired characters; and its theoretical claims were mutually inconsistent, for it held both that germ plasm could be altered by life experiences and that it could pass unaltered to offspring.

Recapitulationism was felled by the same swords of Mendelian genetics and experimental embryology. Embryology suggested that development followed certain patterns for mechanical reasons. Given a chick embryo's previous configurations and the pressures on it, it would change in a particular way—regardless of the acquired structures of its ancestors. Mendelian genetics implied that the law of terminal addition was false, because the genes controlling heredity were present from conception. Further, the discovery of genes that controlled the rate of development cast serious doubt on the law of acceleration or condensation. Mutations in these genes could speed up or slow down development. There was no reason to favor acceleration, but this was crucial to recapitulation (Gould 1977:189, 203–5). Although recapitulationism was not finally buried until the twenties, like Lamarckianism it was in serious decline by the beginning of World War I. As one staunch defender remarked in 1914, "In these days this [biogenetic] law is regarded with disfavour by many zoologists, so that to rank oneself as a supporter of it as to be regarded as out-of-date" (cited in Gould 1977:186).

Even in the thirties, however, Freud clung to Lamarckianism and recapitulationism. In noting that he could not do without Lamarckian inheritance, he was not announcing the fall of his theory. Despite the "difficult position" he had been placed in by "the present attitude of biological science, which refuses to hear of the inheritance of acquired characters . . . [he] must, however, in all modesty confess that [he] cannot do without [it]" (*Moses and Monotheism*, 1939, S.E. XXIII:100). That is, since his theory could not survive without Lamarckian and recapitulationist assumptions, he was, in all immodesty, going to go on believing these theories, whatever the experts said! This move was unfaithful to his own principles of interdisciplinary theory construction. A theory that lived to a considerable degree by the strength of its interdisciplinary support had to be prepared to die by same standard. Since an important part of his original argument for psychoanalysis had been its firm biological foundations, inconsistency with current biological thought had to be acknowledged as a severe setback.

By the thirties, Freud was at the end of his career and near the end of his life, so his defiant attitude may be understandable, if not admirable. The foregoing histories make two crucial points. When he decided to back the twin horses of Lamarckianism and recapitulationism in the 1890s, they looked like very good bets. Both major schools of evolution supported recapitulation, and Darwinians were willing to grant some influence to Lamarckian forces. It is equally clear, however, that twenty years later both theories had become highly controversial. Freud was reshaping some aspects of psychoanalysis during this period. Why didn't he free himself from such dubious entanglements while he still had the chance?

This question has four intertwined answers. It has often been suggested that theorists tend to cling to the ideas of their youth even when they have been clearly superseded. Since most people start building their research programs during their youth, they have a great deal invested in these ideas, so the reluctance to give them up is hardly surprising. As we have seen, Lamarckianism and recapitulationism were integral to the foundations of psychoanalysis. It was these assumptions that gave Freud reason to believe that dream interpretations and clinical evidence could be confirmed by work in historical linguistics, prehistoric anthropology, and child psychology. Critics regard Freudian analyses as wild speculation, because they do not recognize these alleged additional sources of evidence—because they do not accept either recapitulation or the inheritance of acquired characters.

Given the way he had constructed psychoanalysis, Freud had strong motivation for holding on these theories. Within a discipline, there are counterweights to persevering with the ideas of youth, however heavily one has invested in them. Being regarded as out of date is too costly. One problem with Freud's method of organizing the institutions of psychoanalysis, outside the bounds of the academic establishment, was that he was able to evade these pressures.[4] Conversely, one clear advantage of the contemporary system of forming communities of interdisciplinary scholars is that recognition as a full participant requires keeping current.

Freud also persevered with recapitulationism and Lamarckianism because, by his own testimony, he took these theories to be "established beyond question" (*Moses and Monotheism*, 1939, S.E. XXIII:99). Like having more faith in the basic constructs of neighboring discipline than the experts, it is very easy for an interdisciplinary theorist to regard theories in other areas as carved in stone. Local experts may remember the controversies that led to the establishment of these theories and be more acutely aware of current difficulties for them.

From a slight distance, it is harder to see potential weaknesses, particularly when a theory is very much in keeping with shared background assumptions, as recapitulationism reflected the general historicist approach of nineteenth-century science.

The proper response to the crises in recapitulationism and Lamarckianism that threatened the foundations of psychoanalysis was to go back to the home discipline of evolutionary biology and fight the battle there: Draw support from positive developments and try to overturn adverse results. Freud did not do this, but simply stuck with these theories for a third, obvious reason. One problem with interdisciplinary theory construction is that this theoretically correct option is often not practical. Freud had no means of entering the battleground. All he could have done was sit on the sidelines, waiting to see how it would turn out. Further, in a Pickwickian sense, he had no theoretical interest in the debate. For only one outcome was of any use to him. Recapitulationism and Lamarckianism promised him help in filling out the details of psychoanalysis. What could work in experimental embryology or Mendelian genetics tell him in the foreseeable future that would be relevant to psychological development or to psychopathology?

Freud did not try to shore up the foundations of psychoanalysis, but continued to build higher. A look at the general index to the *Standard Edition* reveals that as recapitulation and Lamarckian inheritance became more controversial, his references to "archaic heritage," "phylogenetic inheritance," and "primitive peoples" became more numerous. These reflect the growing influence of anthropology on psychoanalysis after the publication of *Totem and Taboo*. Given Freud's inability to contribute to the debates on evolutionary biology, the response of trying to strengthen the overall case for psychoanalysis is understandable. Nevertheless, it rests on a mistake in interdisciplinary reasoning.

The fourth factor in his continuing support for recapitulationism and Lamarckianism was the one he gave in his "confession" of 1939: As he had constructed psychoanalysis, it implied both recapitulation and the inheritance of acquired characters. Although this was true, strengthening the general case for psychoanalysis could not give any stability to its foundations. Freud's error lay in reversing the epistemic dependencies of the disciplines comprising psychoanalysis. If Lamarck was right and recapitulation true, then it was reasonable to construe childhood and perhaps neurotic behavior in terms of the practices and experiences of primitive humans or even animals. However, support could not run in the other direction. The analogies between neurotic behavior and dreams, on the one hand, and children and prehistoric ancestors, on the other, were much too weak to support specific claims of recapitulation or Lamarckian inheritance. This is especially obvious if consideration is restricted to manifest contents of symptoms and dreams. However, since dream interpretation needed to be supplemented by historical linguistics and prehistoric anthropology—and this procedure was justified on the basis of the two theories in question—it was in no position to provide independent evidence for them.

Placing psychoanalytic psychiatry on one side and recapitulationism and Lamarckianism on the other side, these sets of theories were not mutually supporting. The latter theories gave credence to the former. Psychiatry could provide no serious evidence for these specific biological hypotheses. Hence, when they were cast in doubt, Freud could not parry the threat by pointing to alleged or even real successes of psychoanalysis as a whole. Once a theory is launched and has some real or perceived successes, it tends to take on a life of its own— particularly when it holds the promise of giving a satisfyingly complete picture of the phenomena in question. Lured by this picture and insufficiently sensitive to the fallible theoretical character of the foundations he had borrowed, Freud continued the construction of psychoanalysis. Those who were aware of the raging battle in evolutionary biology must have recognized the precarious state of the foundations of psychoanalysis; in another decade, they would see them crumble altogether.

Current interdisciplinary theorists are protected against some of the mistakes encountered in this episode, but seemingly they can still be enticed into repeating Freud's subtler errors. A recent discussion of connectionism by Jerry Fodor and Zenon Pylyshyn flirts with the error of confusing dependency relations within an interdisciplinary program. "Classical" psychological theories, as they label the position they aim to defend, were made plausible by surprisingly consonant developments in two prima facie unrelated fields, Chomskian linguistics and "classical" theories of computation. I repeat only the bare outlines of these familiar stories. Chomsky offered elegant arguments to show that speakers can enjoy linguistic competence only because they have internalized the complex grammatical rules of their language, which they apply to various levels of internal linguistic representations. At roughly the same time, workers in artificial intelligence and computer simulations showed that machines could carry out complex problem-solving tasks by applying rules specified in their programs to internal symbols. Since language use has long been regarded as a central case of intelligent thought and computer programs were designed to simulate thought at some level of abstraction, these developments made it plausible to model thinking and psychological processes generally in terms of the application of rules to internal symbolic representations.

In a long and influential series of books and papers, Fodor and, more recently, Pylyshyn have elaborated this picture of the mental and its implications for new and traditional issues in philosophy and psychology. The rise of PDP models of computation poses a significant threat to the classical program. This can be seen most easily by recalling a critical lemma in constructing the rules-and-representation model: No computation without representation. Fodor used this implication of classical understandings of computation to argue that any psychological model of thought must posit internal representations (Fodor 1975:31). This, however, is precisely the claim challenged by PDP models. Connectionist networks compute, but not by syntactic manipulations of internal representations (Fodor and Pylyshyn 1988:12; Rumelhart and McClelland 1986:45ff.).

Fodor and Pylyshyn propose to ward off the PDP threat with the following argument:

> Classical psychological theories appeal to the constituent structure of mental representations to explain three closely related features of cognition: its productivity, its compositionality and its inferential coherence. The traditional argument has been that these features of cognition are, on the one hand, pervasive and, on the other hand, explicable only on the assumption that mental representations have internal structure. (Fodor and Pylyshyn 1988:33)

The argument proceeds by showing that connectionist networks cannot model these three features. My concern about this line of reasoning is that Fodor and Pylyshyn appear to be trying to argue from the soundness of their overall approach to the truth of one of its essential assumptions: No real computation or thought-like computation without representation. Again, however, the epistemic dependencies go in the wrong direction. If language and computation require the presence of rules and representations, then it is plausible to regard psychological processes in these terms. Without these assumptions, however, the regularities encountered in thinking are hardly strong enough to imply that any thought-like computation, including the processing or production of language, requires rules and representations. Alternatively, as Fodor and Pylyshyn acknowledge (Fodor and Pylyshyn 1988:48), these three features are variations on the theme of systematicity, and thought is not so clearly systematic as to demand a rules-and-representation account.

Perhaps I have misunderstood the nature of their argument. The evidence for productivity, compositionality, and systematicity comes from Chomskian linguistics. So their point may be to defend one part of their program, a view about thought-like computation, by appealing to another, the truth of Chomskian linguistics: Chomskian linguistics implies that the computation underlying a central part of thought, language use, must involve the manipulation of representations by rules. This line of defense encounters problems of its own, however, since Chomskian linguistics is itself a hotly debated issue among linguists. Given this problem and their remarks about the coherence of the classical doctrine (Fodor and Pylyshyn 1988:7), I suspect that they are trying to argue from their general theory to one of its foundational supports.

This will not work, because the rules-and-representations approach to psychology on the one side and Chomskian linguistics and classical computation on the other side are not mutually supporting. It is the latter doctrines that give plausibility to the former. Perhaps even more than psychoanalysis, the classical approach to psychology is deeply interdisciplinary. It lives by its support from other disciplines. Hence, when one of those theories is brought into question, the general theory cannot come to its rescue. Even though theories tend to take on a life of their own and even though it is tempting to forget that interdisciplinary props are fallible theories, when one of those supports is threatened, the only remedy is to defend it on its own turf or by reference to some neutral source of evidence. Or, if one is in the frustrating position of lacking the disciplinary resources to participate in the defense oneself, pray that someone else defends it.

Interdisciplinary Theory Construction Gone Awry

This chapter has tried to establish three theses. The first is that although Freud's interdisciplinary approach to the construction of psychoanalysis was basically sound, he made some crucial mistakes in carrying out his plan that made his theories more likely to fail. He relied too much on the smooth progress of neurophysiology, took much too great a risk in hoping that physiology would provide an adequate grounding for libido theory, and was overly impressed by the potential unity of his theory of the mental to see that real connections had to be made, not simply assumed. The second is that his reactions to scientific developments in the various fields that he had drawn on—in essence, ignoring them—provide much of the legitimate basis for the perception that psychoanalysis was hopelessly speculative and unempirical. These two points are related. Given the way he constructed psychoanalysis, making it critically dependent on work in several different areas, he had few good options for accommodating adverse developments. He could either give up or deny that fundamental changes were taking place or that they really mattered to psychoanalysis. In availing himself of the latter two options, he opened psychoanalysis to the familiar charges that it was out of date, unscientific, and even pseudoscientific.

My final thesis is that, although some of Freud's errors in interdisciplinary reasoning were willful, other miscalculations were quite natural. It appears to be quite easy to have more faith in a related discipline than its practitioners, particularly when one's theory relies on its basic concepts or needs to be supplemented by its potential results. A related problem is seeing results in another discipline as certain, or as much more certain than claims in one's own field. Finally, harmony between theories in different disciplines is a beautiful thing, and it is also probably quite easy to be gulled into regarding it as nearly conclusive evidence for truth, even in the face of difficulties for the individual theories.

Chapter 7
Changing Times in the Social Sciences

In 1926 Freud offered an optimistic appraisal of the future of psychoanalysis in the social sciences.

> As a 'Depth-psychology', a theory of the mental unconscious, it [psychoanalysis] can become indispensable to all the sciences which are concerned with the evolution of human civilization and its major institutions such as art, religion and the social order. It has already, in my opinion, afforded these sciences considerable help in solving their problems. But these are only small contributions compared with what might be achieved if historians of civilization, psychologists of religion, philologists and so on, would agree themselves to handle the new instrument of research which is at their service. The use of analysis for the treatment of the neuroses is only one of its applications; the future will perhaps show that it is not the most important one. (*The Question of Lay Analysis*, S.E. XX:248)

To some degree, his hopes were realized. Some anthropologists, sociologists, and other students of culture began to apply psychoanalytic concepts to their subjects during the twenties and thirties, and some still do so today. Nevertheless, in this chapter, I will argue that early twentieth-century social science badly undermined the foundations of psychoanalytic theory. For those who understood the important change that had taken place in the direction of the social sciences, the general orientation of psychoanalysis appeared unscientific, even though some believed that its central concept of unconscious motivation might still prove useful.

There is this much truth to the standard view that Freud turned away from biology and physiology and over time gave this theory a more "humanistic" or "purely psychological" character. As he came to realize that advances in neurophysiology were unlikely to corroborate or extend his theory in the near future, he began to look to linguistics and especially to anthropology as more hopeful sources of support. Hence, psychoanalysis assimilated many of the working hypotheses of nineteenth-century social science. The citation above presents only one side of the picture, what the social sciences stood to gain from psychoanalysis. Psychoanalysis also depended on the social sciences as potential sources of evidence—and for some of its key assumptions about the evolution of mental life and civilization. In the opening decades of this century, those assumptions were questioned and rejected, so that the claims of psychoanalysis lost their interdisciplinary moorings in the social as well as the biological sciences.

Like the book as a whole, the chapter has two goals. I use an interdisciplinary understanding of Freud's theory construction to illuminate the course of that theory. In this case, it is a downhill course, the collapse of foundations that stands behind the familiar criticism that psychoanalysis was vague and speculative. I also use Freud's example to bring out some potentially worrying features of current interdisciplinary work in cognitive science and some of the special difficulties faced by institutions of interdisciplinary science.

In Freud's time as now, psychology and psychiatry do not fall comfortably into either the biological or the social sciences. Since it was an important contributor to the theoretical structure of psychoanalysis, I will take a brief look at some developments in early twentieth-century psychology that affected the scientific perception of psychoanalysis. I will then consider in more detail how psychoanalysis fared in its "home" discipline of psychiatry, before turning to the social sciences proper.

Behaviorism and the Rise of Experimental Psychology

Psychoanalysis incorporated five key ideas from nineteenth-century psychology: associationism, developmental psychology, reflexology, evolutionarily and functionally distinct faculties, and the project of tracing human mentality and civilization to its prehistoric origins. Of these, only the first two remained unscathed in the early part of the twentieth century. Associationism endured, because, as E. R. Guthrie observed in 1935, association is probably the only theory of learning that has ever been proposed (cited in Murphy 1949:269). Although it lost the theoretical support provided by recapitulationism, developmental psychology has also remained a vital part of twentieth-century psychology.

Reflexology was challenged in psychology, beginning with John Dewey's important article in the *Psychological Review* in 1896, but the main critique came from neurophysiology. As we saw in the last chapter, prominent neurophysiologists came to doubt the adequacy of reflexes to explain complex integrated neural activity. Under these circumstances, the role of the reflex as the crucial bridge concept between psychology and physiology should have been questioned. It was not. As Hebb has argued, many psychologists who should have known better continued, as Freud did, to accept the reflex as the fundamental explanatory mechanism of the mind/brain (Hebb 1982:2–3, 33). I considered some of the errors involved in Freud's perseverance with the simple reflex doctrine in the last chapter.

The issue of mental faculties is somewhat complicated, because faculties have gone in and out of fashion in psychology. As noted in chapter 2, faculty psychology had often been regarded with suspicion. Through the influence of scientists such as Wundt and Jackson it enjoyed a window of respectability at the time Freud developed the basic plan of psychoanalysis. During the opening decades of the twentieth century, many questions were raised about cerebral localization, culminating in Karl Lashley's argument for equipotentiality in 1929. Freud's program had nothing to fear from this research tradition, however, because he had realized early on that his topographic divisions did not correspond to neat anatomical divisions.

On the other hand, the increasing importance of experimentalism gave added force to the traditional complaint that faculty theories were arbitrary. No series of experiments could confirm that human beings had Freud's triad of faculties rather than many other possible combinations.[1] Should the rise of experimentalism and the distrust of faculties have led him to reevaluate the idea of mental topography? I think that he erred in not being more sensitive to these concerns. If he was willing to invoke the doctrines and methods of psychology when they helped him to construct his unified mental theory, then he had to listen when psychologists pointed to obvious weaknesses in faculty theories. Given psychology's historical ambivalence about faculties, contemporary criticism probably should not have made him reject his mental divisions outright; but it should have led him to rethink his grounds for them.

Freud had two reasons for positing faculties: the idea that different parts of the mind evolved at different times and the view that in certain conditions—dreaming, neurosis, and childhood—mental functioning took on a primitive character that was different in kind from normal adult thinking. The former assumption has never been seriously questioned. Like so many other aspects of his thought, however, the latter relied on recapitulationist thinking: Dreaming and neurotic mental functioning were the result of regressions to childhood thought patterns that were themselves contemporary representations of primitive forms of thought that once characterized the race. Although members of non-Western societies sometimes appear to think differently from Europeans, and children, dreamers, and madmen do think in odd ways, the superficial similarities across these four groups could not justify the claim that they all exhibited one kind of mental functioning. Only recapitulationism gave credence to that theoretical claim, and recapitulation was firmly rejected by evolutionary biology by the twenties.

Freud's final unsuccessful borrowing from psychology was genetic psychology. He always believed that a complete explanation for why people dream and why some develop neurotic symptoms must relate these phenomena to the development of human mentality across eons of time. Wundt had tried to make ethnic psychology and genetic psychology central parts of his new discipline of scientific psychology, but the evolution of human mentality was a much broader nineteenth-century concern. Since questions about the prehistoric origins of mentality did not take root in psychology anywhere near as strongly as they did in the emerging discipline of anthropology, I consider their fate in that context.

Developments in twentieth-century psychology weakened psychoanalysis from two directions. Freud's program suffered from what it had incorporated from the nineteenth century and also from the rise of new schools and methods, in particular, behaviorism and experimentalism. During the teens, psychology in the United States underwent a revolution. Building on Pavlov's important work on reflexes and years of dissatisfaction with the introspective method and the attribution of mental faculties to animals, J. B. Watson successfully launched the school of behaviorism. Introspection was out, faculties were out, and controlled experiments on learning curves and stimulus transfers became the central occupation of large numbers of psychologists.

The rise of behaviorism lessened the credibility of psychoanalysis in three obvious ways. Freud's appeal to the id, ego, and superego parts of the mind was seen as a blatant example of faculty psychology, and behaviorists firmly rejected faculties and every other kind of mental apparatus. Second, behaviorism incorporated the ideal of "operationism" from philosophy of science (Skinner 1953:27ff.). Operationists maintained that terms that did not refer to observable matters were legitimate in science only if they could be given a clear meaning, by defining them in terms of operations that were observable (whence the idea that "IQ" is what an IQ test measures [Hempel 1950]). As Freud and his followers tried to loosen the ties between his theories and particular nineteenth-century sciences, psychoanalytic hypotheses took on a generic character (see pp. 73, 92, 119, and 210) that invited charges of meaninglessness. Given the rich relations among its theoretical claims, psychoanalysis was singularly ill equipped to answer these charges within the operationists' ground rules. Finally, the behaviorists' emphasis on experiment, although not unique to them, led them to take a very low view of psychoanalysis.

Part of the standard scientific lore about Freud's theories comes from the behaviorist critique. In this case, as in others, students of psychology have learned about an earlier school mainly through its critics. From the behaviorist point of view, it would not matter that Freud had developed his basic concepts from reasonably well established neurological, psychiatric, and other theories. Support from above just did not count, even though it provided indirect empirical support, namely, the evidence and experiments supporting the theories on which he drew. Psychoanalytic hypotheses were overly vague, its "data" were unreliable patient reports of dreams and free associations, and there were no experiments.[2] Hence, it followed that psychoanalysis was a theory, or a body of vague speculation masquerading as a theory, that rested on no evidence whatsoever.

The most significant and enduring methodological change in psychology was the rise of experimentalism. Behaviorism flourished in part because it had a flourishing experimental program. Freud was not opposed to experimentation, nor did he think it unnecessary, despite a common interpretation of his position. The idea that he was antiexperiment derives from an oft-quoted letter to an American psychologist. Saul Rosenzweig had written to Freud about some experiments that seemed to provide support for his views. Freud replied, somewhat ungraciously, that he "did not put much value on these confirmations because the wealth of reliable observations on which these assertions rest make them independent of experimental verification" (cited in, e.g., Glymour 1974:286, Grünbaum 1984:101).

Despite its forceful character, this statement is only from a letter. A more definitive source is Freud's explicit, published reply to the criticism that psychoanalysis did not admit of experimental proof in the *New Introductory Lectures*. He began by drawing the stock analogy with astronomy. If experimentation were the required proof of scientific status, then astronomers would have to move the heavenly bodies. Since this was plainly not possible, they had to be content with observation. However, Freud did not leave the matter there. Having argued that the proposed criterion of demarcation for science could not be correct, he went on to note that several experiments had been performed that seemed to confirm various pieces of his dream symbolism, the same experiments that he had added to various editions of the dream book (1933, S.E. XXII:22–23).

Nevertheless, even if Freud did not believe that experiments were a waste of time, he did little to encourage an experimental tradition in psychoanalysis and he put all his own efforts into other methods of verification. In the letter, he mentioned clinical validation; in the *New Introductory Lectures*, he maintained that confirmation could be found in "philology, folklore, mythology, or ritual" (1933, S.E. XXII:24).

Should Freud have guided psychoanalysis in the direction of greater experimentation? Despite Popper's notorious claim to the contrary, psychoanalytic hypotheses can be subjected to experimental testing and were some years after Freud's death (Eysenck and Wilson 1973). Still, it is not clear that he erred in not following the trend toward experimentalism—even though that trend has become a permanent fixture of academic psychology. As Freud's appeal to astronomy showed, experimentation cannot be the sine qua non of all sciences. Experimental testing would have strengthened the scientific credentials of psychoanalysis, had it been done effectively. As Glymour has argued, however, even more recent efforts to test psychoanalytic hypotheses have been disappointing. Experimentalists like easily manipulated features, and these are not readily available in psychoanalysis (Glymour 1974:285). So Freud may have been right that experimental testing was relatively impractical for his theories. Further, Glymour makes a convincing case that psychoanalytic hypotheses could be tested in the clinical setting. In an elaborate analogy with the testing of astronomical hypotheses, he argues that the case history of Ernst Lanzer (the "Rat Man") served as such a test.[3] From the presenting symptoms and several specific psychoanalytic hypotheses, Freud inferred that Lanzer hated his father, because he had interfered with his infantile sexual play. This prediction—and so the hypotheses from which it derived—were disconfirmed by testimony from Lanzer's mother (Glymour 1974:294–302).

Freud was obviously annoyed about the new insistence on experiments (*New Introductory Lectures on Psycho-Analysis*, 1933, S.E. XXII:22). However, psychoanalysis became disengaged from psychology not just because he failed to adopt new methods, but also because he continued to rely on questionable and old-fashioned methods of verification. So, in the passage cited from the *New Introductory Lectures*, he still tried to defend against the charge that free association and dream interpretation were arbitrary by claiming that they could be confirmed by appealing to philology and mythology. Unfortunately, however, recent developments in the social sciences made those appeals seem very dubious, for reasons we will see. Although it is probably unreasonable to criticize Freud for not adopting new methods, he should have paid more attention to the state of his preferred methods. His attempt to fend off the experimentalist challenge must be judged a failure, not because all science must be experimental, but because the methods he proposed in place of experimentation, appeals to folklore and the like, were no longer creditable.

Although nowhere near as devastating as developments in biology, the course of early twentieth-century psychology was largely unfavorable to psychoanalysis. In part, Freud got unlucky. Experimentalism both weakened psychoanalysis and propelled its rivals, principally, behaviorism and Gestalt psychology. Some of Freud's difficulties with scientific respectability were, however, of his own making. The psychological revulsion against faculties had a legitimate basis, and he needed to defend his continuing appeals to the id, ego, and superego systems. In eschewing experimentation, he needed to make sure that his own sources of evidence were acceptable substitutes.

Psychoanalysis has had an odd relationship with twentieth-century psychology. It has been considered both a school of psychology and beyond the pale of academic psychology. To some extent, this was because Freud did not adopt the methods of psychology and also because he continued to focus on motivation, while other schools were concerned with problems of perception, learning, and concept formation (Hebb 1982:65). The separation was also partly deliberate. As we will see in the next section, Freud set up the institutions of psychoanalysis so that it would be independent of medical psychiatry. In doing so, he also insulated psychoanalysis from the other disciplines from which it was constructed, including psychology.

Psychoanalysis in Psychiatry

Just prior to expressing his hopes for psychoanalysis and the social sciences in the passage cited at the beginning of the chapter, Freud explained what he did not want to happen. He did not want psychoanalysis to be "swallowed up by medicine" and become just one more method of treatment, along with hypnotic suggestion, autosuggestion, and the like (*The Question of Lay Analysis*, 1926, S.E. XX:248). Although psychoanalysis was extraordinarily successful as a school of psychiatry, it did not quite avoid this fate. In the United States, where it achieved its greatest success, it became one of a variety of possible methods of treatment.

No dramatic discoveries in psychiatry either confirmed or undermined Freud's basic assumptions. He and others continued to believe in the importance of unconscious ideas; he continued to support sexual etiologies in the face of relatively constant skeptical challenges. The problems of scientific respectability that I discuss in this section came not from external developments in psychiatry but from the institutions of psychoanalysis itself. As psychoanalysis became a preeminent school of psychiatry, Freud and his followers established organizations and procedures intended to promote and safeguard his work. Over time, however, these institutions served psychoanalysis very badly, by allowing it to become out of touch with the rest of science.

Despite Freud's frequent complaints about the poor early reception of psychoanalysis, it was successful virtually from the beginning. Taking *Studies in Hysteria* (1895), *The Interpretation of Dreams* (1900), and *Three Essays on the Theory of Sexuality* (1905) as the classic texts, psychoanalysis began to flourish as a school of psychotherapy almost immediately, in the period from 1906 to 1910 (Ellenberger 1970:793). Ellenberger offers a detailed history of the burgeoning growth of the psychoanalytic movement within psychiatry, noting that as it attracted wider support, it also came in for fairly penetrating criticisms. In 1906, Gustav Aschaffenburg objected to Freud's methods of examining his patients' minds and wondered about the cures, since Freud provided no statistics about his success rates. He also voiced the suspicion that a psychiatrist who devoted that amount of time to patients must produce some improvement, regardless of his theoretical orientation. In 1909, W. B. Parker published an anthology of different approaches to psychotherapy that included a chapter on psychoanalysis written by Freud's first English translator, A. A. Brill. The concluding chapter, contributed by R. C. Cabot, lamented the current tendency to regard Freud's work as the most scientific, an honor he thought belonged to Janet. In 1913, Janet himself offered a critique of psychoanalysis at the Seventeenth International Congress of Medicine in London. He objected that the method of free association was inevitably tainted by therapists' suggestions, that dream interpretation was arbitrary, and that sexuality could not be the unique cause of neuroses. In his own work, he had found that sexual problems were more often the result of neuroses than their cause (Ellenberger 1970:794, 800, 817–18).

Despite such criticisms, the psychoanalytic movement continued to expand. The International Psycho-Analytical Association was founded in 1910, and three journals were inaugurated shortly thereafter. Psychoanalysis survived the teens intact, despite World War I and its own internecine warfare. Alfred Adler, Wilhelm Stekel, and Carl Jung all broke with Freud and, in 1914, the Swiss Psycho-Analytical Association was dissolved (Ellenberger 1970:817, 821). Still, psychoanalysis managed to open its own publishing house and to attract converts in England and America. The first postwar meeting of the International

Association in 1920 was attended by sixty-two people from eight different countries (Fine 1979:89).

A major step in the institutionalization of psychoanalysis was taken in 1920, when Max Eitingon founded the first training institute in Berlin. Although Eitingon set up the curriculum for psychoanalytic training, its central component—a training analysis—was a clear reflection of Freud's own views. Freud had stressed the importance of self-analysis to any practicing psychoanalyst in *The Future Prospects of Psycho-Analysis* (1910, S.E. XI:145). Two years later, in one of his few papers on technique, he made the requirement more stringent: Before becoming analysts, individuals should themselves be analyzed by an expert ("Recommendation to Physicians Practising Psycho-Analysis," S.E. XII:116). The requirement was strengthened again in 1937, when he expressed the view that analysts should periodically submit themselves to analysis again, perhaps at intervals of five years ("Analysis Terminable and Interminable,: S.E. XXII:249). The rationale for this prima facie extraordinary requirement came from his understanding of the dynamics of psychoanalytic treatment. He believed that, in the course of analysis, a neurotic's infantile libidinal urges, originally directed toward the mother and/or father, became attached to the analyst. As a result, the analyst was not merely an observer of the patient's mental dynamics, but an active participant in them (e.g., "The Dynamics of Transference," 1912, S.E. XII:99ff.). Given this assumption, it seemed essential that analysts' words and actions be freed as far as possible from the dominance of their own unconscious impulses. Hence the need to analyze the analysts. After the war, Freud's practice was devoted almost exclusively to training analyses of future analysts (Sulloway 1991:270).

Beyond the training analysis, the curricula of most psychoanalytic institutes included a gesture in the direction of the subjects that Freud specified in the Postscript to *The Question of Lay Analysis:* the mental sciences, psychology, history of civilization, and sociology, and anatomy, biology, and the study of evolution (S.E. XX:252; Lewin and Ross 1960:291–305). Freud described how students were to be taught these subjects by senior members of the profession.

> [Candidates] receive theoretical instruction by lectures on all subjects that are important to them. . . . What is still needed must be acquired by practice and by an exchange of ideas in the psychoanalytical societies in which young and old members meet together. (*The Question of Lay Analysis,* 1926, S.E. XX:228)

A third component was the "control analysis," where students analyzed patients under the supervision of their teachers.

Psychoanalytic education had two other noteworthy features in addition to its curriculum. Both sprang directly from Freud's pronouncements. In his 1910 paper against "wild" psychoanalysis, he had maintained that individuals who were not officially members of the International Psycho-Analytical Association had no business calling themselves "psychoanalysts." As the first psychoanalytic institutes were established, the certification of "training analysts" was taken over by the society (Fine 1979:94). The resulting tight, centralized control of psychoanalytic education has often been suggested as a source of its dogmatism and failure to change with advancing knowledge. Convinced that medical psychiatry was committed to somatic sources and cures for neuroses, Freud also came down firmly on the side of "lay analysis." Whether or not candidates for psychoanalytic training were physicians was "immaterial" (*The Question of Lay Analysis*, 1926, S.E. XX:23). American representatives protested against lay analysts, and after considerable debate, a compromise policy emerged: Although medical training was recommended, it was up to each branch of the society to determine whether it should be required. This meant that American institutes required medical training whereas European ones did not (Fine 1979:97). It also meant that, in the United States, psychoanalysis tended to be assimilated to psychiatry and regarded as one of its methods of treatment.

More than any new developments in psychiatry, its own associations, publications, and especially educational institutions contributed to the erosion of psychoanalysis's scientific credibility. The legendary dogmatism of psychoanalysis was a natural consequence of these institutions. As the International Association grew, the early and often heated encounters with other schools of psychiatry gave way to meetings of relatively like-minded individuals. With its own house organs available, there was no need for psychoanalysts to engage or try to convince editors outside of the fold. Worse still, both critics and Freudians have observed that psychoanalytic training was closer to that of religious novitiate than to education (Hanns Sachs, cited in Fine 1979:93).

Yet, from another perspective, Freud's schemes for psychoanalytic organizations seem perfectly sensible. Professional societies are supposed to facilitate rapid progress in a discipline by bringing together like-minded people for frequent interchanges, and they are often concerned in matters of certifying practitioners and schools. Given the many disciplines relevant to psychoanalysis, a practical educational plan required selection, and the obvious solution was to teach only those aspects of the disciplines that were most relevant to psychoanalysis. Nevertheless, these seemingly reasonable suggestions produced an organization that allowed its members to become dated and dogmatic.

The dogmatism of the institutions of psychoanalysis was partially a reflection of Freud's own dogmatism. He set them up to discourage dissent and then saw that they were run in ways that achieved this goal (Sulloway 1991:266–71). Beyond Freud's personal control, however, two other factors help to explain how organizational structures that might have served other fields reasonably well made psychoanalysis look more like a cult than a science. Both are noted by Henri Ellenberger. Ellenberger distinguishes between "unified" sciences and schools. In previous chapters, I have described psychoanalysis as offering a "unified" theory of the mind, because it had the potential to unify different sciences. When Ellenberger writes of a "unified" science, he means something different. In his usage, "unified science" indicates a situation where there is substantial agreement about the objects and methods of a science. Sciences stay unified in Ellenberger's sense when practitioners are careful to integrate their results into the existing body of theory within the science. In Ellenberger's view, dynamic psychiatry (psychiatry that dealt with unconscious forces) was not a unified science, but a collection of separate schools (Ellenberger 1970:895).

Ellenberger sees the turning away from unified science to schools as a critical, but insufficiently appreciated feature of dynamic psychiatry (Ellenberger 1970:895–96). Although he does not say so, he plainly thinks that the return to schools was an unfortunate development. When a science is largely in agreement about the crucial features of the objects within its purview and about the methods by which further information may be obtained, then highly specialized associations and journals further the cause of knowledge. Even in these cases, however, general journals perform the vital function of keeping the science unified. As psychoanalysis was setting up its institutions, it found itself in a very different situation. Dynamic psychiatry was fragmented. By setting up separate institutions and not trying to integrate its results with those of others, psychoanalysis made itself vulnerable to the charge that it was less than a real science, a school, rather than a part of psychology or psychiatry.

Ellenberger notes a second difference between most modern sciences and dynamic psychiatry: The latter "is not clearly delineated, [but] tends to invade the field of other sciences" (Ellenberger 1970:895). Psychoanalysis was also badly served by the institutions Freud established because of its interdisciplinary character. This can be seen most clearly in the case of its training institutes. Psychoanalysis drew on many different mental and biological sciences, as Freud well understood. Yet in most cases, these subjects were not adequately taught. To see how psychoanalytic theory lost contact with the rest of science, consider more closely how analysts were trained. Most criticism has focused on the training analysis and the supervised analyses, but lack of currency must be traced to the theoretical instruction. This suffered from two interconnected weaknesses. First, candidates were taught history of civilization, anatomy, and so forth, by older analysts, not by specialists in those fields. Lewin and Ross documented this feature of psychoanalytic education for the United States in 1958, but they believe that it characterized the training institutes throughout their history (Lewin and Ross 1960:27ff.). In 1958, training analysts carried on approximately 60 percent of the course instruction, leaving 40 percent for the junior staff. But, except in very rare cases, the junior staff were not themselves trained or practicing historians or anatomists, for example, but simply younger analysts who would one day be training analysts (Lewin and Ross 1960:273, 305). Second, the books used in reading and lecture classes were not primary texts in these subjects, but Freud's own presentations of these matters (Lewin and Ross 1960:292).

Interestingly, there was a much better model for psychoanalytic education available at the time. In 1910, Abraham Flexner had conducted a survey of medical education in the United States and Canada and offered proposals for setting up medical schools. Flexner's report, sponsored by the Carnegie Foundation, became the basis for American medical education. Among recommendations for accrediting medical schools and their faculties, Flexner laid out the fundamental principle that still guides medical education today: Medical students must be taught the basic and specialized sciences relevant to their trade by individuals actively engaged in research in those fields.

> Educationally, therefore, research is required of a medical faculty because only research will keep the teachers in condition. A nonproductive school, conceivably up to date to-day, would be out of date to-morrow; its dead atmosphere would soon breed a careless and unenlightened dogmatism. (Flexner 1910:56)

Instruction by active researchers in basic and secondary sciences is more likely to be current, and students are more likely to be given enough instruction in the fundamental assumptions and methods of these fields to be able to read about new developments with some critical understanding. Of course, in the United States, candidates at psychoanalytic institutes were medically trained psychiatrists. So they should have known enough basic science to realize that Freud was dated. Presumably, some students did know, but did not care, because they were interested not in theoretical foundations but only in acquiring a widely recognized technique of psychotherapy. Others may have realized that Freud's biology was out of date, but believed that he was quite current in areas such as anthropology and philology. This anomaly brings out a third advantage of Flexner's system. Although he wanted the basics of the basic sciences to be imparted before medical school, the more specialized courses of medical school also had to be infused with the basic sciences because "those who would employ it [modern medicine] must trouble to understand it," and the various contributing sciences had to be presented in such a way that students could understand how they all had a bearing on various medical questions (Flexner 1910:53–54, 58; citation from 25). By contrast, even where students in analytic institutes were well trained in the biological sciences, they were never shown how current biology or current social science allegedly related to and underwrote the fundamental principles and practice of psychoanalysis—as Freud believed they must.

I draw no parallels between the mistakes made by psychoanalysis in setting up its institutions and the institutions of contemporary cognitive science—because the latter are just coming into being. Still, the morals from psychoanalysis about how *not* to arrange the institutions of an interdisciplinary science are fairly clear. Interdisciplinary cognitive science has become enormously successful over the last ten years. If it is not yet the dominant approach to the study of mental life, it has attracted a huge following of talented faculty and students. Nevertheless, of its contributing disciplines, at least psychiatry, psychology, philosophy, sociology, anthropology, and linguistics are not unified disciplines, in Ellenberger's sense. Interdisciplinary cognitive science is itself one approach to the study of mental phenomena among others. Under these circumstances, separatism may foster a cult status—even if that cult is very big. Although specialty associations and journals have been founded and will continue to be founded, it is important for cognitive scientists to maintain dialogues with "rival schools." Given its interdisciplinary character, this means serious exchanges with a number of different disciplines.

The implications for education in cognitive science are equally clear. Currently, a number of interdisciplinary programs are turning themselves into departments of cognitive science. What Freud's example shows is that interdisciplinary departments must follow Flexner's ideal, despite the practical and organizational difficulties. Flexner's model has two practical drawbacks. It has made the medical curriculum difficult to coordinate, because basic scientists must be imported to teach many courses, and it has contributed to the enormous expense of medical education. Turning to organizational difficulties, it seems natural for undergraduate and graduate students in cognitive science to be taught by members of the department of cognitive science. And if they don't teach their own students, how are faculty members supposed to fulfill their teaching responsibilities? For the first generation, it makes no difference, because current cognitive science faculty are all practicing members of one of the contributing disciplines and the natural division of labor is to have the former computer scientists teach computer science and so forth. The problem comes in the second generation. Particularly in the case of graduate students, should they be taught linguistics, for example, from a general cognitive science textbook by individuals whose professional training, affiliations, and research are not in linguistics, but cognitive science?

Two solutions seem possible. Faculty could be imported from outside the department, or graduate education in cognitive science could be so structured that future members of cognitive science departments are also specialists in one of the foundational disciplines—meaning that they have received a thorough graduate education in that area and are able to carry out original research in it. Especially in small departments, both strategies will probably be necessary.

Achieving Flexner's ideal would impose a heavy burden on both cognitive science faculty and institutions and may seem unnecessary. It is tempting to think that since departments of cognitive science are located within universities, it could never become dissociated from mainstream science to the degree that psychoanalysis did. Although this is true, University environments probably do not provide sufficient protection against loss of currency. In modern universities, members of different departments are usually colleagues in name only.[4] As educational researchers are prone to ask (rhetorically), how many articles in *Scientific American* can be read, with understanding, by a single faculty member? How likely is it that a faculty member who scored reasonably well on this measure would also be cognizant of recent trends in Russian literature? As long as the rationale for interdisciplinary cognitive science is that the best way to gain a real understanding of mental life is by studying the phenomena and using the methods of a variety of disciplines, then faculty research and student education must have firm anchors in those disciplines. Further, instruction must be sufficiently integrated that students can understand how results from different disciplines bear on cognitive science projects and doctrines. Otherwise, there is no guarantee that theories in cognitive science will remain adequately grounded. In the next three sections, I trace how changes in the approach of the social sciences, more than new results, further undermined the scientific credentials of psychoanalysis, because it failed to keep pace.

Linguistics Leads the Way

Although philological considerations became more important to psychoanalysis over time, they were never as crucial as Freud's borrowings from neurophysiology, sexology, psychiatry, or anthropology. Still, developments in twentieth-century linguistics had a profound effect on the fortunes of psychoanalysis, because it tended to be the model for the social sciences.

The comparative work of nineteenth-century linguistics was not repudiated. At least until very recently, the discoveries of the historical relations among Indo-European languages, epitomized in Schleicher's trees, continued to be regarded as permanent additions to knowledge (Robins 1968:178). But the methodological assumptions began to change in dramatic ways. In 1916, students published a revolutionary set of lectures given by Ferdinand de Saussure. These lectures contained two crucial distinctions. First, Saussure made explicit two different dimensions of language, the synchronic and the diachronic. Although earlier linguists had given some thought to general linguistic theory—trying to understand how languages work and how they are possible—most work was historical (Robins 1968:174). Saussure's second well-known distinction, between *langue* (the language) and *parole* (actual speech), showed the importance of the previously neglected synchronic dimension. If *actes de parole* (speech acts) were the data of linguistics, the *langue* was the underlying structure that accounted for why the *actes* were what they were. A crucial goal for linguistics must then be to unearth the language behind the speech, for different languages (Robins 1968:200). Knowing how different elements in a language had changed over time did not provide much help with this project. The problem was to see how diverse elements could be understood as parts of an interconnected system. After Saussure's *Cours de linguistique générale*, a number of books appeared on synchronic linguistics (Robins 1968:206).

So the historical methods of the nineteenth century were eased aside by a new "structural" approach. The assumption of exceptionless laws of language also gave way to a more realistic understanding of the difficulty of the task. In 1921, the American linguist Edward Sapir explained that

> [s]trictly speaking, we know in advance that it is impossible to set up a limited number of types that would do full justice to the

peculiarities of the thousands of languages and dialects spoken on the surface of the earth. Like all human institutions, speech is too variable and too elusive to be safely ticketed. (1921:121)

Historical linguistics was broadly compatible with the historicist and evolutionary tendencies of the nineteenth century. Schleicher had tried to make that connection more direct. In *Darwinian Theory and Linguistics* (1863), he argued that language was like a natural organism, because its development was independent of the wills of individual speakers. Further, he suggested that the diffusion of different languages around the world was analogous to the struggle for existence among different organisms (Robins 1968:181). Although this particular idea did not catch on, it was natural for linguists to view linguistic change in terms of progressive development. This approach was cast aside in the twentieth century, in Sapir's case, with considerable vehemence.

> It is probably the most powerful deterrent of all to clear thinking. This is the evolutionary prejudice which instilled itself into the social sciences towards the middle of the last century and which is only now beginning to abate its tyrannical hold on our mind. (Sapir 1921:123)

Sapir's complaint against evolutionary thinking was that it inspired linguists to try to classify languages into the "higher" and the "primitive," whereas the real job was to understand how the elements of each language were systematically interrelated so that a language was possible at all.

Leonard Bloomfield's account of the differences between the 1914 and the 1933 editions of his book *Language* indicated another important change in the basic assumptions of linguistics. In the earlier edition, when he had tried to get at the facts that underlay language, he had appealed to the psychological theories of Wilhelm Wundt. Wundt had believed that language, myths, and custom were the joint product of historical conditions and universal psychological laws and hence important evidence about human psychology. By 1933, Bloomfield saw two flaws in his previous tight coupling of language and psychology. First, psychology had changed:

> [T]here has been much upheaval in psychology. . . . The mentalists would supplement the facts of language by a version in terms of mind,— a version which will differ in the various schools of mentalistic psychology. The mechanists [i.e., behaviorists] demand that the facts be presented without any assumption of such auxiliary factors. (Bloomfield 1933:vii)

Bloomfield believed that the mechanists were more scientific, but he also offered a second reason for desisting from references to psychology: "[A]n exposition which stands on its own feet is more solid and more easily surveyed than one which is propped at various points by another and changeable doctrine" (Bloomfield 1933:vii–viii).

In the thirties and forties, Bloomfield was a dominant force in American linguistics, which itself dominated international linguistics. As in most fields at most times, there were different currents in early twentieth-century linguistics. Where Bloomfield eschewed the connection between language and psychology, Sapir and Franz Boas, the two other central figures in American linguistics, tended to view language as part of human life more generally (Robins 1968:207). Still, many key assumptions from the nineteenth century had been vigorously challenged by the European and American traditions, including the progressive character of language, its lawfulness, and most importantly for the purposes of psychoanalysis, the value of historical approaches to language. Freud needed some way of determining the properties of primitive human languages to help anchor his clinical and dream interpretations. But during the first third of the twentieth century, historical linguistics and comparative philology ceased to be central projects in the study of language. To knowledgeable readers, his expectation that philology might confirm his clinical interpretations began to look more and more naive.

The Autonomy of Sociology

Although linguistics probably served as a model in propelling social science away from diachronic studies and toward synchronic research, the history of ideas is never quite that simple. Saussure was encouraged to believe in the extrapsychological reality of languages by Durkheim's similar and much earlier claim for social forces. As noted in chapter 2, Durkheim proposed a separation of sociology from biology and psychology in the 1890s, but this position was not widely appreciated until the second decade of the twentieth century.

It may be easiest to grasp Durkheim's position by considering a particular example, his seminal analysis of the causes of suicide. In *Le Suicide* (first edition, 1897), he argued for the reality of social forces by elimination. He began by delimiting the fact to be explained. This was not individual suicides, but the suicide rate for various societies. Standard psychological theories could not offer acceptable explanations of suicide rates, partly because they appealed to mental faculties, which were no longer recognized by science (Durkheim 1930:61). Next he turned to racial characteristics and local physical conditions, again showing their inadequacy to account for suicide rates. Finally, he considered the possibility that suicide rates could be explained by the effects of imitation. Before offering his positive account, he summed up the earlier argument.

> We have in fact shown that for each social group there is a specific tendency to suicide explained neither by the organic-psychic constitution of individuals nor the nature of the physical environment. Consequently, by elimination, it must necessarily depend upon social causes and be itself a collective phenomenon. (Durkheim 1930:145)

Positively, Durkheim separated suicide into three different classes, egoistic, altruistic, and anomic. Using large numbers of statistics, he argued that egoistic suicide was correlated with lack of integration into family or society, altruistic suicide with dedication to the higher laws of primitive groups, and anomic suicide with sudden changes in the social order that created too much freedom of choice.

Durkheim's argument was far from logically tight, and it has often been criticized for trading on a false dichotomy between social and psychological factors. Despite these flaws, it succeeded in two important respects. It showed the inadequacy of facile psychological and racial accounts, and it opened up the possibility of explanation by social forces by demonstrating the correlation between suicide rates and factors such as religious affiliation and marital status.

By the thirties, Durkheim's approach to sociology had become dominant. In terms of his dates (1858–1917), he was mainly a nineteenth-century sociologist. Still, he is usually regarded as having begun a revolution in sociology that separated it from its nineteenth-century roots and established it as an independent science. Issues of revolution versus continuity are often ambiguous. So, for example, although Durkheim criticized his predecessors and contemporaries for relying excessively on psychology and on the evolutionary perspective, he appealed to collective psychological facts and offered rules for doing evolutionary sociology better (Fletcher 1971, vol. 2:117–18, 271; Durkheim 1895:63–64, 111–12, 130–31). In the context of Freud's borrowings from sociology, however, Durkheim's differences with the nineteenth century were more significant than his similarities.

Freud always assumed the methodological position of evolutionary naturalism: Higher mental achievements, including social institutions, were to be explained by tracing their development through a series of encounters between instincts shared with animals and external conditions. Evolutionary naturalism did not imply that social facts could be reduced by biological and psychological facts, since interactions with external conditions also had to be noted. But it did give psychological and biological facts pride of place in explaining social phenomena. Eventually any social condition had to be tied down to some aspect of human biology or psychology.

Durkheim believed that biology and especially psychology were helpful to sociology, but only up to a point.

> Thus a psychological education, even more than a biological one, constitutes a necessary preparation for the sociologist. But it can only be of service to him if, once he has acquired it, he frees himself from it, going beyond it by adding a specifically sociological education. He must give up making psychology in some way the focal point of his operations, the point of departure to which he must always return after his adventurous incursion into the social world. (Durkheim 1895:135)

That is, it was not necessary always to trace social facts back to psychological facts. Sometimes this could be done and often it was useful, but it was not essential for sociology to be a science. Social facts could be understood by seeing their correlation with other social facts, even when the latter could not be connected to psychology. In emancipating sociology from psychology, Durkheim did not overthrow evolutionary naturalism, but he demoted it from its position of preeminence. Further, in looking primarily for correlations, he made questions of genesis and development secondary to the main enterprise of sociology.[5]

In the twenties and thirties, Freud was turning more of his efforts to explaining cultural phenomena (Postscript to *An Autobiographical Study*, 1935, S.E. XX:72). *Group Psychology and the Analysis of the Ego* appeared in 1921, *The Future of an Illusion* in 1927, and *Civilization and Its Discontents* in 1930. Freud's introductory remarks to his account of *Group Psychology* provide a good indication of how he thought such subjects must be approached.

> [I]t is easy to regard the phenomena that appear under these special conditions [when people have been organized into a group] as being expressions of a special instinct that is not further reducible—the social instinct ('herd instinct,' 'group mind'), which does not come to light in any other situations. But we may perhaps venture to object that it seems difficult to attribute to the factor of number a significance so great as to make it capable by itself of arousing in our mental life a new instinct that is otherwise not brought into play. Our expectation is therefore directed towards two other possibilities: that the social instinct may not be a primitive one and insusceptible of dissection, and that it may

be possible to discover the beginnings of its development in a narrower circle, such as that of the family. (1921, S.E. XVIII:70)

Freud went on to trace phenomena of group psychology to libidinal instincts and the structure of the primal horde (91, 125). In *The Future of an Illusion*, he maintained that a sufficient answer to the absurdities of religious belief and its importance for culture "will be found if we turn our attention to the psychical origin of religious ideas" (1927, S.E. XXI:30). He summarized his approach to culture more generally in *Civilization and Its Discontents*.

And now, I think, the meaning of the evolution of civilization is no longer obscure to us. It must present the struggle between Eros and Death, between the instinct of life and the instinct of destruction, as it works itself out in the human species. (1930, S.E. XXI:122)

As these passages and these works make clear, Freud never wavered in his acceptance of evolutionary naturalism as the proper approach to questions of social organization. He did not even consider the possibility that an institution such as religion might be explained in some way other than by linking its features to modifications of the psychological constitution of human beings that occurred during individual lives and/or during the history of the race. In his methodological assumptions, Freud was oblivious to new developments in sociology, and this led him to believe that his theories about culture were much more plausible than they appeared to others. For evolutionary naturalism sharply limited the space of possible explanations of cultural phenomena to developments from biological or psychological instincts, and Freud had one of the few available, well-articulated theories of instincts. Hence, he wrote with the conviction that although the details were undoubtedly mistaken, something like his accounts of religion and civilization had to be right. For "Historians of civilization appear to be at one in assuming that powerful components are acquired for every kind of cultural achievement by this diversion of sexual instinctual forces from sexual aims and their direction to new ones" (*Three Essays on the Theory of Sexuality*, 1905, S.E. VII:178).

Unlike his problems with early twentieth-century biology and neurology, Freud's persistence in offering psychological explanations for social facts did not place him in direct conflict with scientific authority. Despite Durkheim's somewhat intemperate attacks on psychology, many sociologists continued to believe that there was a place for psychological factors and that Freud had a promising theory (Fletcher

1971, vol. 2:542–74). Further, many distrusted Durkheim's "social facts." Nevertheless, there was an important difference in attitude between Freud and mainstream sociology that accounts for part of the perception that psychoanalysis had an unseemly fanatical streak. The sociologists who resisted Durkheim raised objections to his arguments and assumptions. By contrast, Freud simply took it for granted that the social must be anchored in the psychological and that psychoanalysis offered a correct and comprehensive psychology.

Unless it creates institutions that isolate it from its foundational disciplines, lack of currency is unlikely to be a problem for contemporary interdisciplinary work in cognitive science. It is hard to imagine how a fundamental methodological change in one of the contributing disciplines could be ignored by active cognitive scientists. Still, part of Freud's continued support for evolutionary naturalism derived from a nineteenth-century article of faith: The theory of evolution was the key to the human sciences. In the two next sections, I will argue that such articles of faith both inspire interdisciplinary work and constitute its greatest danger.

Anticipating Anthropology

Freud's attempts to explain various social phenomena were intended to be applications of psychoanalysis. Further, none of his central doctrines or research projects depended on particular sociological theories or discoveries. By contrast, psychoanalysis needed anthropology to corroborate and extend its theories. Freud never seemed to appreciate the degree to which he had built anthropological assumptions into the foundations of psychoanalysis. He conceived of the relation between the disciplines in very different terms: Psychoanalysis was a new tool of research that he offered to anthropology ("The Claims of Psycho-Analysis to Scientific Interest," 1913, S.E. XIII:185).

In fact, his theories depended critically on a substantive anthropological assumption and on the successful completion of the projects of nineteenth-century anthropology. Substantively, he followed nineteenth-century historians of civilization and anthropologists in presuming that primitive human minds were primitive. That is, he assumed that individuals who lived at the very beginning of human life on earth not only were less refined and less knowledgeable than his fellow Viennese, but also had simpler and less developed mental organs. This assumption followed from two others: Mental capacities were subject to evolutionary forces, and evolution was progressive.

To see how important this claim was to Freud's program, consider the support it lent to his views about the id. Casting the id as a survival of primitive mentality made it plausible to characterize its operations in terms of simple association and plausible to see it as the source of irrational actions and wild dreams. Indeed, the background belief that evolutionarily older structures were simple and could survive alongside newer, more sophisticated organs provided a large measure of the scientific plausibility of positing an id at all. When combined with recapitulationism, this belief also contributed the rationale for trying to test hypotheses about infantile, neurotic, and primitive mental states by comparing each with the others.

Early twentieth-century anthropology did not discover that prehistoric humans were intellectually sophisticated, but it came to doubt the presumption that civilizations and their inhabitants could be lined up in a steady and slow progression from prehistoric times to the present. In 1937, Robert Lowie explained the inadequate basis for the earlier conception.

> [T]he idea of progressive development from savagery to civilization was much older than Darwin or even Lamarck. However, when evolution became not merely an approved biological principle but a magical catchword for the solution of all problems, it naturally assimilated the earlier speculations about cultural changes as obviously congruous with its own philosophy. Similarly, the discoveries of prehistory neatly fitted into the evolutionary picture. (Lowie 1937:19; cf. Boas 1920:281)

Like the changes in the direction of linguistic and sociological research, this change in the background assumptions of anthropology undercut Freud's position and his scientific respectability. For although anthropologists came to question the facile equation between "ancient" and "primitive," his arguments never ceased to trade on it.

Changes in the projects and expectations of anthropology were, however, far more devastating to Freud's program. Like many nineteenth-century thinkers, he assumed that prehistoric archaeology would eventually permit a reconstruction of the characteristics of primitive human minds. Wundt had captured this view explicitly in his presentation of the methods of *Völkerpsychologie*. Since myths, symbols, literature, and artifacts were the joint products of historical conditions and universal psychological laws, they could be used to uncover the latter at particular stages of human development. This assumption was extremely important to psychoanalysis. As Freud was well aware, psychoanalysis was primarily a genetic psychology. It explained current conditions by tracing them back to earlier events in the life of the individual—or in the history of the race. Over time, as he came to believe in the increasing complexity of mental dynamics, he felt that psychoanalysis had to rely more and more on explanations that appealed to the "archaic heritage" of the human race (e.g., *Moses and Monotheism*, 1939, S.E. XXIII:99; *An Outline of Psycho-Analysis*, 1938, XXIII:167,241). Even more importantly, the mind's instinctual endowment, the course of psychosexual development, and "the nucleus of the unconscious mind" itself were all to be explained in part by the long course of human history ("Instincts and Their Vicissitudes," 1915, S.E. XIV:131; *Introductory Lectures on Psycho-Analysis*, 1917, XVI:362; *Moses and Monotheism*, 1939, XXIII:75; "A Child Is Being Beaten," 1919, XVII:203–4).

In 1896, Franz Boas published an elegant critique of the comparative method in anthropology that was to provide enlightenment about primitive minds. The problem with this method was simple. It was circular. What was to be proved was that the human mind was uniform and everywhere developed along similar paths. By comparing different societies, especially those that appeared to lack direct contact, anthropology was going to fathom the universal laws that govern the human mind, its development, and the consequent uniform development of civilization. But this project encountered an insuperable obstacle.

> [T]he point of view is taken that if an ethnological phenomenon has developed independently in a number of places its development has been the same everywhere; or, expressed in a different form, that the same ethnological phenomena are always due to the same causes. This leads to the still wider generalization that the sameness of ethnological phenomena found in diverse regions is proof that the human mind obeys the same laws everywhere. It is obvious that if different historical developments could lead to the same results, that then this generalization would not be tenable. . . . It must, therefore, be clearly understood that anthropological research which compares similar cultural phenomena from various parts of the world, in order to discover the uniform history of their development, makes the assumption that the same ethnological phenomenon has everywhere developed in the same manner. (Boas 1896:273)

That is, suppose that similar cultural phenomena (e.g., totems) could arise from quite different causes. If this is possible, then it was fallacious to infer from the similarity of phenomena alone to the same cause, namely, the uniform working of the human mind and laws of cultural evolution. But how could this possibility be ruled out?—except by assuming that there were universal laws of development governing the production of cultural artifacts, which was the point at issue.

Anthropology had no other resources for furnishing the required proof (Boas 1896:273). Further, the comparative method had been almost completely devoid of results (Boas 1896:280).

Like Durkheim's critique of the methods of previous sociologists, the effect of Boas's attack was not immediate. From this time forward, however, evolutionary anthropology began to lose ground, as other critics joined him in objecting to its sloppy and superficial comparisons. By the early teens, it was no longer a dominant force in any country, although there were still numerous practitioners (Wallace 1983:121). Boas also offered a positive program. Consonant with the new directions in linguistics and sociology, he stressed the importance of "understanding a culture as a whole" (Boas 1938:5). The best way to do this was to postpone possible comparisons and concentrate on the study of particular cultures (Boas 1896:276). So, in anthropology, as in linguistics and sociology, diachronic studies were replaced by vigorous attempts to understand the interconnections among the elements of individual cultures. In this climate, the old project of history of civilization and Wundt's fledgling sciences of genetic psychology and *Völkerpsychologie* simply withered.

Right in the middle of this fundamental shift in the direction of anthropology, Freud published *Totem and Taboo* (1913). It did not begin to attract serious critical attention in anthropology until 1920, at which point it was soundly criticized. Professional anthropologists were appalled at Freud's sources: Atkinson, Darwin, and Robertson Smith were regarded as both out of date and speculative (Wallace 1983:132, 141). Further, Edward Sapir argued bluntly that anthropology could not be used for the purposes Freud intended.

> [T]he psychoanalyst has confused the archaic in the conceptual or psychologic sense with the archaic in the literal chronologic sense. Cultural anthropology is not valuable because it uncovers the archaic in the psychological sense. It is valuable because it is constantly rediscovering the normal. (cited in Wallace 1983:145)

Despite such negative professional reactions to *Totem and Taboo*, psychoanalysis became highly influential in anthropology during the twenties, thirties, and forties. This was partly because of Boas's view that the fundamental question of how cultural forces interact could only be given an adequate answer by psychology (Boas 1938:4–5) and partly because anthropologists despaired of finding rational explanations for cultural phenomena. The reaction of the British anthropologist W. H. R. Rivers in 1918 was typical. Although unimpressed by Freud's anthropology, Rivers thought that the ideas of psychoanalysis were intriguing and might be usefully applied in anthropology (Wallace 1938:136). Boas's own criticisms of Freud indicated the same ambivalence.

> While I believe some of the ideas underlying Freud's psycho-analysis studies may be fruitfully applied to ethnological prob-lems, it does not seem to me that the one-sided exploitation of this method will advance our understanding of the development of human society. (Boas 1920:288)

A number of other major anthropologists adopted the same attitude, including Seligman, Marett, and Malinowski in Britain, and Radin, Goldenweiser, and Herskovits in the United States (Wallace 1983:chap. 4, passim). Thus, psychoanalysis attracted the attention of anthropol-ogists, as Freud had hoped—but not in a way that advanced his cause. To see the problem, consider the issue that became the focal point for discussions of psychoanalysis in anthropology, the universality of the Oedipal complex. Freud needed anthropology to establish that this complex and various associated social structures were present in "primitive" societies that were themselves contemporary representa-tives of ancient societies. By contrast, anthropologists used the pres-ence or absence of the Oedipal complex in remote societies to test the universality or cultural relativity of social arrangements (Spiro 1982:x; Wallace 1983:3–4).

The classic case was Bronislaw Malinowski's study of the Trobriand Islanders, which argued that the male Oedipal complex was absent among this group (Spiro 1982:1–11). Of course, if the Oedipal complex was not universal among human beings, then a central piece of Freud's theories had to be wrong. However, the deeper difficulty for psycho-analysis was that even if Malinowski had found the male Oedipal complex among the Trobriand Islanders, that would not have been particularly helpful, because anthropologists were no longer prepared to take such results as evidence about the social life of primeval hu-mans. In a later discussion, Malinowski mocked this inference of nineteenth-century anthropology.

> [Anthropology] has so far been merely playing at problems, con-structing fairy tales about primitive man. . . . For a long time the main anthropological game was the search for origins. "Primitive man," that is primeval man, the missing link, had to be recon-structed. Modern savages provided us with the stage properties by which this reconstruction was carried out. (Malinowski 1962:94)

Given the new attitudes, even positive evidence provided by psycho-analytic anthropologists could not support Freud's hypothesis that the social arrangements of ancient ancestors helped to explain the presence of particular unconscious urges and repulsions in contemporary humans. It could only support generic claims, such as the universality of the Oedipal complex, and not his more detailed, causal explanation of why this complex was both universal and extremely powerful among contemporary human beings.

Like his reaction to the fall of the biogenetic law, Freud dealt with the changes in anthropology and the criticisms of his own work by stubborn defiance. In response to the nearly unanimous decrying of his sources, he maintained that

> [t]o this day, I hold firmly to this construction. . . . I have not been convinced either of the correctness of these innovations or of Robertson Smith's errors. A denial is not a refutation, an innovation is not necessarily an advance. Above all, however, I am not an ethnologist but a psycho-analyst. I had a right to take out of ethnological literature what I might need for the work of analysis. (*Moses and Monotheism*, 1939, S.E. XXIII:131)

But this was clearly wrong. He had no right to take theories that were no longer considered sound by expert opinion and present them as scientific evidence in favor of his own position.

While visiting at Clark University in 1909, Freud had attended a lecture by Boas and was obviously aware of the new antievolutionary direction in anthropology, as well as its doubts about psychical unity (Wallace 1983:177). But he never appreciated the devastating impact of these changes on the project he had envisioned for anthropology. Commenting on *Totem and Taboo* in 1938, he clung firmly to hope.

> It must be admitted that this historical survey has gaps in it and is uncertain at some points. But anyone who is inclined to pronounce our construction of primeval history purely imaginary would be gravely under-estimating the wealth and evidential value of the material contained in it. . . . There is nothing wholly fabricated in our construction, *nothing which could not be supported on solid foundations*. (*Moses and Monotheism*, 1939, S.E. XXIII:84; my emphasis)

Where was the evidence of the killing of the primal father to come from? In another part of this passage, Freud alluded to the possibility of survivals, but he never answered the serious questions that had been raised about their possibility. Writing in 1921, Sapir had noted that "if the history of culture teaches us anything, it is that while forms tend to persist, the psychic significance of these forms varies tremendously from age to age and from individual to individual. There is no permanence of psychic content" (cited in Wallace 1983:136). One year earlier, Boas had observed that "[s]tudies in the dynamics of primitive life [show that] . . . [i]t is exceedingly improbable that any customs of primitive people should be preserved unchanged for thousands of years" (Boas 1938:286). As already noted, the idea that contemporary tribes could provide evidence about archaic or primitive human mental structures had also been severely questioned. Further, Sapir had criticized Freud's equation of neurotics with primitive peoples, and Marett had denied that primitives could be regarded as infantile (Wallace 1983:145, 137). In 1915, Boas's most outstanding student, Alfred Kroeber, had crushed any suggestion that study of contemporary children or neurotics might provide clues to primeval mental life. "*Heredity by acquirement is equally a biological and historical monstrosity*" (cited in Stocking 1968:259).

The superficial successes of psychoanalysis in anthropology mask the magnitude of the problems caused by changes in the latter's goals and assumptions. It was all very well for anthropologists to engage in lively debates about the universality of the Oedipal complex, but Freud needed far more from anthropology than its refraining from contradicting his generalizations about familial structure. He needed anthropology to underwrite the scientific plausibility of claiming that within the mind there was a primitive portion that was especially evident in childhood, dreaming, and neurosis. He also needed anthropology and historical linguistics to corroborate his claims about dream symbolism and so finally to silence the continual criticisms that his interpretations were arbitrary. He needed anthropology to provide important parts of the explanation for the peculiar sexual constitution that he maintained was the source of all human achievements and miseries. But what professional anthropologists were telling him was that they no longer believed that their discipline was capable of illuminating problems about the uniform development of human mentality or the earliest origins of culture. They could provide no support at all for his theory of the origins of human mental life that underlay so many of his specific claims about dreams, neurosis, society, and the structure of the mind.

As the social sciences recognized their limitations in reconstructing the distant past, Freud's historical hypotheses began to look like fairy stories. He had always acknowledged their speculative character, but had taken them to be scientific speculations, because he believed that some account of roughly the kind he was offering had to be right. Perhaps Freud's faith in the ability of historical linguistics and anthropology to shore up and fill out crucial parts of psychoanalysis was always unjustified. By the time he began sketching the broad outlines of his theories in the 1890s, evolutionary anthropology was already being criticized. Still, it is hard to say that professional anthropologists had given up on this project, since anthropology was in the process of becoming a discipline and the line of demarcation between amateurs and professionals was still blurred. In any case, by the twenties and early thirties, Freud realized that the approach of anthropology had changed and, wrenching as this would have been, he should have recognized that he had to draw back from his numerous phylogenetic claims. He did not, but persevered in the belief that the evolutionary project of nineteenth-century anthropology would someday be brought to fruition.

Freud's attitude toward anthropology displayed most of the errors in interdisciplinary reasoning already encountered in previous contexts. He had more faith in the power of the discipline than practitioners, and he failed to stay current, in the sense of having current views influence his work. When anthropology seemed to promise help, he listened, but when it sent up warning signals, he turned a deaf ear. As with sexual chemistry, he bet his theory on quite specific future discoveries in other disciplines and then ignored the mounting evidence that these discoveries would never be forthcoming. He thought the approach, if not the results, of nineteenth-century social science was carved in stone. Having built the assumptions of social science into the foundations of psychoanalysis, he became so accustomed to them that he no longer recognized that he was dependent on them. Hence, he reversed the epistemic dependencies: Psychoanalysis stood on its own and offered hints to anthropology and sociology about how to understand the origins and basis of cultural phenomena.

Beyond the errors already cited, two further problems noted in earlier contexts were major factors in Freud's mishandling of social science. He mistook the promise of interdisciplinary fit for the reality and then compounded the error by taking fit as evidence for truth in the absence of independent support for either of the comporting theories. The accounts provided by historians of civilization about how various institutions might have arisen from simpler practices grounded in instincts never moved beyond the realm of conjecture; nor did the claim that there were behavior-guiding instincts that could be linked to physiology. So the fact that such accounts—had they been provided—would have dovetailed nicely should not have persuaded him that a unified theory of the mental was at hand.

Although these last two errors have contributed to the many negative judgments about Freud's work, the historical circumstances of his theory construction provide some mitigation and are instructive for current interdisciplinary efforts in cognitive science. In the latter half of the nineteenth century, different sciences appeared to be converging on a common account of human mental life. The mind was the brain, and the human mind/brain, like those of other animals, came to have its current properties through a long process of evolution involving both physical and social environments. Through these interactions, the lowly human animal endowment was changed in two ways. The organs of thought themselves evolved, and experiences of previous humans were passed on to their descendants, either by some unknown process of social evolution or by the inheritance of acquired characters, leading to the sophisticated and complex social creatures of today. Hence, it seemed fruitful and necessary to approach the study of the mind/brain in two complementary ways, by fathoming its neural wiring and by tracing its lengthy history.

As Lowie noted, archaeological discoveries gave added credence to the idea of evolutionary progress. Further, the discovery of common myths and common social practices such as marriage and exogamy across widely separated societies made it reasonable to think that there were regularities governing the development of human mental life, regularities that could be used to fill in gaps when actual data were unavailable. Historical linguistics had provided an impressive example of the possibility of extracting and using such laws to trace the development of a key aspect of mentality. The theory of evolution strongly suggested, even though it did not imply, that sexual and self-preservative instincts were likely to be heavily favored by evolution, and evolutionary sociologists and anthropologists had offered plausible scenarios about the development of human institutions from these instincts. Sexology had revealed a wealth of such instincts available for co-option for social purposes. Finally, the two approaches to the mind/brain, the neurological and the historical, were perfectly consonant, since the brain itself was a product of evolution and since the bases of social evolution were always instincts that seemingly could be tied to physiology.

Thus, as Freud was coming to intellectual maturity, a number of diverse sciences agreed on what was needed to understand the human mind—a reconstruction of its organic and social evolution—and each seemed able to contribute a complementary piece. Given the dramatic consilience of the sciences and their evidence, it was natural to hope that a unified, tolerably complete story of the origins of human mentality could be told and that it would be true. Further, genetic approaches had an obvious logic. With something as baroque as human social life, it made sense to try to understand it as a series of incremental changes, each building on what came before to produce a complexity that could not be achieved in a single creative step.

The problem with this consilience was its source. Although comparative anatomy's discovery of older brain structures shared with lower animals was independent of linguistics' discovery of a common and ancient root of European languages, both research projects came out of the same nineteenth-century tradition of historical explanation. To see the issue more clearly, consider a more limited case. The agreement in approach among evolutionary sociology, evolutionary anthropology, and evolutionary biology was no coincidence. The former disciplines began with the premise that the biological theory of evolution was true and must be used as a benchmark for research in the social sciences. Historical linguistics predated Lamarck and Darwin, but—like the theory of evolution itself—was very much a product of nineteenth-century historicism. Biological evolution seemed attractive, in part, because it was a historical doctrine. When it emerged as a major scientific achievement, it reinforced the preexisting historical predilections of contemporary theorists and created a much tighter correspondence among the explanatory frameworks of the social and biological sciences. Toward the end of the nineteenth century, different sciences appeared to be converging on a unified approach to the problem of mentality, because they were all being guided by the same dominant intellectual force: basic historicism dramatically invigorated and made specific by the theory of evolution. The correspondences among the sciences were largely a reflection of this zeitgeist.

That different sciences operated under the sway of the powerful zeitgeist of evolutionary historicism did not diminish the validity of their results. But it undercut the probative value of their consilience. Under these circumstances, the agreements among the sciences could not be credited to their correct, independent depictions of a common reality. Understandably, Freud did not appreciate this point. A devout evolutionist and system-builder, he looked for ways of integrating different branches of knowledge. When he found them, he did not question their source or recognize their common ancestry, but took them as prime indications that a unified theory of the mental was possible along evolutionary lines. Hence, although he always conceded the likelihood of errors of detail, he found it impossible to believe that the search for laws governing the development of human mental and social life from the beginning of civilization to the present might itself be completely barren.

Zeitgeists and Interdisciplinary Science

It is no accident that Freud proposed his unified theory of mental life during a time of great intellectual hegemony. A dominant zeitgeist creates two complementary pressures for adopting an interdisciplinary stance. When there is substantial agreement among the disciplines about the important questions to ask and the range of acceptable or plausible answers, then collaboration seems much more likely to be fruitful. Second, a dominant zeitgeist makes the inevitable success of current research appear more certain, for different sciences will employ similar approaches and so appear to confirm each other's methods. Further, all the advances will come out of the common approach, since there is no rival. If it is assumed that, in the end, the various mental sciences must converge on a consistent and integrated story of mental life and if it seems likely that current theories are at least roughly right, then it should be possible to begin integrating those theories in a unified account. So considerations of both short-term gain and long-term objectives make interdisciplinary strategies more attractive in a time of an overarching zeitgeist.

As the predominance of evolutionary explanations led Freud to believe that the time was ripe for integrating the mental sciences, so the proliferation of computational or information-processing approaches has inspired the contemporary ideal of a unified, interdisciplinary cognitive science. It would require another book to detail the rise of computationalism, but the basic outlines are clear enough. During the thirties, important results in logic demonstrated the power of formal methods. In particular, Alonzo Church proposed that any decidable function (that is, any function whose values can be computed in a finite number of steps) could be computed by a very simple device called a Turing machine (after Alan Turing).[6] Alan Turing proved that it was possible to construct a universal Turing machine that could emulate the behavior of any particular Turing machine. Putting these results together, it followed that a universal Turing machine could, in principle, solve any problem that was decidable.

When these and other results in computational theory were supported by technological advances in the fifties, it became possible to build computers and so to demonstrate their enormous practical utility in managing information. At about the same time, Noam Chomsky started a revolution in linguistics. In *Syntactic Structures* (1957) and later writings, Chomsky offered convincing arguments for understanding linguistic competence in terms of an internalized set of rules for manipulating linguistic symbols. As the theory of evolution made nineteenth-century historicism both more precise and more powerful, the theory of computation has given both tremendous impetus and recognizable shape to the twentieth-century inclination for formal or at least precisely defined theories. As historical linguistics seemed to provide an existence proof for the possibility of finding laws of development for human mentality, so Chomskian linguistics made it seem possible to fathom the actual rules and representations involved in human information processing. Further, like evolutionary approaches to complex mental and social structures, the idea that thinking is computing enjoys considerable plausibility independently of advances in particular disciplines. It is completely natural to characterize problem solving, for example, in terms of starting with one symbolic structure (the question) and trying to transform it into another (the answer).

By the second half of the fifties, the information-processing approach was beginning to take hold in the central discipline of psychology. Behaviorism, whose hallmark had been the rejection of inner mental states, was being supplanted by a "cognitive" psychology that took internal information-bearing states as its central theoretical construct (Mandler 1985:7–13). Thirty years later, the proliferation of computational approaches across the mental sciences is evident in the listings of university catalogues. At the University of California, San Diego, for example, there are courses in computational (or information-processing) psychology, computational anthropology, computational linguistics, and computational neuroscience.

Part of the current appeal of interdisciplinary strategies in the cognitive sciences derives from the prevailing computationalist zeitgeist. Different disciplines agree on many of the central questions of mental life and on the general shape of plausible answers: Individual and collective mental processes are most perspicuously described as computational processes. Hence, it seems useful to share results and techniques. The computationalist zeitgeist also contributes to optimism about contemporary research, because the disciplines appear to be converging on an integrated account, and more and more results are being generated by the computationalist approach. (Even where there are significant disagreements in cognitive science, as between those who favor classical computational architectures and the new school of parallel distributed processing, they occur within the common framework of computationalism.)

The parallel with psychoanalysis is obvious. Beyond his own personality quirks, Freud was confident that a complete interdisciplinary theory of mind was within his grasp because he was fooled by the spurious consilience of evidence produced by evolutionary historicism. Contemporary cognitive scientists may be making the same mistake, for the agreement among recent results is not a matter of independent sciences converging on a common reality, but of them all sharing a common belief in computationalism.

There are further, disturbing parallels between Freud's situation and contemporary cognitive science. Although the evolutionary mode of explanation showed great promise, not a single well-confirmed law of the development of mentality or civilization over the course of human history was ever established. Freud and his followers persevered on the conviction that such laws must exist, because they were strict determinists, because Darwin had showed that human mentality evolved over eons of time, and because common sense suggested that civilization must have been built up by gradual accretion. The problem is that, although the last two assumptions were entirely reasonable, they did not imply that the evolution of either mentality or civilization was sufficiently orderly that it could be captured in developmental laws. To date, it has not been possible to establish that any computational description of an actual human mental process is true. Many hypotheses have been proposed about the sorts of processing that might underlie various cognitive capacities, but there is no firm evidence that any of these theories is correct.[7] Contemporary cognitive scientists believe that it will be possible to provide computational descriptions of actual mental processes, because work in artificial intelligence has demonstrated that extremely complex problems can be solved by computational means and it is natural to describe thinking in terms of information processing. But the possibility remains that although both these points are true, the mechanisms of human thinking are most perspicuously described, not in terms of computational processes, but by reference to distinctive properties of the nervous system, emotional factors, previous conditioning, other currently unrecognized factors, or all of the foregoing.

Freud's forceful personality and the institutions of psychoanalysis he established led to an unhealthy homogeneity and stagnation of views. Today, it is unlikely that any individual or any group could exercise this kind of domination. Unfortunately, however, an interdisciplinary approach to research may itself produce excessive homogeneity. As a dominant zeitgeist fosters an interdisciplinary approach, so an interdisciplinary approach leads to greater commonality of beliefs and attitudes. Thus, the adoption of an interdisciplinary research strategy increases the hegemony of a zeitgeist, which further encourages interdisciplinary integration, and so on. An interdisciplinary research strategy also tends to preserve existing views, because it sacrifices an important mechanism for change. As work in related (but independent) fields can offer important confirmation, it can also cast doubts on accepted theories and offer hints about more fruitful approaches. The great danger in utilizing an interdisciplinary research strategy in the presence of a dominant zeitgeist is theoretical stagnation. Or, putting the point in the jargon of contemporary computationalism: Given a dominant zeitgeist, an interdisciplinary approach runs the risk of forcing research into a "local minimum" by depriving it of any sources of energy that would enable it to climb out. For this reason, and to maintain an adequate theoretical grounding, the institutions of cognitive science need to encourage constant contact with its foundational disciplines.

Conclusion

Given the tenor of these last two chapters, I should repeat the point made at the outset: My purpose has been neither to disparage nor to discourage interdisciplinary work in cognitive science. Since neurophysiological, developmental, linguistic, psychological, social—and very probably computational—factors are all involved in cognition, a complete theory must include them all in a more or less unified whole. Hence, it is reasonable to integrate work in these fields as far as possible. What I have argued in this chapter and throughout the book is that there are some subtle and not so subtle dangers in this approach that contemporary cognitive science needs to avoid.

Although the devout will never believe me, neither has my purpose been to add yet another sin to the growing list of Freud's alleged scientific transgressions. His example is illuminating, because he made relatively few careless or silly mistakes in interdisciplinary theory construction. He built assumptions from various fields into the foundations of psychoanalysis and then paid the price when those fields underwent substantive or methodological changes. But it is not clear how to develop detailed interdisciplinary theories (as opposed to theory sketches) without utilizing fallible work from other fields. His example shows the futility of two tempting precautions. First, there is little point in asserting that a borrowed theory is merely provisional. The status of that theory within the other discipline must be constantly monitored. Even this may be insufficient, however, since it is easy to underestimate the difficulties of a theory or a program of research from outside the field. Second, it may not be helpful to assume merely that the rough direction of a field is correct and so borrow only generic versions of theories. Although this strategy offers some protection against change, it also lays an interdisciplinary theory wide open to the charge that it is vague and ill supported.

Freud erred, I believe, because although he understood the rationale for an interdisciplinary theory of mind very well, he did not grasp how fully psychoanalysis realized the ideal. Hence, when the biological and social sciences underwent significant changes, he failed to appreciate the dire implications for his program and reacted inappropriately. By his reactions, he raised the price of failure. Psychoanalysis was not only bypassed by the course of other sciences, but made to appear unscientific. Beyond problems with clinical validation, the unsavory reputation of psychoanalysis is due largely to Freud's misunderstanding of the interdisciplinary structure of his theory—and to his tremendous overconfidence, fueled by the apparent evolutionary synthesis of the mental sciences at the end of the last century.

Contemporary cognitive science shares Freud's dream of a science of the mind in which the contributions of all the relevant disciplines illuminate each other and finally do justice to the complexities of mental life. But it does not wish to share either the reputation of his theories or, if possible, their fate. Freud hoped that his theories would become indispensable to all the mental sciences and that he was inaugurating a new era of scientific psychology. Perhaps psychoanalysis still has substantive insights to offer in the fields of personality and motivation, and even in anthropology and sociology. But, however that turns out, his bold attempt to construct an interdisciplinary theory of mind should enable his successors to achieve a more critical understanding of this necessary and exciting project—and so to proceed much more cautiously.

Notes

Chapter 1

1. Although it is sometimes used more broadly, I use "psychoanalysis" to indicate Freud's own theories.
2. For a clear discussion of reduction, see Schaffner 1967.
3. For a more extended discussion of supervenience, see Kim 1978.
4. Here I exclude the sort of indirect insight popular in tales of scientific creativity, for example, Kekule's dream of snakes biting their tails leading to the idea of the structure of benzene.
5. Since computer science is a branch of mathematics, this does not change the order of the disciplines, but it is a major difference between Freud's time and the present.
6. See Rapaport 1960, Sulloway 1979, Amacher 1965, Pibram and Gill 1976, Fancher, ms., and Wallace 1983. Peter Machamer drew my attention to Rapaport's monograph after I had completed the penultimate draft of the book. Although Rapaport had no inkling of the contemporary movement in cognitive science, he saw a number of nineteenth-century sciences and scientific attitudes as critical to understanding the development of psychoanalysis.

Chapter 2

1. One field is conspicuous by its absence. Freud believed that medical training was unnecessary for the practice of psychoanalysis. I discuss then current medical practice only in connection with Freud's classifications of neuroses, which he admitted that he borrowed from medicine ("Lay Analysis," S.E. XI:9–11; see chapter 4). In both text and notes, I use "S.E.," volume, and page number to give references to Freud 1953–74.
2. Freud cited the first (1874) edition of Wundt's *Principles of Physiological Psychology*. I will sometimes refer to the more expansive (and occasionally different) discussions of the fifth edition (1902) to describe the state of various questions at this time, because Wundt is a standard authority and was widely influential. I do not mean to suggest that Freud read the precise discussions I cite.
3. This principle will be discussed at greater length in chapter 4.
4. Although I have consulted Krafft-Ebing 1903 and Ellis 1897, this section is heavily indebted to Frank Sulloway's extensive discussion of Freud's precursors and contemporaries in the field of sex (Sulloway 1979:chap. 8, passim).
5. Although "perversion" was the term used in these discussions, I put it in scare quotes, because I doubt the reasonableness of applying it in many cases.

Chapter 3

1. Note, however, that the distinction between directive and doctrine is relative. The directive to understand characters in terms of descent with modification is itself a reflection of the substantive position that characters do not emerge completely de novo, but evolve. Nevertheless, relative to claims about the development of particular characters, it is a principle for theory construction.
2. I owe this way of expressing the point to Peter Machamer.
3. Given Freud's efforts to differentiate these aspects, I think that Sulloway errs in identifying them quite closely, although his interpretation rests on strong textual evidence. In his *Autobiographical Study*, Freud wrote:

   [I]t introduces a dynamic factor, by supposing that a symptom arises through the damming-up of an affect, and an economic factor, by regarding that same symptom as the product of the transformation of an amount of energy. . . . (1925, S.E. XX:22)

   Although "damming-up of an affect" suggests that a quantity of some substance is being blocked from flowing, I think the phrase is simply a mistake. One year later, he presented the *economic* point of view in terms of the metaphor of "damming-up" ("Psychoanalysis," 1926, S.E. XX:265–66).
4. Functional and evolutionary considerations need not always go together. But like many thinkers today, Jackson and Freud tended to think they would.
5. When citing Freud, I follow the editors of the *Standard Edition* in using the anachronistic "neurone" rather than "neuron."
6. "We must call the Witch to our help after all!" The citation is from Goethe's *Faust*, part I, scene 6.
7. In a passage in *Beyond the Pleasure Principle*, Freud expressed the hope that some of the language of psychoanalysis would be replaced by that of physiology or chemistry: "We . . . [are] obliged to operate with the scientific terms, that is to say with the figurative language, peculiar to psychology. . . . We could not otherwise describe the processes in question at all, and indeed we could not have become aware of them. The deficiencies in our description would probably vanish if we were already in a position to replace the psychological terms by physiological or chemical ones" (1920, S.E. XVIII:60). In this work, Freud speculated about the biological forces that underlay certain clinical syndromes, in particular, the compulsion to repeat. He tried to tie this to what he took to be a basic trait of living matter: its tendency to return to a previous state. Freud described this tendency, somewhat awkwardly he realized, as a "death" instinct. Thus, what he expected someday to be replaced were terms that were always intended to capture biological forces, and not basic psychoanalytic concepts such as "repression" or "ego-ideal."
8. For a more thorough discussion of the relation between "reduction" and "explanatory extension," see the work of Philip Kitcher (1984, 1989), from whom I borrow the latter notion.

Chapter 4

1. The origin of this view is probably Freud's own confessional remark in the Preface to the second (1908) edition of *The Interpretation of Dreams* that his self-analysis of his reaction to his father's death was critical to the dream book, a book he described as containing his greatest and most original insights (S.E. IV:xxvi, xxxii). See also Jones 1961:209ff. and Gay 1988:87ff. The distinction between Freud's early work in

physiology and his later allegedly pure psychology has also become entrenched in psychoanalytic circles because of the decision of the editors to include only a few pieces of his early "scientific" work in the "*Standard Edition*" of the *Complete Psychological Works of Sigmund Freud.*

2. It is also possible to see these as two closely related but slightly different principles, with the pleasure principle dictating that the level of energy be kept as low as possible, the constancy principle requiring only that it be kept relatively constant. Nothing in my discussion turns on whether these principles are regarded as related or identical.

3. I connect a mental state with a system of neurons, because Freud never fell for a simple "grandmother neuron" picture. See "On Aphasia," 1891, S.E. XIV:206ff. for a discussion.

4. Ellenberger (1970:479) notes that Brücke, Meynert, and Freud's early coworker Sigmund Exner all described processes indifferently in physiological or psychological terms. Perhaps as a reaction against this trend, Breuer began his theoretical discussion in *Studies in Hysteria* by noting that he would not use "excitation of the cortex" in place of "idea," since the former term would only have any meaning insofar as readers recognized an old friend under that cloak and tacitly reinstated "idea." The substitution of one term for another would seem to be no more than a pointless disguise (1893–95, S.E. II:185).

5. I translate Freud's term "*Vorstellung*" by "representation" because I find the *Standard Edition's* choice of "presentation" quite confusing. Since a *Vorstellung* can be unconscious, it is not necessarily present to anything; on the other hand, it always represents something beyond itself.

6. See below for further discussion, p. 94.

7. Glymour (forthcoming) drew my attention to this passage.

8. Briquet's study was inadequate, since it considered only the percentage of offspring of neurotics who were neurotic. It was also necessary to consider the frequency in individuals with no evidence of familial neurosis. Further, as Freud observed ("The Aetiology of Hysteria," 1896, S.E. II:209), even when family members shared neuroses, that did not show that the mode of transmission was genetic.

9. Grünbaum (1984) argues convincingly that, since Freud did not rule out suggestion, placebo effects, or spontaneous cures, alleged cures were no evidence for the truth of his etiological claims. Again, however, my concern is with the reasonableness of Freud's belief that he was amassing evidence. The sad fact is that standards for accepting medical hypotheses are shockingly low. To take a very recent example, thousands of patients were subjected to unnecessary operations before a controlled study was finally carried out comparing the relative effectiveness of coronary bypass surgery versus medication. Thus, by the standards of his profession, Freud's position was not unreasonable.

10. I agree with Sulloway that Freud's awareness of normal adult victims of childhood seduction was what forced the issue and that Albert Moll's work and, perhaps, a brief collaboration with Felix Gattel (Sulloway 1979:513–15) were crucial, but I dissent on the time frame. Assuming that Freud read Moll before writing to Fliess, it is reasonable to believe this accounted for the letter's dramatic announcement. But did this represent his considered position? He went on to observe that "now I have no idea where I stand" (Masson 1985:265). It seems reasonable to assume that, on reflection, he was not prepared to be stampeded by Moll, given his own (apparent) contrary findings, but came to accept the position as inevitable only as Moll's work was confirmed and assimilated into the scientific community—and only as he figured out where he stood.

11. Glymour (forthcoming) argues that the collapse of the seduction theory led Freud to doubt his methods, which is why he postponed admitting the failure in print. For reasons I give in the text, I do not believe that Freud's doubts spread very far, although his *Autobiographical Study* (1925) presents this episode as a great crisis of faith, resolved by the discovery of childhood sexuality and the Oedipal complex (S.E. XX:34–35).

12. Freud took "*Instinkt*" to indicate the presence of complex, fixed, innate forms of behavior. By contrast, "*Trieb*" merely denoted an innate impulse that experience could channel into different behaviors. Besides the comparative complexity and fixity of *Instinkte*, Freud assumed that they were intermittent, whereas he regarded *Triebe* as continual sources of excitation. See Nagera et al. 1970:15–50.

13. At this point, Freud had no very clear idea of how the societal norms became incorporated into individual psychology, an issue that was finally resolved in *The Ego and the Id*. See below, *The Development of the Ego*.

14. I enclose "perversion" in quotation marks, because I do not wish to endorse the classifications I discuss. See chapter 2, note 5.

15. Again, I use quotation marks to avoid appearing to endorse the characterization of contemporary tribes as "primitive."

16. Although, as will be apparent, the attachments were never quite this simple.

17. Siblings or nursemaids might also be present, but Freud also allowed them to be part of the Oedipal complex. See note 18.

18. Two changes were quite significant. In early discussions, the "Oedipal complex" referred only to the attachment of children for parents or parent-substitutes of the opposite sex (e.g., *The Interpretation of Dreams*, 1900, S.E. IV:260–61; *Three Essays on the Theory of Sexuality*, 1905, VII:56; *Five Lectures on Psycho-Analysis*, 1909, XI:47). Later, his convictions about bisexuality led him to see a four-way attachment of sons and daughters to mothers and fathers (*The Ego and the Id*, 1923, S.E. XIX:33). He also realized that it followed from his own view of the importance of nursing that girls would take their mothers as their first love-objects. His way of dealing with this change is instructive.

> [This can be handled in two different ways.] On the one hand, we can extend the content of the Oedipus complex to include all the child's relations to both parents, or on the other, we can take due account of our new findings by saying that the female only reaches the normal positive Oedipus situation after she has surmounted a period before it that is governed by the negative complex. ("Female Sexuality," 1931, S.E. XXI:226)

Despite appearances, the first option was not an ad hoc move to save the importance of the Oedipal complex. Freud had already presented this complex as a "family" complex, including brothers and sisters (*Introductory Lectures on Psycho-Analysis*, 1916–17, S.E. XVI:333ff.) and as "comprising a child's relation to his parents" ("From the History of an Infantile Neurosis," 1918, XVII:119).

Chapter 5

1. I compare Hobson's and Freud's theories at the end of the chapter.

2. Later, "regression" took on a more specific sexual meaning, referring to earlier phases of sexual development. See *Introductory Lectures on Psycho-Analysis*, 1916–17, S.E. XVI:341–42 for an explanation of the early and late terminology.

3. This point can become confused. Freud sometimes wrote as if the id "intended" to have a dream. Given his own description of this mental system, however, it was

incapable of having "intentions," as we normally use the word, namely, to indicate rationally derived instrumental goals. It had "purposes" only in the Pickwickian sense that it served nature's purpose of procreation.

4. One difficulty with Freud's analysis is that his friend's wish to avoid impregnating his lover was not repressed, but conscious. Presumably Freud would reply to this objection by claiming that the analysis was very partial—that behind this conscious wish were other unconscious infantile wishes.

5. I discuss Freud's attempts to confirm reversals below.

6. I discuss this issue from a somewhat different angle in chapter 7.

7. See below for further discussion of Freud's use of literature to support psychological hypotheses.

8. At this point, it may seem as if too many factors are implicating sex. Is the latent content of dreams sexual, because dreaming is always instigated by unconscious sexual wishes or because the archaic language in which dreams are expressed is inherently sexual? Freud would deny the antithesis between the alleged rivals, I believe, and would argue that they are complementary claims. The language of the unconscious is sexual, because it is the repository of unconscious sexual wishes.

9. Freud referred several times to experiments performed by Herbert Silberer. As Silberer was getting sleepy, he would think of an intellectual task. Apparently because of his tiredness the thought would then be replaced by a picture that seemed to represent it. Freud's point in noting these experiments was to demonstrate the possibility of finding such relations and not to confirm particular interpretations (e.g., *The Interpretation of Dreams*, 1900, S.E. V:344–45).

10. For a survey of this controversy, see Strum 1987. Some feminists see this episode in terms of the flaws of male-dominated science. Even if this is part of the story, it is hard to believe that the research program would have gotten off the ground in the absence of plausible evolutionary arguments.

11. I use these examples rather than the more familiar cases of phlogiston and the overlooking of novas by Western scientists, because I do not wish to endorse the strong Kuhnian position that theory commitment affects visual capacity. (See Kuhn 1970:62–65, and, for criticism, Fodor 1986). My point is much weaker: Data usually require interpretation; interpretation is guided by theory; hence, spurious confirmations will happen.

12. In chapter 7, I consider how the institutions of psychoanalysis allowed it to become isolated and dogmatic. However, these factors cannot explain Freud's success. If anything, they should have driven people away from psychoanalysis.

Chapter 6

1. Many of my examples from current cognitive science deal with arguments for or against PDP or connectionism. This is not because I wish to criticize this school, but because it is widely discussed and potentially extremely important.

2. In logic, this is known as a "quantificational fallacy," because it involves changing the positions of the quantifiers "every" and "some." Compare: "For every person, there is some woman who is his or her mother" and "There is some woman who is every person's mother."

3. I should note that McClelland and Rumelhart argue that PDP models are consistent with both prototype and exemplar models of concept use. I do not discuss this complication in the text because it is irrelevant to the point I wish to make.

4. I discuss the institutions of psychoanalysis at some length in chapter 7.

Chapter 7

1. In his forthcoming book on Freud and computational theories of mind, Clark Glymour argues that the top-down, functional decomposition approach is the common flaw of both programs. As Glymour notes, however, Freud was a top-down theorist by necessity, not choice. He would have welcomed neurophysiological support for his mental divisions. Glymour's complaint against functional decomposition is that there is no way to tell which of many possible combinations of faculties is the one we actually possess.

2. As we will see, this was not strictly true. Freud occasionally appealed to experimental results, but experimentation was not the focus of psychoanalysis as behaviorists believed it had to be.

3. Glymour refers to the Rat Man as "Paul Lorenz," but his true identity was Ernst Lanzer. See Sulloway 1991:255.

4. Fortunately, this is not always true. I am grateful to my medical school colleague, Darrel Fannistel, for recommending Flexner's enlightening report to me.

5. I owe this point to Peter Machamer.

6. A Turing machine has three parts: a tape divided into squares that are either blank or have a symbol written on them, an executive unit that can move, that scans one square at a time, and that can change what is written on the square it is scanning, and a program that tells the executive unit what to do, for example, move three squares to the left and if there is a certain symbol in the square at that place, erase it and write a different symbol. For a more extensive and very clear discussion, see Boolos and Jeffrey 1974:19ff.

7. As Glymour (forthcoming) argues, one serious difficulty with computational approaches is that since there are many different ways to perform the same task, it may be impossible to tell which of the ways is actually being used by purely computational means. See note 1.

Bibliography

Alexander, Franz (1948). *Fundamentals of Psychoanalysis.* New York: W. W. Norton, 1963.

Amacher, Peter (1965). "Freud's Neurological Education and Its Influence on Psychoanalytic Theory." In *Psychological Issues,* vol. IV, no. 4. New York: International Universities Press.

Antilla, Raimo (1972). *An Introduction to Historical Linguistics.* New York: Macmillan.

Bernfeld, Sigfried (1949). "Freud's Scientific Beginnings." *American Imago* 6:163–96.

Bloomfield, Leonard (1933). *Language.* New York: Holt, Rinehart and Winston. Reprinted, 1966.

Boas, Franz (1896). "The Limitations of the Comparative Method of Anthropology." Reprinted in Boas 1940.

Boas, Franz (1917). "Introduction to *International Journal of American Linguistics.*" Reprinted in Boas 1940.

Boas, Franz (1920). "The Methods of Ethnology." In Boas 1940.

Boas, Franz, ed. (1938). *General Anthropology.* San Francisco: D. C. Heath. Reprinted by Johnson Reprint Corporation, 1965.

Boas, Franz (1940). *Race, Language and Culture.* New York: The Free Press.

Boolos, George S., and Richard C. Jeffrey (1974). *Computability and Logic.* Cambridge: Cambridge University Press.

Bowler, Peter J. (1983). *The Eclipse of Darwinism.* Baltimore, Md.: The Johns Hopkins University Press.

Brazier, Mary A. B. (1988). *A History of Neurophysiology in the 19th Century.* New York: Raven Press.

Brentano, Franz (1874). *Psychology from an Empirical Standpoint.* Antos C. Rancurello, D. B. Terrell, and Linda L. McAlister, trans. New York: Humanities Press, 1973.

Buckle, Henry Thomas (1857–61). *Introduction to the History of Civilization in England.* With an introduction by John M. Robertson. London: Routledge, 1904.

Bullock, Theodore Holmes (1977). *Introduction to Nervous Systems.* San Francisco: W. H. Freeman.

Burghardt, Gordon M. (1973). "Instinct and Innate Behavior: Toward an Ethological Psychology." In John A. Nevin and George S. Reynolds, eds., *The Study of Behavior.* Glenview, Ill.: Scott, Foresman.

Carey, Susan (1983). "Cognitive Development: The Descriptive Problem." In M. Gazzaniga, ed., *Handbook for Cognitive Neurology.* Hillsdale, N.J.: L. Erlbaum Assocs.

Chomsky, Noam (1957). *Syntactic Structures.* The Hague: Mouton.

Churchland, Paul M. (1989). *A Neurocomputational Perspective: The Nature of Mind and the Structure of Science.* Cambridge, Mass.: MIT Press.

Clark, Peter, and Crispin Wright, eds. (1988). *Mind, Psychoanalysis and Science.* Oxford: Basil Blackwell.

Clarke, Edwin, and L. S. Jacyna (1987). *Nineteenth-Century Origins of Neuroscientific Concepts*. Los Angeles: University of California Press.

Cohen, R. S., and L. Laudan, eds. (1983). *Physics, Philosophy and Psychoanalysis: Essays in Honor of Adolf Grünbaum*. Boston: D. Reidel.

Crews, Frederick (1988). "On the Irrelevance of Psychoanalysis to Literary Criticism." In Clark and Wright 1988.

Crick, Francis, and Graeme Mitchison (1983). "The Function of Dream Sleep." *Nature* 304:111–14.

Crick, Francis, and Graeme Mitchison (1986). "REM Sleep and Neural Nets." *The Journal of Mind and Behavior* 7:229–50.

Cummins, Robert (1975). "Functional Analysis." *Journal of Philosophy* 5:102–22.

Darwin, Charles (1859). *On the Origin of Species*. Cambridge, Mass.: Harvard University Press, 1976.

Darwin, Charles (1872). *The Expression of the Emotions in Man and Animals*. Chicago: University of Chicago Press, 1965.

Darwin, Charles (1874). *The Descent of Man and Selection in Relation to Sex*. Chicago: Rand, McNally, 1974.

Dewey, John (1896). "The Reflex Arc Concept in Psychology." *Psychological Review* 3:357–70. Reprinted in Herrnstein and Boring 1965.

Diagnostic and Statistical Manual of Mental Disorders (1987). 3d ed., rev. Washington, D.C.: American Psychiatric Association.

Durkheim, Emile (1895). *The Rules of Sociological Method*. W. D Halls, trans. New York: The Free Press, 1982.

Durkheim, Emile (1930). *Suicide: A Study in Sociology*. John A. Spaulding, trans. New York: The Free Press, 1951.

Edelson, Marshall (1975). *Language and Interpretation in Psychoanalysis*. Chicago: University of Chicago Press.

Ellenberger, Henri (1970). *The Discovery of the Unconscious*. New York: Basic Books.

Ellis, Havelock (1897). *Studies in the Psychology of Sex. Vol. I: Sexual Inversion*. With J. A. Symonds. London: The University Press.

Encyclopaedia Britannica (1910). 11th ed. New York: Encyclopaedia Britannica Company, Handy Volume Issue.

Eysenck, Hans J., and Glenn D. Wilson, eds. (1973). *The Experimental Study of Freudian Theories*. London: Methuen.

Fancher, Raymond E. (1973). *Psychoanalytic Psychology: The Development of Freud's Thought*. New York: W. W. Norton.

Fancher, Raymond E. (ms.). "The Neurological Origins of Psychoanalysis."

Feldman, J. A., and D. H. Ballard (1982). "Connectionist Models and Their Properties." *Cognitive Science* 6:205–54.

Fenichel, Otto (1945). *The Psychoanalytic Theory of Neurosis*. New York: W. W. Norton.

Feyerabend, P. K. (1962). "Explanation, Reduction, and Empiricism." In H. Feigl and G. Maxwell, eds., *Minnesota Studies in the Philosophy of Science III*. Minneapolis, Minn.: University of Minnesota Press.

Fine, Reuben (1979). *A History of Psychoanalysis*. New York: Columbia University Press.

Fletcher, Ronald (1971). *The Making of Sociology*. 2 vols. London: Michael Joseph.

Flexner, Abraham (1910). *Medical Education in the United States and Canada: A Report to the Carnegie Foundation for the Advancement of Teaching*. New York: The Carnegie Foundation for the Advancement of Teaching. Reproduced in 1960.

Fodor, J. A. (1975). *The Language of Thought*. New York: Crowell.

Fodor, J. A., and Z. W. Pylyshyn (1988). "Connectionism and Cognitive Architecture." In Steven Pinker and Jacques Mehler, eds., *Connections and Symbols*. Cambridge, Mass.: MIT Press.

Freud, Sigmund (1915). *A Phylogenetic Fantasy*. Axel Hoffer and Peter T. Hoffer, trans. Cambridge, Mass.: Harvard University Press, 1987.

Freud, Sigmund (1953–74). *The Standard Edition of the Complete Psychological Works of Sigmund Freud*. 24 vols. Translated from the German under the General Editorship of James Strachey. In collaboration with Anna Freud. Assisted by Alix Strachey and Alan Tyson. London: The Hogarth Press and the Institute of Psycho-Analysis.

Gay, Peter (1988). *Freud: A Life for Our Time*. New York: W. W. Norton.

Gelman, Susan A. and Ellen M. Markman (1987). "Young Children's Inductions from Natural Kinds: The Role of Categories and Appearances." *Child Development* 58:1532–41.

Gillispie, Charles Coulston, ed. in chief (1970). *Dictionary of Scientific Biography*. "Ernst Brücke," vol. II. New York: Scribner.

Glymour, Clark (1974). "Freud, Kepler, and the Clinical Evidence." In Richard Wollheim, ed., *Freud: A Collection of Critical Essays*. New York: Anchor Books.

Glymour, Clark (1983). "The Theory of Your Dreams." In Cohen and Laudan 1983.

Glymour, Clark (forthcoming). *Necessary Connections: Freud and the Foundations of Cognitive Science*.

Gould, Stephen Jay (1977). *Ontogeny and Phylogeny*. Cambridge, Mass.: Harvard University Press.

Gould, Stephen Jay (1989). *Wonderful Life: The Burgess Shale and the Nature of History*. New York: W. W. Norton.

Grünbaum, Adolf (1984). *The Foundations of Psychoanalysis*. Los Angeles: University of California Press.

Hebb, D. O. (1982). "Drives and the C. N. S. (Conceptual Nervous System)." Reprinted in Henry A. Buchtel, ed., *The Conceptual Nervous System*. New York: Pergamon Press.

Hempel, Carl G. (1950). "Empiricist Criteria of Cognitive Significance: Problems and Changes." Reprinted in Carl G. Hempel, *Aspects of Scientific Explanation*. New York: The Free Press.

Herrnstein, Richard J., and Edwin G. Boring (1965). *Sourcebook in the History of Psychology*. Cambridge, Mass.: Harvard University Press.

Hexter, J. H. (1979). *Reappraisals in History*. 2d ed. Chicago: University of Chicago Press.

Hobson, J. Allan (1988a). *The Dreaming Brain*. New York: Basic Books.

Hobson, J. Allan (1988b). "Psychoanalytic Dream Theory: A Critique Based upon Modern Neurophysiology." In Clark and Wright 1988.

Holt, Robert R. (1965). "Freud's Biological Assumptions." In Norman S. Greenfeld and William C. Lewis, eds., *Psychoanalysis and Current Biological Thought*. Madison, Wisc.: The University of Wisconsin Press.

Holt, Robert R. (1989). *Freud Reappraised*. New York: Guilford Press.

Horgan, Terry, and John Tienson (1989). "Representation without Rules." *Philosophical Topics* 17:147–74.

Jackson, John Hughlings (1873ff.). *Selected Writings of John Hughlings Jackson*, vol. I. James Taylor, ed. New York: Basic Books, 1958.

James, William (1892). *Psychology: The Briefer Course*. Gordon Allport, ed. New York: Harper and Row, 1961.

Jones, Ernest (1961). *The Life and Work of Sigmund Freud*. New York: Basic Books.

Jung, C. G. (1906). *Studies in Word Association*. M. D. Eder, trans. New York: Russell and Russell, 1918.

Keil, Frank (1989). *Concepts, Kinds, and Cognitive Development*. Cambridge, Mass.: MIT Press.

Kemeny, J. G., and P. Oppenheim (1956). "On Reduction." *Philosophical Studies* 7:6–17.

Kim, Jaegwon (1978). "Supervenience and Nomological Incommensurables." *American Philosophical Quarterly* 15:149–56.

Kitcher, Patricia (1988). "What Is Freud's Metapsychology?" *Proceedings of the Aristotelian Society Supplement* 62:101–15.

Kitcher, Philip (1984). "1953 and All That. A Tale of Two Sciences." *Philosophical Review* 93:335–73.

Kitcher, Philip (1989). "Explanatory Unification and the Causal Structure of the World." In Philip Kitcher and Wesley Salmon, eds., *Scientific Explanation*. Minneapolis, Minn.: University of Minnesota Press.

Klein, George S. (1976). "Freud's Two Theories of Sexuality." In Merton M. Gill and Philip S. Holzman, eds., *Psychology versus Metapsychology*. *Psychological Issues*, vol. IX, no. 4. New York: International Universities Press.

Krafft-Ebing, Richard von (1903). *Psychopathia Sexualis*. Translated from the 12th edition (1903) by Franklin S. Klaf. New York: Stein and Day, 1965.

Kuhn, Thomas (1970). *The Structure of Scientific Revolutions*. Chicago: University of Chicago Press.

Laplanche, J., and J.-B. Pontalis (1973). *The Language of Psycho-Analysis*. Donald Nicholson-Smith, trans. London: The Hogarth Press and the Institute of Psycho-Analysis.

Laudan, Larry (1983). "The Demise of the Demarcation Problem." In Cohen and Laudan 1983.

Leibniz, Gottfried Wilhelm (1714). "The Monadology." In *Philosophical Papers and Letters*. Leroy E. Loemker, trans. and ed. Boston: D. Reidel, 1976.

Leopold, Joan (1987). "Friedrich Max Müller." In H. Aarsleff, L. G. Kelly, and H.-J. Niederche, eds., *Papers in the History of Linguistics*. Philadelphia: John Benjamins.

Lewin, Bertram D., and Helen Ross (1960). *Psychoanalytic Education in the United States*. New York: W. W. Norton.

Lloyd Morgan, C. (1910). "Instincts." In *Encyclopaedia Britannica*, 1910, vol. 14, 648–50.

Lowie, Robert H. (1937). *The History of Ethnological Theory*. New York: Holt, Rinehart and Winston.

McClelland, James L., and David E. Rumelhart (1986). *Parallel Distributed Processing*. Vol. 2: *Psychological and Biological Models*. Cambridge, Mass.: MIT Press.

Malinowski, Bronislaw (1962). *Sex, Culture, and Myth*. New York: Harcourt, Brace and World.

Mandler, George (1985). *Cognitive Psychology*. Hillsdale, N.J.: L. Erlbaum Assocs.

Masson, Jeffrey Moussaieff (1985). *The Complete Letters of Sigmund Freud to Wilhelm Fliess 1887–1904*. Cambridge, Mass.: Harvard University Press.

Mill, John Stuart (1843). *A System of Logic*. London: Longmans, 1970.

Müller, F. Max (1861). *Lectures in the Science of Language*. New Delhi: Oriental Publishers and Booksellers, fifth reprinting, 1965.

Müller, F. Max (1897). *Contributions to the Science of Mythology*. London: Longmans, Green.

Murphy, Gardner (1949). *Historical Introduction to Modern Psychology*. New York: Harcourt, Brace and World.

Murphy, G. L., and D. L. Medin (1985). "The Role of Theories in Conceptual Coherence." *Psychological Review* 92:289–316.

Nagel, Ernest (1961). *The Structure of Science*. New York: Harcourt, Brace and World.

Nagera, Humberto, et al. (1970). *Basic Psychoanalytic Concepts on the Theory of Instincts*. New York: Basic Books.

Nietzsche, Friederich (1887). *The Genealogy of Morals*. Francis Golffin, trans. New York: Doubleday, 1956.

Nisbett, Richard, and Lee Ross (1980). *Human Inference: Strategies and Shortcomings of Social Judgment*. Englewood Cliffs, N.J.: Prentice-Hall.

Nordenskiöld, Erik (1917). *The History of Biology*. New York: Tudor Publishing Company.

Pedersen, Holger (1962). *The Discovery of Language*. John Webster Spargo, trans. Bloomington, Ind.: Indiana University Press.

Porte, Helene Sophrin (1988). "The Analogy of Symptoms and Dreams: Is Freud's Dream Theory an Impostor?" In Clark and Wright 1988.

Pribram, Karl, and Morton Gill (1976). *Freud's 'Project' Re-Assessed: Preface to Contemporary Cognitive Theory and Neuropsychology*. New York: Basic Books.

Rapaport, David (1960). *The Structure of Psychoanalytic Theory: A Systematizing Attempt*. *Psychological Issues*, vol. II, no. 2, monograph 6. New York: International Universities Press.

Robins, R. H. (1968). *A Short History of Linguistics*. Bloomington, Ind.: Indiana University Press.

Rumelhart, David E., and James L. McClelland (1986). *Parallel Distributed Processing*. Vol. I: Foundations. Cambridge, Mass.: MIT Press.

Sapir, Edward (1921). *Language: An Introduction to the Study of Speech*. New York: Harcourt, Brace and Company, 1960.

Schaffner, Kenneth (1967). "Approaches to Reduction." *Philosophy of Science* 34:137–47.

Sejnowski, T. J. (1986). "Open Questions about Computation in Cerebral Cortex." In McClelland and Rumelhart 1986.

Sherrington, Charles S. (1906). *The Integrative Action of the Nervous System*. New Haven, Conn.: Yale University Press.

Sherwood, Michael (1969). *The Logic of Explanation in Psychoanalysis*. New York: Academic Press.

Singer, Charles (1959). *A History of Biology*. New York: Abelard-Schuman.

Skinner, B. F. (1953). *Science and Human Behavior*. New York: The Free Press.

Smith, E. E., and D. L. Medin (1981). *Concepts and Categories*. Cambridge, Mass.: Harvard University Press.

Smolensky, Paul (1988). "On the Proper Treatment of Connectionism." *Behavioral and Brain Sciences* 11:1–23.

Spiro, Melford E. (1982). *Oedipus in the Trobriands*, Chicago: University of Chicago Press.

Stich, Stephen P. (1988). "From Connectionism to Eliminativism." *Behavioral and Brain Sciences* 11:53–54.

Stocking George W., Jr. (1968). *Race, Culture, and Evolution*. Chicago: University of Chicago Press, 1982.

Strum, Shirley C. (1987). *Almost Human*. New York: Random House.

Sulloway, Frank (1979). *Freud: Biologist of the Mind*. New York: Basic Books.

Sulloway, Frank (1991). "Reassessing Freud's Case Histories." *Isis* 82:245–75.

Tinbergen, Niko (1968). "On War and Peace in Animals and Man." Reprinted in Arthur L. Kaplan, ed., *The Sociobiology Debate*. New York: Harper and Row, 1978.

Tylor, Edward B. (1891). *Primitive Cultures: Researches into the Development of Mythology, Philosophy, Religion, Language, Art and Custom*. 2 vols. 3d ed. London: John Murray.

Wallace, Edwin R., IV (1983). *Freud and Anthropology: A History and Reappraisal*. *Psychological Issues*, vol. XIV, no. 3. New York: International Universities Press.

Wilm, E. C. (1925). *The Theories of Instinct*. New Haven, Conn.: Yale University Press. Reprinted by University Microfilms, Ann Arbor, Michigan, 1980.

Wollheim, Richard (1971). *Freud*. London: Fontana.

Wundt, Wilhelm (1874). *Grundzüge der physiologischen Psychologie* [*Principles of Physiological Psychology*]. 1st ed. Leipzig: Wilhelm Engelmann.

Wundt, Wilhelm (1902). *Principles of Physiological Psychology, Vol. 1.* 5th ed. Edward Bradford Titchener, trans. New York: Kraus Reprint, 1969.

Wundt, Wilhelm (1916). *Elements of Folk Psychology* [*Elemete der Völkerpsychologie*]. Edward Leroy Schaub, authorized trans. London: George Allen & Unwin.

Index